Rings

DIANA SCARISBRICK

Rings

Symbols of wealth, power and affection

HARRY N. ABRAMS, INC., PUBLISHERS

Library of Congress Cataloging-in-Publication Data

Scarisbrick, Diana.

Rings: symbols of wealth, power, and affection by Diana
  Scarisbrick.
    p.   cm
Includes bibliographical references and index.
ISBN 0–8109–3775–1
1. Rings—History.   I. Title.
NK7446.S32   1993
739.27'8—dc20   92–29626
                                           CIP

Published in 1993 by Harry N. Abrams, Incorporated, New York
A Times Mirror Company

Printed and bound in Singapore

CONTENTS

Introduction

The desire to encircle the finger with a ring combining beauty, value and a distinctive character is a human impulse which can be traced back to the Sumerian civilization of the 3rd millennium BC. During its long history many of the functions, materials, techniques and motifs familiar to the people of antiquity have been revived and reinterpreted.

The role of the ring to signify the transfer of power and to designate an heir is recorded in the Bible and in classical literature. When Pharaoh made Joseph ruler of Egypt he 'took off his ring from his hand and put it on Joseph's hand'. During the Roman Empire, a man's professional status and success were judged by the number of rings on his fingers. Juvenal said they were essential for barristers, since 'no litigant would give Cicero himself 200 pence nowadays unless a huge ring were blazing from his finger.' Women wore rings to enhance the beauty of the hand and as the finishing touch to the toilette. The funeral effigy of an Etruscan woman shows her wearing no fewer than six rings, on both upper and lower joints of her fingers. The passion for rings continued into the Early Christian period, when we find the 3rd-century Church Father Tertullian inveighing against the ostentatious parade of rings other than signets and marriage tokens.

Signets hold first place among rings made to serve a practical purpose. At a time when the art of writing was known only to a few, signets, which bore a distinguishing mark or badge that could be impressed on clay or wax to authenticate correspondence, documents, and seals on property, were essential for governments and commerce.

Signet rings found in Egypt in Middle and New Kingdom tombs, of the 2nd millennium BC, are in the form of scarabs carved from hardstone, with the device engraved on the underside. A gold wire running through binds the scarab to the finger and allows it to revolve when required for use. That style was succeeded by a massive stirrup-shaped ring with the device engraved on a fixed metal bezel. The goldsmiths of Greece in the 5th century BC produced signets with fixed round or oval bezels, engraved either on the metal or on an inset hardstone with miniature versions of the masterpieces of contemporary painting and sculpture. Gradually, Greek and Roman gem-engravers added subjects from mythology, history, nature, sport, genre, literature and the theatre. The choice of motif reflected the taste of the owner, and was immediately recognized by friends.

Iron signets were the common wear of Romans of all classes during the Republic. (The Renaissance goldsmith Benvenuto Cellini records that he copied some of these rings, discovered when he was in Rome in 1524.) As the Romans became richer, gold supplanted iron, except among slaves and soldiers: the general Marius, we are told, riding in triumph after his defeat of Jugurtha in 104 BC, wore an iron ring just like the slave behind him. During the Empire the custom lapsed, and military valour was rewarded by massive gold rings set with coins – the first in a long line of which the latest is the Bulgari coin ring, introduced in the 1960s. As for the custom of the iron soldier's ring, it was echoed in early 19th-century Prussia, among patriots in the fight against Napoleon.

A particular type of signet is that engraved with a portrait. Scipio Africanus sealed with the portrait of the father he admired, and his son did the same. Alexander the Great commissioned cameo and intaglio portraits of himself from the court artist Pyrgoteles, and thereafter rings bearing the image of the ruler, given as rewards for services, were worn as badges of loyalty. Julius Caesar, who claimed descent from the goddess Venus, wore a ring with her image, armed; but his successor, Augustus, soon followed Alexander's model in commissioning a portrait of himself, by the gem-engraver Dioscourides. Succeeding emperors continued this tradition, using the portrait of Augustus or their own, as did all loyal subjects. Private individuals, too, had themselves and their families depicted. The custom survived the decline in gem-engraving during the Dark Ages: the signet of Childeric I, King of the Franks, buried with him in AD 481, has a gold bezel engraved with his portrait. The portrait signet was revived at the end of the medieval period, and retained its appeal well into the 19th century.

No poet of the ancient world wrote more eloquently of the essentially personal character of the ring than Ovid, who in lines full of feeling addressed the signet he gave his beloved: 'May she receive thee with glad heart and straightway slip thee on her finger; mayst thou fit her as well as she fits me, and press her finger with aptly adjusted circle! ... to help her seal her secret missives, and to keep the dry, clinging gem from drawing away the wax, I should first touch the moist lips of my beautiful love ...' Nowhere does Ovid disclose the device on the signet, but unless it was the portrait of himself or the lady, it is likely to have shown Cupid engaged in his all-conquering activities.

The 2nd-century Church Father Clement of Alexandria, while acknowledging the usefulness of signets, proposed to replace the pagan divinities and erotic subjects with symbols of the new faith: 'many of the licentious world', he observed, 'wear engravings of their naked minions or mistresses in their rings so that not even if they wish it can they at any time enjoy a respite from the torments of desire'; for Christians, instead, 'let the engraving of the gem be either a dove or a fish or a ship running before the wind ... or a ship's anchor ... And if it represent a man fishing the wearer will be put in mind of the Apostles ...' Byzantine signets bore these Christian emblems, and also pictures of saints, the Chi-Rho monogram of Christ, crosses surrounded by personal monograms, and pious acclamations in Greek. Monograms are a feature, too, of Merovingian and Frankish signets. Much prized in the Dark Ages were signets set with ancient gems, rimmed in a gold border which might be inscribed with the owner's name.

If signets were important, so wedding rings have been for much of history. At the Sponsalia which preceded marriage in ancient Rome, the guardian of the future bride made a solemn promise on her behalf and in return her future husband gave a ring as a pledge. At first these rings were plain iron circles, but they came to bear the symbol of the *dextrarum iunctio*, or two right hands clasped. The device was wrought in relief in gold or engraved on hardstone intaglios, and often accompanied by the Greek word OMONIA (concord). This symbol of mutual trust had reappeared in rings by the 12th century; known in Italy as a *fede* and in France as a *bonne foi*, it retained its appeal for the next seven centuries. Plaited wire Hercules or reef knots also symbolized the tie of marriage; they too reappear on love rings of the medieval period.

Rings played an important part in the marriage ritual in early Christian times. Isidore of Seville in the 7th century asserted that the ring was 'given by the spouser to the spoused either for a sign of mutual fidelity or still more to join their hearts by this pledge and that therefore the ring is placed on the fourth finger because a certain vein is said to flow from thence to the heart'. The iconography was also Christianized. The typical Byzantine marriage ring is engraved with a depiction of the couple standing before Christ who gives them His blessing. Another Byzantine gold ring, with architectural bezel, prefigures the characteristic Jewish marriage ring.

The pattern of Roman and Byzantine double-portrait rings, showing a man and a woman facing each other in profile, was taken up for love rings in Renaissance Italy and was also adopted by post-classical royalty. A cameo ring of the future Louis XVI and his bride Marie-Antoinette commemorates their marriage, and in 1840 Queen Victoria and Prince Albert chose a similar device, but mass-produced in stamped gold for a wide distribution.

Greek and Latin messages of affection anticipate the later posy ring. Usually the mottoes are either inscribed on the metal bezel or cut on cameos and intaglios for insertion within it, but in the 3rd century AD a more complex form emerged, consisting of a wide openwork hoop where the motto – to the effect of 'Good luck' or 'Live happily' – may be wrought amidst scrolls, tendrils or ivy leaves. Christian influence is seen in rings inscribed with pious acclamations, prayers and quotations from the Gospels, which foreshadow those on rings of the 15th and 16th centuries. Another type of posy introduces the name of the owner, sometimes with a greeting and good wishes. One Anglo-Saxon hoop ring includes the name of the goldsmith as well.

Just as the author of Ecclesiastes enjoined good Jews to 'Remember thy end', so Greek and Roman philosophers urged their followers to consider death, and we find rings set with gems showing symbols of mortality: Cupid with the torch of life extinguished, skulls, skeletons, and butterflies representing the soul. The theme was revived in jewelry in the Renaissance, and assumed the greatest importance during the 17th century.

Plato tells the story of the shepherd Gyges who could make himself invisible by turning his ring upside-down, and many feats were performed by King Solomon using a magic ring. Rings which could avert misfortune and heal the sick are mentioned in classical literature as customary for ordinary citizens. Their powers derived from the metal or stone of which they were made and from symbols and inscriptions. Although Pliny ridiculed the idea that amethysts prevented drunkenness, he agreed that the diamond prevented poisoning and brought victory to the wearer. Lapidaries listing the virtues of stones were compiled. Other apotropaic rings incorporated amulets, such as the Hercules knot, phallus and frog.

Besides signets and those rings associated with power, love, marriage, religious belief and magic, there is the large category of rings which were worn only for their value and beauty. Those set with plain unengraved stones began their long reign in the Hellenistic period and reached a zenith of popularity under the Roman Empire. The smaller gems are grouped into clusters or set in a circle studding the hoop, prefiguring the modern 'eternity' ring. In addition to pearls and coloured stones, particularly amethysts, garnets and plasma, there were octahedral diamonds, set as solitaires and in 'gimmel' (from *gemellus*, twin) bezels. The commonest form of gem-set ring in the Dark Ages has slices of garnets in a wheel pattern.

Some Byzantine rings have cloisonné enamel bezels; far more numerous are those decorated with niello. This late Roman technique of fusing a black substance into the lines of a pattern cut into the metal was adopted by both Byzantine and Northern European goldsmiths. Ornament provided by the metal itself ranges from the sophisticated motifs wrought in filigree and granulation by the goldsmiths of classical Greece to the primitive coils, knots, spirals and plaits on Viking and Anglo-Saxon rings.

While most sculptural motifs wrought in gold or carved from hardstones in relief as cameos have a significance beyond the purely decorative, there are some whose status is hard to define. An ancient Egyptian ring inscribed with the name of Ramesses IV has a bezel surmounted by two ducks in the round. It is followed by a succession of examples from Hellenistic, Etruscan, Roman, Byzantine and Anglo-Saxon sources, where the bezel itself is modelled in relief as a bust, bird, dragon or snake, or is supported by figures – the shepherd boy Atys, lions, panthers, crouching hares. Like the other themes we have traced from the ancient world, this too had an afterlife, in the tours-de-force of the Renaissance goldsmith and, in our own day, Cartier's famous panther ring.

1

1100–1500:
the Middle Ages
and the early Renaissance

D uring the Middle Ages more rings were worn than any other jewel, and many have survived, found in tombs, or in the ground, usually singly, but sometimes hidden in hoards. The ring was a sign of affluence and rank. It could be used as a seal, a pledge of contract, a token of love, a diplomatic credential, a mark of religious faith, an amulet to drive away misfortune, and a badge of political and party allegiance. Several functions could be combined in a single ring.

TYPOLOGY

Popular throughout the Middle Ages, especially for small stones, was the stirrup shape, so called because of the manner in which the bezel rises from the shoulders to the point which contains the gem. Larger stones are mounted in little boxes, sometimes called 'pie-dish' bezels; the sides may be ornamented with small motifs such as eagles which possibly allude to the arms of the first recipient or donor. From about 1300, tall flared bezels, sometimes supported by heads at the shoulders, emerge: this was to be the typical Gothic gem-set ring. Settings may be strengthened by claws, either applied or formed by drawings up the metal edge at intervals. In the 14th century this developed into cusping, a quatrefoil shape being the most common. In the 15th century that was combined with arcading, prefiguring the standard 16th-century pattern. p. 26 p. 25 p. 29 p. 30 pp. 26, 30 p. 38 p. 29

The hoops, which may be rectangular, square, round or oval in section, are usually engraved with a motto or device. They may also be reeded; and from the late 14th century writhen (twisted) hoops are ornamented with flowers, foliage, and sunbursts, sometimes combined with mottoes, all picked out in enamel or black niello. Similar designs occur on signet rings with the hoops expanding to broad firm bezels from which the device can be impressed in warmed beeswax. p. 37 p. 31

Shoulders may be angled, in a form going back to late Roman rings, or decorated with discs, shields, initials or portrait heads. Sometimes the bezel is held by hands or by animals resembling the creatures in manuscripts. p. 26

Every stone – whether precious, semi-precious, or one of several strange substances such as unicorn horn (narwhal tusk) and toadstone (from the fossilized fish *Lepidotus*) – had a 'vertu' or magical power attributed to it, sometimes enhanced by inscriptions. Some of these were derived from the Jewish cabalistic tradition, such as TETRAGRAMMATON (for the name of Jehovah) and TEBAL GUT GUTDANI which was a cure for toothache. Venerated phrases from the Gospels were used against other misfortunes. Merchants fearing to meet thieves on their travels relied on IESUS AUTEM TRANSIENS PER MEDIUM ILLORUM IBAT (But He, passing through the midst of them, went His way; Luke 4.30), alluding to Christ's escape from His enemies, and sailors used the last words of Christ on the cross, CONSUMMATUM EST (It is finished; John 19.30), to calm tempests. These and the magical properties of gems were listed in lapidaries – from the Latin for stone – of which the most important was the treatise compiled by Marbode, Bishop of Rennes in France (d. 1123). From the minute size of so many stones it seems p. 14

A ring for the age of chivalry, with a projecting bezel in the form of a spur with revolving rowel. From the venetian colony at Chalcis in Euboea, 15th century.

their power was effective regardless of scale or colour. So that the 'vertu' might be transmitted more easily to the wearer some are set transparent, without a solid back.

Coloured gems were treated as cabochons – left uncut in their natural irregular shape and merely polished. To improve colour and lustre, a paper-thin sheet of metal might be placed behind them: this was the process known as foiling. Involving considerations of the type of metal and fixative used, it was a test of the goldsmith's skill.

DECORATIVE RINGS

Diamond

p. 28

p. 29

The prestige of the diamond stood so high that it was often given as a diplomatic gift: Edward III of England gave 'one ring with a great diamond' to the King of France at Calais in 1362. Whereas the earliest cuts – octahedron or point-cut – were set in stirrup-shaped rings, by the 14th century both faceting and settings had evolved. The inventory of Charles V of France (1364–80) lists not only point-cuts but also irregular triangular shield shapes, a table-cut, and a diamond fleur-de-lis, all set off by white, blue and red enamels. Valentina Visconti, the heiress who married the Duc d'Orléans in 1387, brought from Milan a ring enamelled with her initials and set with a small table-cut diamond. The inventory made after the death in 1469 of Marguerite, Duchess of Brittany, lists diamonds rings enamelled with daisies – alluding to her name – and with the red and white ermine, badge of the Breton dukes. Another ring with heraldic ornament is recorded in the will of Jeanne de Laval (d. 1498): the diamond was cut as a fleur-de-lis and the ring bore the arms of her husband, Duke René of Anjou.

Under the patronage of the art-loving dukes of Burgundy new cuts, the lozenge and hogback, were produced for setting in yet more elaborate patterns such as the letters of the alphabet. A ring associated with Mary of Burgundy (d. 1482) bears the initial M – for herself and for the Virgin – in diamonds flanked by crowns at the shoulders. The rosette, formed by precisely cut lozenges arranged like a star round a gold point with triangular cuts set between the tips to complete the circle, was another tour-de-force, surviving today in a late 15th-century pendant in the Grünes Gewölbe, Dresden.

Ruby

p. 26

In the 14th-century *Vision of Piers Ploughman*, Lady Meed, the personification of wealth and worldly success, is splendidly attired, crowned, and be-ringed with many rich red rubies, synonymous with luxury. Balas rubies or spinels, which have a slight blue tint, were a less expensive alternative to the Oriental ruby proper. Most of those mentioned in the inventory of Charles V were cabochons in rough square, round and triangular bezels, but one was shaped as a heart and another as a shield; the royal emblems of crown and fleur-de-lis ornamented the shoulders with, in one instance, an angel replacing the crown. Enamels were usually white or russet, though exceptionally a heart-shaped ruby ring belonging to Marguerite of Brittany was enamelled blue. The most important survival is from the Chalcis Hoard, with a tall bezel ornamented with scrolls and niello.

Emerald

Pope Innocent III sent four symbolic gems in rings to Richard I of England (1189–99), explaining that the sapphire stood for hope, the topaz for duty, the garnet for love and the emerald for faith. Those listed in the inventories of Charles V were cut into square, lozenge and heart shapes in settings left plain or enamelled red and white. Survivals are rare. One in the British Museum has a conical bezel supported by scrolls; the hoop is inscribed QUI PLUS DESPENT QUA LI NAFIERT SANS COLP FERIR A MORT SE FIERT (He who spends more than he has kills himself without striking a blow; D 929*).

Sapphire

A sapphire stirrup-shaped ring in the pictorial inventory of the treasury of St Albans Abbey, north of London, compiled in 1257 by Matthew Paris bears the initials of Richard Animal, who had been given it by his childhood friend, Queen Eleanor of Aquitaine (d. 1204), so it is securely dated. Another type, of late 13th- or early 14th-century origin, is represented by a remarkable series of silver rings from graves outside the cathedral of Murano in the Venetian lagoon. The sapphires are set in tall octagonal bezels with incurved sides and milled borders; projecting high above the hoops, they are buttressed by pierced supports rising from the mouths of dragons guarding the shoulders. The stones varied in origin: one of Charles V's rings was set with a sapphire from Puy in the Haute Loire, whereas Louis of Anjou's large faceted stone was imported from the East.

Pearl

Pearls, both Oriental and freshwater, which required no faceting or polishing, were either secured by claws or fixed to pins. Larger specimens could be worn as solitaires, smaller ones as clusters around a gem in the centre. The inventory of Charles V records 'a silver ring with a Scottish pearl held by two men'. The two largest pearls in the collection of Louis, Duc de Guyenne (d. 1415) – la Grosse Perle de Berry and la Grosse Perle de Navarre, both named after their donors – were set in black and gold rings. The elaboration and refinement of 15th-century pearl rings are illustrated by the group from p. 27 Chalcis. Some are secured to flat plates on cable twist hoops, while others are fantastic structures rising high above hoops wrought with scrolls and rosettes. They vividly evoke the elegant world of the Venetian expatriates in this fortress on the island of Euboea, where the continual round of balls and tournaments always impressed visitors.

Semi-precious stones

An amethyst was found in the hoard of 12th-century rings at Lark Hill, near Worcester in England (D 1744), and another appears in the inventory of Charles V. Most elegant of all the surviving examples is a ring from Chalcis with stone set in a simple cup-shaped bezel high above the slender hoop. Peridot rings occurred in the collection of Charles V; a contemporary example, probably of English make, found in 1940 in a hoard at Thame near Oxford, has a hexagonal cusped bezel flanked by sprays of flowers at the shoulders

* For an explanation of the abbreviations, see the Bibliography.

(Ashmolean Museum, Oxford). A turquoise, very simply set in an oval bezel on a plain gold hoop, was among the late 13th- and early 14th-century rings discovered on the site of the old Jewish ghetto at Colmar in Alsace. Others were more elaborate: Charles V owned a turquoise in a rose-shaped bezel, and a turquoise in the fully developed 15th-century style with polyfoil bezel was found in England as part of the Fishpool Hoard (British Museum, London). Garnets, topazes, aquamarines, chrysoprases and catseyes are all recorded in the collection of Charles V, confirming that a far wider range of stones was used for rings than in any other type of medieval jewel.

Multiple-gem-set rings
Although the French royal inventories indicate that pearls and coloured stones were combined into elaborate patterns, most mixtures were set very simply. A sapphire and a ruby are set in the bezels of a twin or gimmel ring, the two stirrup-shaped hoops lying side by side (D 1816). Clusters were composed of a large central stone – perhaps a sapphire – surrounded by small rubies or diamonds in detached collets, sometimes with small stones actually mounted on the gold claws securing the large one. Two stones of contrasting colour but approximately the same size might be set horizontally or vertically across the bezel, or five set in a row as a half hoop. This last developed into the bold harlequin style with a sapphire, an amethyst and a turquoise set in a band between strips of filigree to catch the light.

Substitutes for gems
The presence of a silver ring set with transparent yellow paste in the Lark Hill Hoard (D 1745) proves that people of modest means wore jewels too. Varieties of glass were produced in a wide range to imitate not only transparent and opaque coloured stones but also marble. By 1334, and perhaps long before that, the glassworkers of Venice were making 'stones for rings of white glass, both tinted red and not'. Paris too had a reputation for glass stones and also for doublets, of tinted rock crystal (see below, p. 47). Efforts were made to regulate the trade in precious stones and their substitutes, and the general rule was that doublets and paste were not to be set in gold.

Cameos
Precious and semi-precious stones, both monochrome and multi-layered, carved with images in relief were highly prized for rings. Some of these cameos may have been ancient but others were carved in Europe from 1200 onwards when the classical art of gem-engraving revived, first in Sicily, then in Paris, boosted by French royal patronage. The medieval engraver made a speciality of portraits and Christian subjects for which there was no classical precedent. Surviving examples include a Roman plasma bust of a woman set in a plain gold 13th-century ring found at Witney in Oxfordshire (O 247) and a 15th-century Italian sardonyx dog (D 920). Two splendid 15th-century portrait cameos are also known: one has a lady in profile with turban headdress, the hoop

inscribed DUNG SEUL REGART VOUS DOIT SUFFIRE – You must be happy with just one glance (Victoria and Albert Museum, London), while another shows the profile bust of Jean Sans Peur, Duke of Burgundy. That ring was buried with the Duke after his p. 33 murder in 1419.

Decorative rings without gems

Not all decorative rings were set with stones, real or counterfeit. Two early examples were found in the 12th-century Lark Hill Hoard: one is made from twisted silver wire, in a design similar to Viking Age examples that survived well into the 14th century (D 1741); the other is a flat silver band widening out to form a bezel divided into three, each section nielloed with a cross amidst quatrefoils. These motifs as well as linear patterns and chevrons are also nielloed on stirrup-shaped rings found in Ireland. Gold, silver and base metal rings might be cast with raised elements simulating point-cut diamonds and domed cabochons. Another group is ornamented with naturalistic motifs – crossed dragon heads (D 1858), a carnation, and a stag at speed framed in leafy branches (O 271). Two rings from Chalcis, in the form of a miniature knightly belt and a spur rowel, reflect p. 10 the concerns of the age of chivalry.

SIGNETS

Whereas a cameo stands out in relief, an intaglio is cut into the surface of the stone so that an impression can be taken from it to use as a seal, guaranteeing the authenticity of a document. Some of the earliest medieval signets were set with Roman intaglios, reflecting the interest in classical culture which developed in the 12th century.

Drawings of the bezel, shoulders and hoop of the signet ring of the 14th-century Italian merchant Noario de Petruchio.

When the owner's name appears on the rim framing a classical intaglio it is sometimes possible to associate surviving signets with particular individuals. Richard I of England is believed to have worn a ring of simple design set with a plasma intaglio of Minerva p. 32 framed in the inscription S[IGILLUM] RICHARD RE[G] P[PRIVATUM] (The private seal of King Richard). Designs become more elaborate in 14th-century Italy, when the inscriptions are carried round the hoop. One ring, set with a sard intaglio of a youth, framed in a rim inscribed NOARIU DE PETRUCIU MERCATAT, bears on the shoulders the distinctive mark by which the owner identified his goods; the hoop carries the Biblical phrase used as a talisman against robbers, IESUS AUTEM TRANSIENS PER MEDIUM ILLORUM IBAT (see above, p. 10), and also the invocation IESUS NOMINE TUO S[ALUS] (Jesus, in thy name is safety). The rims may also be left plain or may bear inscriptions that are magical or devotional or allude to the signet itself, such as TECTA LEGE LECTA TEGE (Read what is written, hide what is read).

Some signets are set with contemporary portrait intaglios, counterparts of the more decorative cameos. Engraving on precious stones was a speciality of the artists patronized by the French monarchs and nobility. Ruby, spinel and sapphire signets of Charles V bore the royal devices: a king's head, a dolphin with the fleur-de-lis, a crowned rose with the name Charles, and his own full-length figure in armour bearing a shield charged with three fleurs-de-lis crowned by an angel. One French royal signet survives in the original setting: it is a sapphire intaglio of a crowned and haloed king holding orb and sceptre, between the letters s and L (for *sigillum Ludovici*, the seal of Louis); the stone is set in a plain square bezel supported by a hoop nielloed with fleurs-de-lis and inscribed within C'EST LE SINET DU ROI SA[I]NT LOUIS (This is the signet of the King St Louis).

p. 30
p. 31
In the 15th century engraved gems continued to be used for signets but the settings are ornamented more profusely, with naturalistic motifs of leaves and flowers. Another change was the adoption of the angular Gothic script, though Italian signets, such as those from Chalcis, retained Lombardic lettering.

Heraldic signets
With the rapid spread of heraldry in the 13th century from kings and nobles to churchmen and merchants, armorial signets became increasingly current. Most were engraved on gold, silver or bronze. It is rare to find a name around the arms, but devotional, magical or personal inscriptions often occur on the hoop. While the early designs are just oval or round bezels on plain hoops, by the 14th century more finely wrought octagonal bezels with chasing and niello on the hoop and shoulders were available.

p. 32
French 14th-century rings are of fine quality. One of them, the massive gold signet of Jehan de Grailly, Captal de Buch (d. 1367), companion in arms of the Black Prince, appointed to the Order of the Garter in 1364, has a massive gold polyfoil bezel engraved with his shield of arms and the letters E[ST] [SIGILLUM] I[OHANNIS] D[E] GRE (This is the seal of Jehan de Grailly), and cable-twist ruby-studded shoulders. A Spanish signet with round bezel engraved with a shield of arms charged with six quatrefoils and inscribed with the name PETRI MOZARICO is supported by a hoop expanding to shoulders finely nielloed with dragons, heads turned backwards (Harari Collection 123). Italian families are well represented. One of the best belonged to John of Goltario, whose name frames his shield of arms; smaller shields are engraved on the shoulders (D 258). Several
p. 31
signets of typical Venetian form, with octagonal bezels and dragons or leaves at the shoulders, come from the Chalcis Hoard. None of the arms has yet been identified.

An interesting group of massive gold signets found on the sites of battles between the Yorkist and Lancastrian parties contending for the British throne during the Wars of the Roses of the later 15th century bear the crests of the leading protagonists. A ring said to have been removed from the body of Richard Neville, Earl of Warwick, after the battle of Barnet in 1471 has on the bezel the Warwick badge of a bear chained to a ragged staff
p. 31
(OBR 40E). Another signet, allegedly taken after the defeat and death of Richard III at the battle of Bosworth, bears his badge, the white boar.

Merchants' marks

While some merchants used arms all had marks to identify their goods. These had to be easily recognized, and made by just a few simple strokes of the brush. In England most were like mastheads or vanes designed round an inverted V, a double X or W base, sometimes surmounted by a cross, a reversed 4, or a combination of all these elements. p. 67 Whereas the Italian merchant Noario de Petruchio, as we saw, sealed with a classical p. 14 gem and put his mark on the shoulders of his signet, many preferred to seal with the mark itself, engraved directly on the bezel. Most merchants' rings carry talismanic inscriptions. A signet with swivel bezel, the mark on one side, the monogram SR on the other, bears two: IESUS AUTEM TRANSIENS PER MEDIUM ILLORUM IBAT (see above, p. 10) on the hoop, and IHESUS NAZAR[E]NUS REX IUDEORUM (Jesus of Nazareth, King of the Jews; Matt. 27.37) with the names IHESUS MARIA JOHANNES on the shoulders. Sometimes the name of the owner is inscribed in the border framing the mark on the bezel itself; sometimes it is on the hoop. An Italian variant made of silver, the mark encircled by flowers, has profiles of young women nielloed on the shoulders.

Occupational symbols

Some devices referred to the owner's occupation. A 15th-century bronze ring has a mason's hammer between two stars surmounted by a palm branch and the name GUILLE MACON – William the Mason (D 419). Another, of silver, is engraved with a pair of shears and the word GRACE, perhaps for a tailor of that name (T&S 354).

Rebuses

In one type of 15th-century signet ring the owner's name is expressed by means of a rebus – one or several objects whose names, when pronounced, make the same sound as the proper name. There are numerous English examples including a key and a bell for Keble, and the letter I and a fish for John Pike. An Italian gilt bronze rebus ring for an owner named Campana (bell) bears a shield charged with a bell and the name GUILEM DE CAMPA (T&S 315).

Initials

Very often signets of bronze, and more rarely signets of gold or silver bear an initial, usually in Lombardic capitals surmounted by a crown and flanked by palm branches. Some have two or more initials, side by side or woven into a monogram. Those made of precious metal have more elaborately wrought hoops in the usual late medieval styles and p. 30 are often inscribed EN BON AN, the traditional greeting accompanying a New Year's gift.

Miscellaneous devices

A wide range of other devices can be found on signet rings. Many of them are also charges in heraldry but in this context they were not necessarily intended to refer to particular coats of arms. A cockatrice ring found in Norfolk compares with the 'signet of gold with a cocatryx' mentioned in the will of John Bondy, a London stationer, in 1479. Sporting subjects were popular: they include a hunting horn, a hawk's lure, and a dog which also symbolized fidelity and vigilance. The ship device occurs frequently, referring to maritime trading and voyages abroad. The squirrel, a favourite pet, alluded to the virtues of thrift and husbandry.

p. 31

A further category of signet rings, bearing religious imagery or inscriptions, is discussed on pp. 19–20 and 22–23 below.

RINGS OF POLITICAL AND PARTY ALLEGIANCE

The inscription DE LOIALTE NOS HONE VIN (Our honour comes from loyalty) on a ring in the museum at Lincoln sums up the prime virtue of chivalry – loyalty to the pledged word and the feudal lord. Each lord had a distinctive badge which retainers wore as a livery or uniform, and whoever wore the livery was bound in honour to follow the cause. Most badges were brooches, or links of collars for the neck, but some appear on rings. In England, for instance, we find the Bourchier knot and Pelham buckle, and in Hungary the Tarnoczy family Gordian knot. The device of the dukes of Burgundy, a carpenter's plane, is engraved within the cameo portrait ring of Jean Sans Peur. Henry IV's Lancastrian livery, the collar of Esses, appears on a gold hoop ring; the connection is further reinforced by the inscription inside, SOVEREYNLY, echoing the motto SOVERAIN on his seal of ostrich feathers used on documents in 1399. The Yorkist faction, who fought the Lancastrians during the Wars of the Roses, took the falcon on a fetterlock as their device: this was also engraved on signets (T&S 339).

p. 33

p. 33

Serjeants' rings

It was customary for barristers called to the status of Serjeant-at-Law, and therefore eligible to become judges, to present gold rings to the king, princes of the blood, the chief lords spiritual and temporal, and certain officials. The custom is first referred to in Sir John Fortescue's vindication of the laws of England, *De Laudibus Legum Angliae*, written in exile on the Continent after 1463 though not printed until the reign of Henry VIII; it continued until 1875. The rings were flat bands inscribed on the outside with mottoes in Latin. Although a huge number were made for distribution over five centuries so many were consigned to the melting pot that the number of surviving rings is very small.

LOVE AND MARRIAGE

The lovers in Chaucer's *Troilus and Cryseyde* (c. 1375) exchanged rings, and the giving of such pledges is also illustrated in manuscripts. Amorous symbols and inscriptions – *chançons* in French, posies (poesies, or little poems) in English – distinguish the rings used in the ritual of courtship and marriage. Those bearing the ancient Roman device of two hands clasped together as a pledge of plighted troth are known as *fede* rings, from the Italian word for trust. To judge by the example found in the Lark Hill Hoard (D 1025) they were worn in 12th-century England; certainly they remained in fashion throughout the medieval period and beyond. In the 15th century the hands emerge from billowing sleeves with buttoned cuffs, and may clasp a heart that is crowned or has flowers blooming from it. The *fede* may also be placed at the base of the hoop of a signet, iconographic or decorative gem-set ring. In a 14th-century diamond ring of this type the hands emerge from full sleeves inscribed with the affectionate message IO SUI EN LIU DAMI ODCEST PRESENT (I am here instead of a friend with this gift; D 1006).

All who could afford it chose a wedding ring with a stone. Dante notes in the *Purgatorio* (*c.* 1310) that the murderous Nello dei Pannocchieschi wed the Sienese heiress Pia dei Tolomei with a gemmed ring. The stones varied. In 1445 Henry VI of England married Margaret of Anjou with his ruby coronation ring, remodelled for the occasion, and the 1474 will of Dame Edith Scott mentions 'a Ryng of gold with a Safyour that was my wedding ryng'. Paintings of the Mystic Marriage of St Catherine occasionally show the ring in detail: in Filippino Lippi's version the infant Christ places a ring set with a very large round white pearl on the fourth finger of the saint's left hand (S. Domenico, Bologna). According to a transcript in the Vatican Library recording the marriage of Camilla of Aragon and Costanzo Sforza in 1475, they chose a diamond ring because the stone's extraordinary hardness signified permanent abiding love and fidelity. The sumptuous pageantry of that wedding is echoed by a fine 15th-century Italian diamond-set ring inscribed at the shoulders LORENSO A LENA LENA (From Lorenzo to Lena; D 984). The inscriptions VERGIS MIN NIT (Forget me not; D 959) on a 13th-century German ring and AMOURS (Loves) on a French emerald ring indicate that they, too, were p. 40 used for weddings.

Knots were used to symbolize the union between man and woman; they are placed at intervals round the hoop of a sapphire ring from Chalcis and alternate with scrolls in a p. 40 ring inscribed PENCEZ DE MOY (Think of me; D 979).

Gimmel rings (from the Latin *gemellus*, twin), with twin bezels and hoops joined at the base, were a natural choice to represent two lovers, side by side, hearts united. DE MOY PENCEZ appears on the surviving half of one example (D 993); a complete ring, set with a ruby and a turquoise, is inscribed with the Angelic Greeting, AVE MARIA (Hail, Mary; D 691). Gimmel rings also represented pledges of friendship between men: when Henry III of England met the Count of Gynes in 1204 he gave him a gimmel ring set with a ruby and two emeralds.

In 1376 Francesco Datini, merchant of Prato, married his wife Mergherita with two plain gold bands, almost certainly inscribed with posies. These are the commonest surviving love ring. Made of gold, silver or gilt bronze, the hoops may be twin interlaced ribbons, have channelled borders, or consist of thorned stems or lopped branches. The words or letters may be divided by leaves and flowers of sentimental significance – pansies, pinks, roses warmed by sun rays, once bright with enamel. Most posies are plain statements of love such as AUTRE NE VEUX (I wish for none other) and the reassuring DE MON AMOUR SOIEZ SURE (Be confident of my love). Sometimes the ring itself speaks: for example, WHEN YOU LOKE ON THIS THINK ON THEM YT GAVE YOU THYS.

Two highly individual love rings with broad bands have survived. One is remarkable for the inscription, which is a play on the rules of grammar that may be approximately translated: 'A nominative report has made me her dative, by the genitive word, in spite of the accusative./ My love is infinitive; I want to be her relative.' The message is punctuated by roses, pansies and forget-me-nots; accompanying it is a depiction of a woman holding a bouquet and a chained squirrel. The second broad band ring was found at Godstow Priory in England. The outside is engraved with lozenge-shaped panels of the Virgin, the Trinity and a saint; inside is a message of farewell, placed between trailing flowers: MOST IN MYND AND YN MYN HERT LOTHEST FROM YOU FER TO DEPART. It belongs to the category of 'iconographic' rings (see below), many of which were inscribed with love mottoes and used at weddings. This is confirmed by the 1508 will of William Rede of Boston in Lincolnshire, which mentions his mother's 'wedding ring with two images and enamelled'.

✠ vne fame nominatiue
a fait de moy son datiff
par la parole genitiue
en depit de lacusatiff

✠ ⓐ amour est
infiniti u e ge veu
est r e son relatiff

The inscription and image on the hoop of a 15th-century love-token ring, set with a sapphire.

Jewish marriage rings

The ring used at Jewish weddings had a character of its own. It was inscribed with the Hebrew MAZZAL TOV (Good luck), usually on the roof of a building perched on the bezel. This distinctive roof represents either the Temple of Jerusalem or the home which the couple will build together, recalling the Talmudic phrase, 'his house is his wife'. Several survive of which the most notable is an enamelled filigree and beaded ring from a 14th-century hoard discovered in the ghetto at Colmar in Alsace; each of the six parts of the pyramidal roof is inscribed with a letter in Hebrew and at the shoulders are dragons swallowing long-stemmed flowers (Cluny Museum, Paris). The general type survived into post-medieval times.

p. 66

The Umbrian group

p. 40

Traditionally ascribed to 15th-century Umbria in Italy is a group of silver rings nielloed with profiles of a woman alone, or facing her lover with a flower between them. The heads are similar to those decorating maiolica dishes. Sometimes there is a *fede* at the base of the hoop, or the hoop is nielloed with simulated interlaced ribbons inscribed with posies such as AMORE VOLE VOLE FE (Love flies; it wants fidelity).

ECCLESIASTICAL AND DEVOTIONAL RINGS

Papal rings

The 'Fisherman's Ring' which has become the investiture ring of the popes is first referred to in a letter from Clement IV written in 1265 to his nephew Pietro Grossi of St Gilles: 'Greet my mother and brothers: we do not write to you or your familiars under the bull but under the seal of the Fisherman which the Roman Pontiffs use for their private letters.' Neither the subsequent history of the usage nor the iconographical development of the Fisherman's Ring during the Middle Ages has been fully studied. According to Edmund Waterton, Papal Chamberlain and antiquary, it bore the device of St Peter seated in a boat and drawing a net from the waters, a view substantiated by an entry for 'working the sapphire of the *navicella* [little boat]' in the accounts of Paul II (1464–71).

No Fisherman's Ring proper has survived from this early date, but another signet used by Pope Paul – who as Cardinal Pietro Barbo was one of the great connoisseurs of his day – has come down to us. This is a sardonyx intaglio superbly engraved pp. 34–35 with the bearded heads of SS. Peter and Paul, face to face, a processional cross between them, and on the back the name PAULUS II PONTIFEX MAXIMUS inscribed in relief as a cameo.

Victorian collectors gave the name 'Papal' to a group of massive gilt-metal rings set with paste and bearing the arms of popes from Martin V (1416–31) to Innocent VIII (1484–91) as well as those of a few cardinals, bishops and secular princes. Their purpose has yet to be discovered. The hoops are so huge that they could only have been worn over a glove, and the theory that they were used as a *laisser passer* has gained some acceptance. C. W. King in his *Antique Gems* (1860) accepted their use as credential rings, noting that with two exceptions they would all have belonged to ecclesiastics, but warned that they were being forged in Germany and that only those with an authenticated pedigree should be considered genuine.

Cardinalitial rings

The earliest mention of a ring given by the pope to a new cardinal at the conclave at which he was appointed occurs in 1294. Although such rings are listed in 14th-century documents there is no detail given until 1450, when the papal goldsmith was paid for those given to the Cardinal Archbishop of Taranto and Cardinal Alberto degli Alberti – both set with sapphires, though not of equal value.

Cardinal Pietro Barbo, whose collection at the Palazzo S. Marco (now Palazzo Venezia) in Rome was recorded in an inventory of 1457, seven years before he became pope, owned important rings to wear over his liturgical gloves when celebrating High Mass. Several were set with sapphires, huge and table-cut; another was set with a large square-cut garnet; and there were two clusters – a large spinel framed in emeralds and pearls, and a sapphire bordered by four rubies alternating with pearls. Two of the sapphires and a spinel were engraved with religious subjects, as signets (see below, p. 23).

Episcopal rings

The ritual of conferring a ring on a bishop at his consecration is first referred to in 590, when Pope Gregory the Great stipulated that the episcopal dignity and authority should be symbolized by a ring worn on the third finger of the right hand, as well as by a crozier. There does not seem to have been any uniformity of design until 1194, when Innocent III specified that it should be of gold, solid, and set with a precious stone in which nothing was to be cut. It is only because bishops were interred in their vestments as for Mass, holding chalice and paten and be-ringed, that these official rings have survived, for most other episcopal valuables went to the Crown as a form of death-duty.

p. 28 Most of the rings in church treasuries are solitaires set with sapphires; a few are set with rubies, fewer still with amethysts. Settings compare with those made for the laity. The majority are stirrup shapes or have pie-dish bezels with rosettes or dragons at the shoulders, evolving into cusped settings with shoulders engraved and enamelled with long sprays of flowers and leaves – as in the ring of William Wytlesey, Archbishop of Canterbury (d. 1374). More elaborate episcopal rings are set with many stones and pearls clustered round a large central gem amidst filigree scrollwork. Two of this type are illustrated in Matthew Paris's inventory of the St Albans Abbey treasury: they had been presented by Henry of Blois, Bishop of Winchester (d. 1171), and Stephen Langton, p. 36 Archbishop of Canterbury (d. 1228). Others survive at Evreux, Trier and York.

Some bishops' rings show devotion to a particular saint or doctrine. Bishop Grandisson of Exeter (d. 1369), a great patron of the arts, owned a gold ring engraved with the Virgin on a blue enamel ground; the hoop was inscribed AVE MARIA GRACIA PLENA (Hail, Mary, full of grace), and the monograms IHS and XPS (from the Greek letters for 'Jesus' and 'Christ') appeared on the back of the bezel. A silver-gilt ring said to have pp. 38–39 belonged to William of Wykeham, Bishop of Winchester (d. 1404), set with a pale green stone, has what appears to be St Vitus on the shoulders, worn to avoid epilepsy and St Vitus's dance.

Nuns' rings of profession

The English royal accounts for 1291–92 include an entry for 'one small gold ring with a sapphire which was one of the small gold rings for the nuns of Amesbury against [i.e., used at] their profession'. The use of a gem ring might have been exceptional, for most nuns chose plain gold bands as more appropriate to a renunciation of the things of this world. This is the type represented by a ring of c. 1300 which is inscribed O CEST : ANEL : DE CHASTETE / SEV : ESPOSE : A IHESU CRIST – This is the ring of chastity / I am the spouse of Jesus Christ (D 712). Similar rings were worn by those widows who took vows of perpetual chastity: Lady Alice West, for instance, in her will of 1395 left her son 'a ryng wherewith I was espoused to God'.

Devotional images

Confraternities were established in the 14th and 15th centuries to spread devotion to the cult of the Five Wounds – on His hands, feet and side – suffered by Christ on the cross. Each wound was described as a well, dripping with blood from which flowed mercy, wisdom, grace, godly comfort and everlasting life. Sir Edmund Shaw, a former Lord Mayor of London, left instructions in his will of 1497 for sixteen rings to be made as keepsakes for his friends. The most important survival of this type, from Coventry, is a massive gold band depicting Christ in the tomb, with the instruments of the Passion around Him and the weeping Wounds individually identified; inside is a three-line inscription combining appeals to the Five Wounds, the Cross and the Passion of Christ with magical formulas (cf. above, p. 10):

+ WULNERA QUINQ' DEI SUNT MEDICINA MEI PIA
+ CRUX ET PASSIO XPI SUNT MEDICINA MICHI JASPAR
+ MELCHIOR BALTASAR ANANYZAPTA TETRAGRAMMATON

Some rings with hearts allude not to profane love but – like funerary monuments showing the deceased holding a heart – to the Biblical prayer, 'Create in me a clean heart O God and renew a right spirit within me' (Ps. 51.10). They may have flowers issuing from them; the accompanying inscriptions, however, are devotional monograms and prayers, not amorous posies.

The Tau cross, emblem of St Anthony, who carried a crutch of this shape when he lived as a swineherd, was worn as protection against St Anthony's fire or erysipelas. It often appears on rings, sometimes with the cockle shell, emblem of St James of Compostella.

Devotional inscriptions

When captured by the English in 1430, Joan of Arc was wearing a latten ring inscribed with the names of Jesus and the Virgin. Many such rings have survived, on which the names of saints, Biblical quotations and monograms are engraved, nielloed or wrought in relief. The letter M was used by those devoted to the Virgin Mary. The letters IHS show a desire for Christ's protection; the Sacred Monogram was worn particularly by followers of the cult of the Holy Name preached by St Bernardino of Siena (d. 1444). Christ's name appears also as IESUS, IHESUS NAZARENUS REX IUDEORUM, and in conjunction with other inscriptions such as EST AMOR MEUS (Christ is my love), IN NOMINE DOMINI (In the name of the Lord), and the lengthy QUI P[RO] ALIIS ORAT P[RO] SE LABORAT (He who prays for others aids his own salvation). The most popular Biblical phrases are AVE MARIA, ADIUVA NOS DOMINE [SALUTARIS] (Help us O God of our salvation; Ps. 79.9), and ANIMA MEA IN MANIBUS TUIS (Into Thy hands I commend my spirit; Luke 23.26). A ring in the collection of Cardinal Barbo was inscribed in Latin from the Vulgate DNS REGIT ME ET NICHIL MIHI DEERIT (The Lord is my shepherd, I shall not want; Ps. 23.1). Also found are invocations such as that addressed to the Virgin, MATER DEI MEMANTO MEI (Mother of God, remember me), and, more unusually, CHRISTUS PASSUS EST (Christ has died), which was engraved on a gold ring mentioned in the 1499 will of Robert Hunt.

p. 33

Devotional signets

Images and inscriptions were also used as seals by the devout. Surviving signets indicate the most popular subjects: the Greek, Latin, Tau and St Andrew's crosses, the Agnus Dei, the Pelican in her piety, and the Host with chalice. We find again IHS and the initial M referring to the Virgin Mary. For pilgrims to Rome who had witnessed the solemn exposition of St Veronica's Veil on Good Friday, signets reproduced the image of Christ's face impressed on the Veil (the Vernicle). From the *Paston Letters* we learn that Sir John Howard of Norfolk had presented one to his wife in 1467–68: 'my master gaff her a great sygnet of goolde with the vernycle.' Some liked to seal with the image of a patron saint, for instance the Frenchman Jacques Bouchier, whose name is inscribed on a signet engraved with the figure of St James holding staff and book, framed on the shoulders by cockle shells (O 588).

The cameo cutters placed their art at the service of the Church, engraving episodes from the Bible and depictions of the saints with their attributes. Such gems are recorded only in the collections of the richest art-lovers, such as Charles V of France and Cardinal Barbo. On Fridays – the traditional day of fasting and commemoration of Christ's death on Good Friday – Charles wore a ring that contained an important cameo of the Crucifixion flanked by the Virgin and St John, with angels standing on the arms of the Cross; the setting was nielloed and bore black crosses on the shoulders. Cardinal Barbo's inventory includes three signet rings: a table-cut spinel showing St Catherine, identified by the initials SC, holding a palm; a sapphire of St Paul holding his sword in one hand, book in the other; and a portrait of a cardinal wearing robes and hat, also engraved on a sapphire.

A 15th-century Italian gold signet ring engraved with a depiction of the Vernicle. St Veronica's Veil, believed to have miraculously retained the image of Christ when she wiped His face with it on the road to Calvary, was one of the most prized relics to be seen in Rome.

Iconographic rings

Victorian collectors applied the term 'iconographic' to a distinctive type of gold (and rarely, silver) ring found only in England and Scotland, because the engraving was always religious in theme. The Crucifixion, the Trinity, the Annunciation, the Virgin and the Evangelists are most frequently represented, together with a group of saints, of whom the most popular are St John the Baptist and the military St George and St Michael, followed by SS. Christopher, Barbara and Margaret. Each protected from a particular disaster: SS. Christopher and Barbara saved from sudden death, so that the wearer had time to prepare the soul for the next world. The rings are first mentioned in 1378 in a delivery made by a London goldsmith of 'twelve rings of Christophers'.

The bezels are either single or divided into two or three panels, each with a different image. The quality of the settings varies but most are finely made of gold, once bright with enamel. Some iconographic rings are swivels, with a different saint on each face. P. 37 There is one surviving tryptych: the cover of the bezel is engraved with SS. Catherine and George; it opens to reveal the Trinity within, flanked by the Angel Gabriel and the Virgin of the Annunciation.

The rings are known to have been used for weddings, and also to have been given as New Year presents, being often inscribed EN BON AN on the shoulders or at the back. In 1477 Margaret Paston reminded her husband, 'I pre you wyl were the ring with the emage of Seynte Margrete that I sent you for a remaumbrance tyle ye come home.'

Reliquary rings

According to the influential 12th-century Abbot Suger of St-Denis, 'men's eyes are set under a spell by reliquaries ... they see the shining image of a saint and in their imagination ... his saintliness is proportioned to its brilliance.' Privileged people who owned relics, such as Charles V, set them in jewelled lockets, crosses and rings. Three

The Flemish lady in Rogier van der Weyden's portrait, painted *c.* 1450–60, wears rings on both the lower and the upper joints of her fingers. The bezels of the ornamental rings are adapted to the shapes of the gems, which are uncut and simply polished. The plain hoop rings would have been inscribed with religious, magical or amorous mottoes. Since the sitter was a person of high rank, her rings and way of wearing them must represent the latest Netherlandish fashions of the time.

Typical also of medieval forms is a 13th-century English gold ring with a plain hoop and oval bezel set with a star sapphire. Box-like settings of this kind, with solid sides, are also called 'pie-dish' bezels.

A 15th-century *memento mori* ring, with the letters CMU, for 'C'est mon ure' (i.e., heure) on the bezel, and a plea for prayers on the writhen hoop.

rings in his collection were set with pieces of stone alleged to have come from the tombs of St Catherine and of Christ and from the pillar at which He was scourged, all identified by inscriptions on the hoops. The finest belonged to the dukes of Burgundy and were set with diamonds, engraved and enamelled with miniature tableaux. Their quality is suggested by a reliquary ring from the Thame Hoard which enclosed a relic of the cross. p. 37

CRAMP RINGS

As a charm against epilepsy, convulsions and other spasmodic disorders, cramp rings were worn. A 14th-century medical treatise set out their manufacture: while prayers were recited, they were to be inscribed with the names of two of the Magi accompanied by a magic charm – IASPER BATASAR ATTRAPA – and with the Holy Name, IHS NAZARENUS. Similarly, apotropaic gold and silver rings were hallowed by the kings of England at a service held on Good Friday, from the time of Edward II (1307–27) to that of Elizabeth I (see below, p. 56). The curative power of these royal rings derived from the coronation unction, as Sir John Fortescue explained in the 1460s:

> the kings of England at their very annointing receive such an infusion of grace from heaven that by the touch of their annointed hands they cleanse and cure those infected of a certain disease that is commonly called the King's Evil [i.e., scrofula] though they be pronounced otherwise incurable. Epileptics too and other persons subject to the falling sickness are cured by means of gold and silver devoutly touched and offered by the sacred annointed hands as has been proved by the trial of rings made of gold and silver and placed on the fingers of sick persons in many parts of the world.

In his will of 1463, John Baret of Bury bequeathed 'a rownd ring of the Kynges silver . . . and my crampe ryng of blak innamel and a part silvir and gilt'.

MEMENTO MORI RINGS

In the 15th century inscriptions reminded of the approach of death and the need to prepare for it. This is the message conveyed on a ring by the initials CMU, for 'C'est mon ure' (My hour has come), placed on the lobes of a trefoil; it is reinforced by a plea for prayers, ESPOIRIER DE MY SANS FYNE (Pray for me always), on the shoulders. A silver signet of the same date engraved with the arms of the Genoese family Poggio da Cibo bears the advice RESPICE FINEM SAPIENS ESTO – It is wise to contemplate the end (Ashmolean Museum, Oxford, Fortnum Collection 83).

Even more admonitory were symbols, particularly the death's head. Two flank a heart applied to the bezel of a silver-gilt hoop inscribed on the outside with the name IOHES GODFRAY (O 718). A worm between the two parts of the name alludes to the Biblical passage: 'For when a man is dead he shall inherit creeping things, beasts and worms' (Eccl. 10.11). This was presumably a memorial ring. The subject of *memento mori* was to remain vivid and popular for the next three hundred years, and the custom of wearing memorial and mourning rings did not die out until the early 20th century.

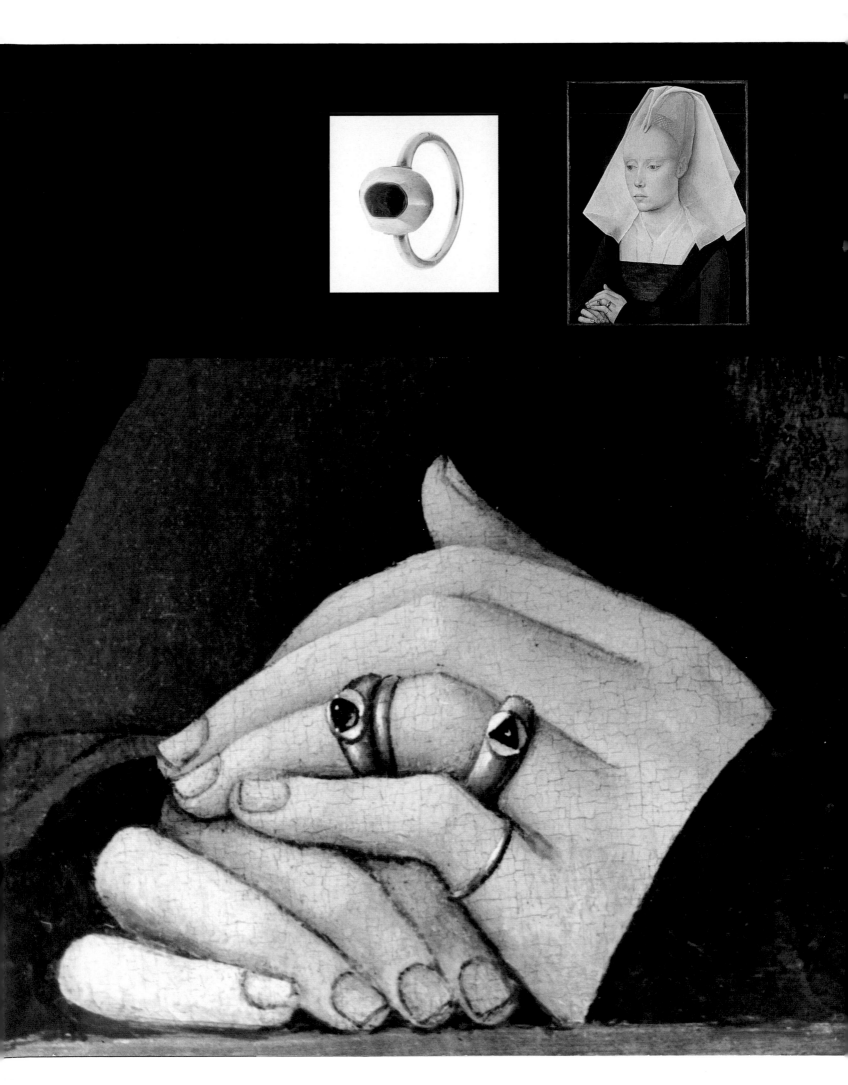

Far left: A stirrup ring, of gold, with a small sapphire set in a projecting bezel, a design dating from the 12th century. *Left*: A gold ring set with a ruby secured by claws in a pie-dish bezel.

Below and opposite:
Chalcis was a Venetian colony on the Greek island of Euboea, likened by a visitor in 1395 to the court of King Arthur. Here in 1840 a rich hoard of rings was discovered, made in the early 15th century in Veneto-Byzantine style. Some of the settings are exceptionally tall and fantastical and have niello decoration, such as that of the important ruby *below*, with inverted pyramidal bezel flanked by scrolls held by dragons at the shoulders. Venice was famous for pearls. Among the pearl rings found at Chalcis (*opposite*) are a solitaire guarded by stylized dragon shoulders (*above left*), a cluster resting on a twisted gold and silver wire hoop (*above right*), and a pyramid rising above dragons (*below*).

MEDIEVAL SIMPLICITY

RINGS FROM CHALCIS

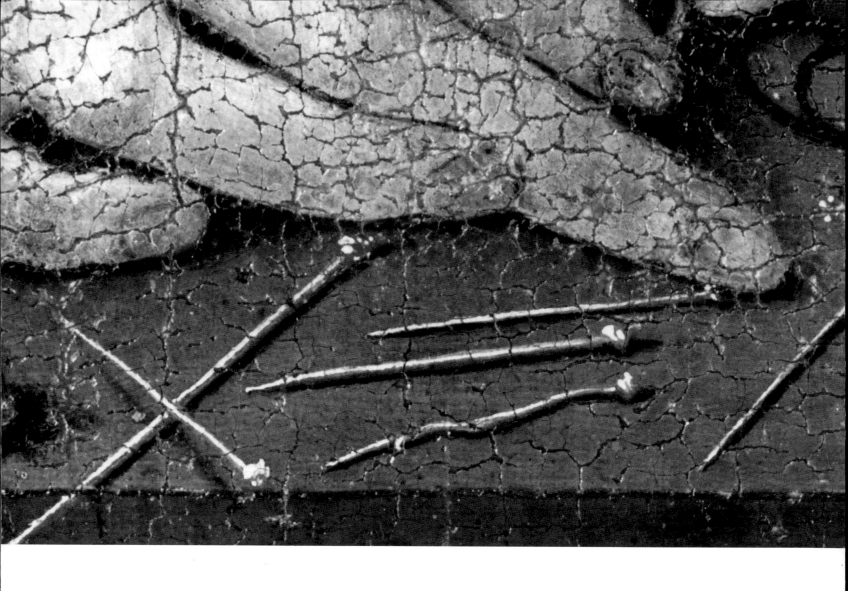

ROMANESQUE TO RENAISSANCE

Above: Still Romanesque in style is a gold ring (*inset*) made in the 13th century in England or France, perhaps for a bishop. It is set with a sapphire, held in claws; the sides of the bezel are cut out in the shape of eagles, and dragon heads terminate the hoop at the shoulders. The hoop is inscribed in Lombardic letters, AVE GRATIA PLENA DM – Hail [Mary] full of grace, Mother of God.

The jewels in the painting are those of Costanza Caetani, born a Medici, who was portrayed by Ghirlandaio *c.* 1490. Her rings, placed on a parchment roll, are set with a pearl and table-cut stones in quatrefoil bezels, which were to be a standard 16th-century pattern.

MEDIEVAL DIAMONDS

Right: Three views of a 15th-century gold ring set with a stone in its natural octahedral form. The square box bezel is flanked by moulded shoulders decorated with nielloed quatrefoils, while the hoop is finely inscribed with a Biblical quotation believed to protect travellers.

Far right: Hogback-cut stones used to highlight the letter M, for the Virgin (seen in front and back view). Together with the crowns at the shoulders of the wide hoop, the initial suggests that this ring was made for Mary of Burgundy, who married the Archduke Maximilian of Austria in 1477.

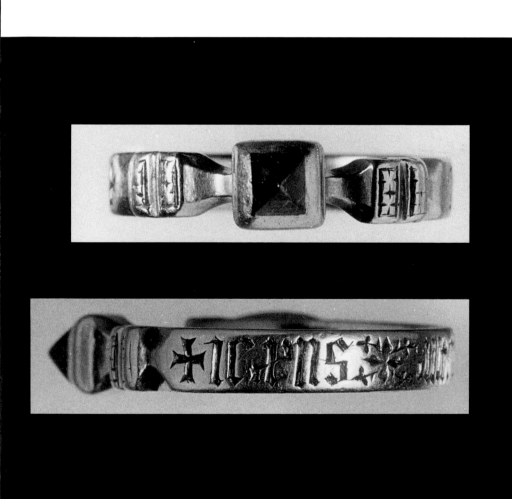

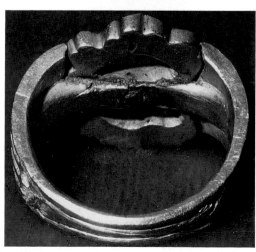

SIGNET RINGS

Signets served as their owner's signature or as a sign of allegiance. Individuals might choose an ancient intaglio, a heraldic device, or a personal emblem such as an initial or an animal of no heraldic significance.

Left: Silver signet engraved with a Lombardic letter A, 15th century. Initial signets were usually made of bronze; silver and gold ones are rare.

Below: Two views of an early 15th-century gold ring from Chalcis, set with an ancient amethyst intaglio of Abundantia holding her cornucopia. The hoop is inscribed in Lombardic letters VERBUM CARO FACTUM EST (The Word was made flesh), a Biblical phrase supposed to avert fits.

Opposite page:

Above left: Gold signet engraved with the arms of an unidentified noble family. The shoulders are nielloed with dragons. The octagonal shape of the bazel (here very rubbed) is characteristic of Venetian signets. From Chalcis, 15th century.

Above right: Gold signet set with an ancient cornelian intaglio of Nemesis holding a branch and standing on a wheel. The gem is framed in a gold rim inscribed MANASSEUS PINZASTRU, the name of the owner. Italian, 13th–14th century.

Below left: Silver signet engraved with a squirrel and the owner's initial, T; 15th century.

Below right: Gold signet with a boar (originally enamelled white), the badge of Richard III of England. It was found on the field of the Battle of Bosworth, where the King was killed in 1485.

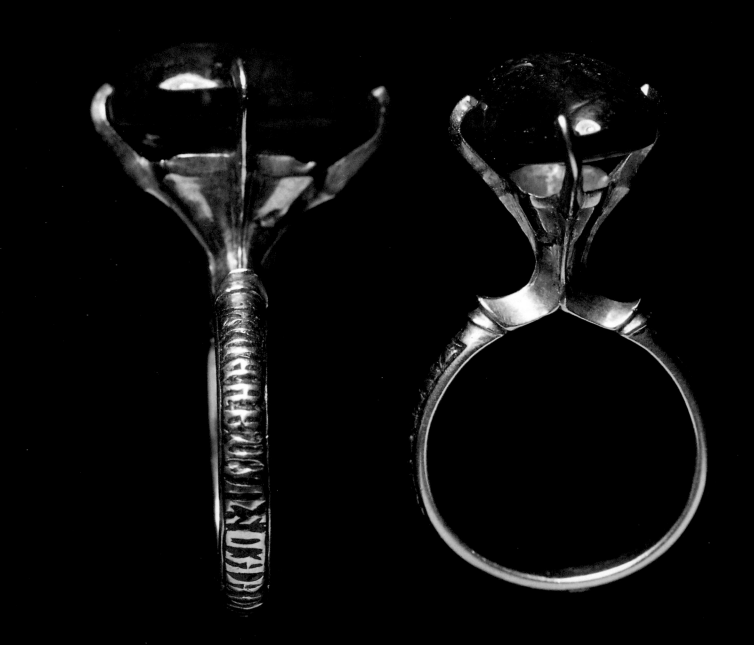

SIGNETS OF THE POWERFUL

Above right: Gold signet associated with Jehan de Grailly (d. 1367), a famous soldier who campaigned with the Black Prince. It is engraved with the arms of Grailly and the letters E I D GRE, for 'Est [sigillum] Iohannis de Grelly' – this is the seal of Jehan de Grailly.

Right: A signet that may have been made for Richard I, king of England (d. 1199). It is set with an ancient plasma intaglio of Minerva, goddess of wisdom. The surrounding inscription, S RICHARD RE P, suggests that it was King Richard's private seal.

Below: Detail of a portrait of Alexander Mornauer, an important late 15th-century dignitary in the town of Landshut in Bavaria, showing his signet worn on the thumb. The device, a moor's head, alludes in rebus form to his surname.

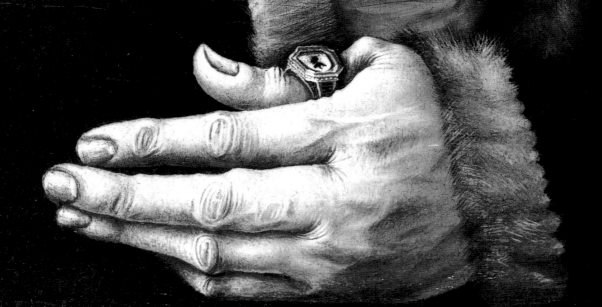

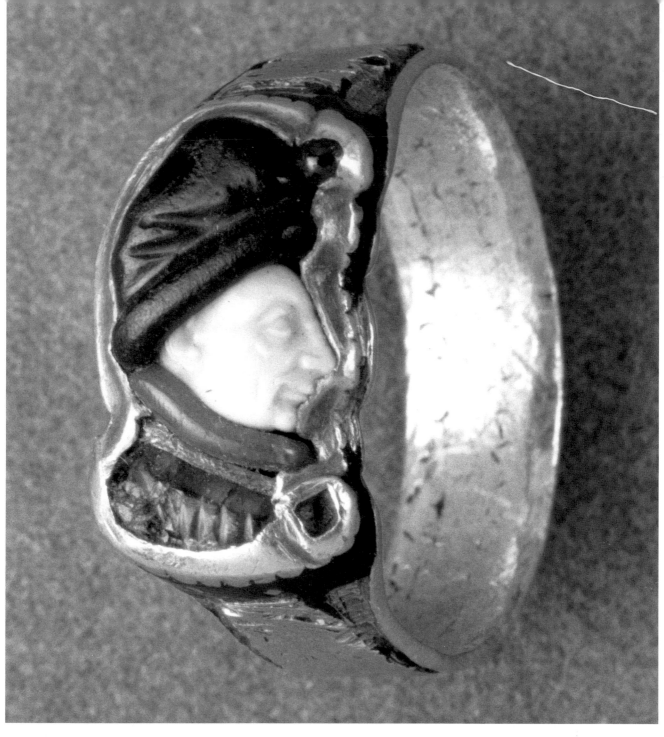

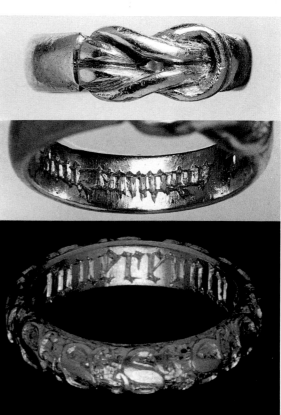

RINGS OF POLITICAL AND PARTY SIGNIFICANCE

Above: A gold ring set with the cameo portrait of Jean Sans Peur, Duke of Burgundy (1371–1419); he is wearing a black hat, emerald green tunic, and ruby brooch. The hoop, which bears his device of a carpenter's plane, is inscribed with the magical phrase VERBUM CARO FACTUM EST (see p.30).

Right: Gold ring with a bezel in the form of a reef knot, badge of the influential English family of Bourchier. The hoop is inscribed with the initials of the owner, EW, and the phrase ADIUVA NOS DEUS (Help us O God) from Psalm 79.

Below right: Gold hoop engraved on the outside with a chain of Esses, badge of the house of Lancaster. Inside this 15th-century ring is the word SOVEREYNLY, which echoes Henry IV's motto, SOVERAIN.

THE SIGNET OF POPE PAUL II

Pietro Barbo, who became pope as Paul II (1464–71), was an
aristocratic Venetian prelate who assembled a cabinet of eight hundred
cameos and intaglios, arranged like a miniature gallery. After his death
the greater part of the collection was acquired by Lorenzo de' Medici.

His signet is set with a three-layered sardonyx, and makes ingenious
use of the stone's pale outer layers and dark core. The reverse is cut in
relief, the Pope's name and title standing out pale against the dark

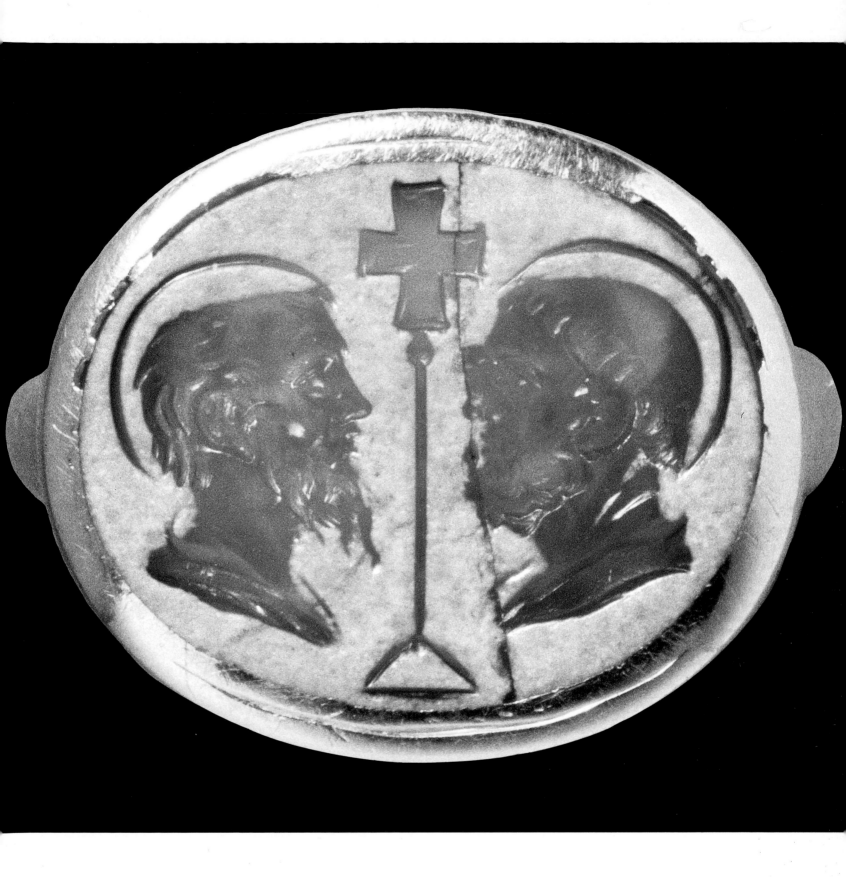

ground. The front is cut in intaglio, through the upper pale layer, so that the design here appears dark against light. St Peter (right) and St Paul face each other, divided by a processional cross. This iconography goes back to Early Christian art, occurring on a signet of 4th-century date, and was taken up again in the Middle Ages. The engraver has transformed the conservative image into a splendid example of Early Renaissance art. The heads of the two founders of the Church are alive,

full of spiritual power and dignity, combining classical idealization with Christian piety.

Among the various contemporary artists whose names are recorded in the accounts of Pope Paul, only one, Giuliano da Scipione, can be connected with a gem which has survived, the cornelian intaglio portrait of the Pope in the Museo degli Argenti, Florence. This signet, used for sealing private correspondence, is of comparable quality.

ECCLESIASTICAL AND DEVOTIONAL RINGS

Left: Two views of the ring of Bishop Arnold II von Isenburg (d. 1259), found in his tomb in Trier Cathedral. The front is set with chrysoprases, while the back is nielloed with a portrait of a man. A similar ring, with the figure of a bishop on the back, belonged to the late 13th-century Pope Boniface VIII.

Opposite page:
Above: A remarkable reliquary ring of late 14th- or early 15th-century date, perhaps made by a Burgundian goldsmith, found in a hoard at Thame in England. The rectangular bezel, which enclosed a relic of the True Cross, is set with a large amethyst cut into a double-armed cross and surrounded by the inscription MEMANTO MEI DOMINE (Remember me, O Lord). The back is engraved with the Crucifixion outlined on a red enamel ground. The relic itself was placed between a plate engraved with a spray of flowers and the inner side of the back, which is similarly decorated. Seven amethysts round the hoop echo the cross on the bezel.

Below: A unique surviving triptych ring, of gold, made in England in the 15th century. When shut, it shows St George and St Catherine with their attributes of dragon and wheel. These twin panels open to form a miniature equivalent of an altarpiece, in which wings with the Angel of the Annunciation and the Virgin flank the Trinity. The shoulders are ornamented with sprigs of flowers warmed by sunrays, and the hoop is inscribed JOY SANS FIN (Unending joy). This is an unusually elaborate example of the genre of engraved 'iconographic' rings made in England and Scotland.

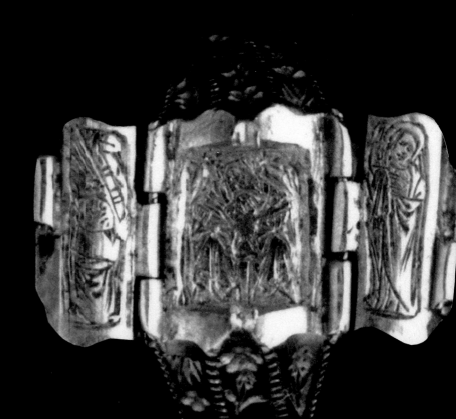

Because of its size and striking design, this ring is believed to have been worn by William of Wykeham, Bishop of Winchester (d. 1404), when officiating at High Mass. It is of silver gilt, set with a green crystal in a triangular bezel with scalloped sides and six claws. The cast figures at the shoulders may represent St Vitus, the Early Christian martyr tortured by boiling in a cauldron, who was thought to protect those who fasted on his feast day from epilepsy and from St Vitus's dance.

RINGS FOR LOVE AND MARRIAGE

Above left: A gentleman, hawk on wrist, holds out a ring set with a large gem to a lady with her pet squirrel. The dog between them symbolizes fidelity. (From the Ormesby Psalter, English, *c.* 1310–25.)

Left: A wedding, depicted in a 13th-century English legal manuscript. The bishop holds the hands of the bride and bridegroom while the ring is placed on her finger.

Below left: A loving couple face-to-face, a flower between them, appear in niello on a silver ring made in the 15th century in the north Italian province of Umbria.

Framing that ring, and seen in profile beside it, are engraved views of a contemporary French ring whose shoulders bear cubes pierced on three sides with letters forming the message AMOURS (Loves).

Below: The hoop of this gold ring, set with a sapphire, is divided by reef knots centred on a star, symbolizing the union of man and woman in marriage. Like the other rings from the Chalcis Hoard (see p. 26), it dates from the early 15th century.

2

The 16th century:
the age of the virtuoso goldsmith

According to the Lorrain designer Pierre Woeiriot, in his virtuoso *Livre d'Aneaux d'Orfèvrerie* (The Book of Rings of Goldsmith's Work, 1561), the ring, requiring the precision of the sculptor and the taste of the painter, was the masterpiece of the Renaissance goldsmith. He takes technical pp. 56, 61 skills of the highest order for granted, setting stones – cut and uncut, cameos and intaglios – in high bezels on bases ornamented with classical motifs or in the midst of flowers, each petal elaborately wrought. Sometimes there is a frieze of grotesque masks, fruit or flowers decorating the sides of the bezel, which is flanked by shoulders chased with strap-work or volutes, or supported by figures – dolphins, rams, eagles, snakes, winged satyrs, p. 64 turbanned Turks, men and women acrobats – derived from contemporary as well as from ancient Roman sources. One particular tour-de-force condenses a vast bacchanal round the minute dimensions of the bezel. Notwithstanding their complexity, Woeiriot's designs are kept in perfect balance, with each element – bezel, shoulders and hoop – making an equal contribution to the whole. Those rings finely chased with figurative motifs that have survived still echo these imaginative creations even though the resplendent enamels have mostly worn away.

Men and women liked to wear rings in quantities: when the Venetian ambassador met p. 72 the twenty-five-year-old Henry VIII he noted that his fingers were 'one mass of jewelled rings'. This was thought in bad taste in Italy: Mario Cavalli, another Venetian diplomat, recommended in his *Informatione dell'offitio dell'ambasciatore* (Guide to the Conduct of an Ambassador, 1550) that just one or two rings, perfect of their kind, the stones remarkable for quality rather than for size, were preferable to a whole array. That attitude was p. 57 exceptional and elsewhere in Europe most people were anxious to show off their possessions – even when wearing gloves, as Bishop Hall noted in his *Satires* (c. 1600): p. 72

> Nor can good Myen weare on his left hand
> A signet ring of Bristol diamond
> But he must cut his glove to show his pride
> That his trim jewel might be better spy'd.

Portraits show that the practice of wearing rings on the second joint of the finger had ceased; but they are often seen on the thumb. They were also hung from a ribbon on the ears and on the hat as well as on cords round the neck, wrists and sleeves. Many would have been tokens of remembrance and good will, like the heart-shaped diamond ring which Mary Queen of Scots sent to Queen Elizabeth of England in 1564. The Scottish humanist George Buchanan wrote a Latin poem explaining that the ring represented Queen Mary's heart and had been given in the hope that it would bind the two women in a bond which 'neither suspicion, nor rivalry nor envy nor hatred nor old age' would dissolve! Queen Elizabeth reciprocated with another ring and her ambassador, Thomas Randolph, described how Queen Mary wore it 'dressed in black and white and no other jewel but the ring I brought her from the Queen's Majesty hanging at her breast with a lace of white and black about her neck'. The custom is also illustrated by Antonio Mor in his portrait of Queen Elizabeth's Champion, Sir Henry Lee, whose rings are worn not only on his fingers but hanging from a cord round his neck and sleeve.

Shakespeare alludes to the role of the ring as a token in *All's Well that Ends Well*:

> This ring was mine; and when I gave it Helen
> I bade her if her fortunes ever stood
> Necessitied to help, that by this token
> I would relieve her

In *Richard II* it guaranteed the authenticity of a message, as the Duke of York gives orders to his servant:

> Sirrah, get thee to Plashy to my sister Gloucester,
> Bid her send me presently a thousand pound.
> Hold, take my ring.

DECORATIVE RINGS
The late 15th-century trefoil, quatrefoil and hexafoil bezel forms are elaborated. From 1540 the plain petals are subdivided into double arches, of which the lower tier is ornamented with scrolls, arabesques and ribbonwork filled with enamels harmonizing with the gems set in the bezel.

Diamond
Because of its remarkable properties the diamond was adopted as an emblem by kings and queens to epitomize the ideals with which they wished to be associated. The first to do so was the Florentine Cosimo de' Medici (1389–1464), followed by his son Piero (1416–69) and grandson Lorenzo the Magnificent (1449–92), whose device was a diamond ring with three feathers – green, white and red – accompanied by the motto SEMPER (Always). According to Paolo Giovio's *Dialogo dell'Imprese* (1559), this signified the virtues of Hope (green), Faith (white) and Charity (red) which the Medici always possessed and through whose aid they would arrive at the Kingdom of God.

Jacopo Typotius in *Symbola Divina et Humana* (1603) analysed the three interlaced diamond rings with the motto SUPERABO (I shall overcome) of Cosimo I, who became Grand Duke of Tuscany in 1569:

p. 61

> As the diamond surpasses in fortitude, endurance and valor all other gem stones, so Cosimo, Grand Duke of Tuscany, wished to show with his three rings set with diamonds that he was determined to excel all other princes in fortitude, endurance and valor.... Furthermore, the rings set with diamonds are intertwined to show that these virtues are conjoined so that they may not be separated. Indeed the fortitude of the diamond, by which it can wear down all stones and gems, and the endurance by which it resists fire and iron, and the dignity by which it surpasses all other gems in valor are well known to all.

The emblematic ring was not confined to the Medici. Borso d'Este, Duke of Modena and Ferrara, used the diamond as his *impresa* or device with the motto NEC IGNE NEC FERRO (Neither by fire nor by the sword) signifying the pursuit of constancy, the chief virtue of princes. Mathias Corvinus, King of Hungary (1458–90), took as his device a sparkling diamond ring with the motto DURAT ET LUCET (Enduring and shining), p. 60 which referred to his escape from prison and subsequent ambition to rule with brilliance. Henri II of France (1547–59) declared his undisputed sovereignty in a badge incorporating a crowned dolphin carrying a globe and encircled by a solitaire. The *impresa* of John Casimir, Duke of Bavaria and Count Palatine (1583–92), was a diamond ring terminat- p. 60 ing at the base of the hoop with clasped hands and framing a coat of arms with branches of laurel and palm. According to Typotius, this emblem demonstrated the Count's hopes for the success of his family in war and peace.

With these associations the diamond ring had a prominent place in coronation ceremonies. It also marked the encounters of monarchs. In 1535, for instance, the Emperor Charles V sent Pope Paul III a diamond ring, acquired in Venice, as a token of good will after the Battle of Tunis. It was by means of that particular diamond that Benvenuto Cellini demonstrated his mastery of foiling. By this technique the internal flaws could be disguised and each stone could appear perfect. After removing the diamond from the Venetian setting Cellini concealed its imperfections so successfully that even his rivals had to concede that he had increased the value from 12,000 to 18,000 crowns. When the Pope asked him to tell them his secret he refused, saying it would take at least three hours to explain. He does however include advice on foiling transparent stones in his *Treatise on Goldsmith's Work* (1568). Whereas this was a straightforward technique for coloured gems, diamonds presented more of a challenge since each required a foil individually created for its own particular lustre or water. Some foils were tinted hard, some soft, some dark, some light. Black was best, enhancing a thousandfold the most beautiful and limpid stones. For this reason when diamonds are depicted in 16th- and 17th-century paintings they are always shown black. Exceptionally, some stones were so perfect they could be set *à jour* without foil: the inventory of Queen Elizabeth includes 'a ring of gold enamelled black with a point-cut diamond set without foyle like four claws'.

An analysis of diamond rings in inventories indicates that although some settings were enamelled black with white and a few white or red the majority were plain black. Exceptionally, another of Queen Elizabeth's rings was 'of gold enamelled green like snakes with a pointed diamond in it and six sparks of diamond about it'. Snakes are not so widely used as other motifs of classical origin – grotesques, masks, cornucopias, fruit and putti – all wrought in relief. Only the greatest masters could execute sculpture in gold on this miniature scale. The Grand Duchess of Tuscany was so impressed by a diamond ring ornamented with four masks and four putti made by Benvenuto Cellini that she sent it at once to Philip II of Spain as a gift.

Unless the diamond was set as a solitaire it was mounted into a cluster composed of stones varying in size and cut. Three of the grandest surviving examples are designed round a central point-cut set above triangular-cuts with flat facets, in a cluster supported by shoulders studded with small table-cuts. All have royal provenances. One (in the Grünes Gewölbe, Dresden) belonged to the Elector of Saxony, another was a gift from p. 59 Charles I of England to Sir Nicholas Kemeys, and the third bears the name and motto of Queen Isabella who married John Zápolya of Hungary in 1539. In a variant of this p. 61 design the central point-cut is set like a star above four smaller point-cuts. Pierre Woei- p. 61 riot's extravagant version is set with a large point-cut supported by twin cornucopias on a hoop studded throughout with small triangular-cuts: the closest surviving parallel is the 'hedgehog' locket ring with domed bezel paved with small point-cuts in the Kunsthistoriches Museum, Vienna. Comparable with Queen Elizabeth's 'ring of gold p. 61 enamelled red with a great diamond cutt with diverse triangles' is a ring with triangular bezel mounted with four triangular-cuts into one great rock secured by claws supported by volutes standing out at the shoulders on a hoop studded with a continuous band of table-cuts. The inside of the hoop is enamelled with white interlaced ribbonwork on black and the back of the bezel with spiral twists.

p. 66 Diamonds were also arranged into ambitious rosette patterns. There was a 'ring of gold with a rose of diamonds' in the Countess of Oxford's will of 1537, and another in the 1595 inventory of the Dame de Saint-Aulaire, Jeanne de Bourdeille: 'ung austre bague faicte en rose ou il y a 9 diamants'.

The lily and initial rings of the Burgundian goldsmiths have their 16th-century counterparts. Outstanding is a locket ring in the Chequers Collection set with table-cut stones forming the letter E accompanied by a blue R, mounted on a mother-of-pearl hoop with rubies round the sides of the bezel and on the shoulders; it is associated with Queen Elizabeth, whose enamelled portrait is enclosed inside with that of another woman, perhaps Anne Boleyn. The Seymour phoenix at the back of the bezel suggests that the ring may have been a gift from a member of that family.

Table-cut stones were clustered together on the bezel of another ring known to have been in Queen Elizabeth's collection: 'a verye great table diamond garnished rounde about with small diamonds being in a box of gold'. The majority of table-cuts were set as solitaires – either in quatrefoils with subdivided and ornamented petals, or in square box bezels on moulded bases.

Around 1600 designs become much simpler. The box bezels are plain and the shoulders are no longer emphasized but merge with the hoop. Such a ring was found at Lauingen on the Danube in the grave of the Count Palatine Philip Ludwig (1547–1614): the box bezel with arcaded sides filled with black enamel is set with a point-cut stone. (The Lauingen rings are now in the Bayerisches Nationalmuseum, Munich.)

Coloured stones

Rubies were the most expensive of all stones, according to Benvenuto Cellini: 'a ruby for instance of five grains of wheat and of as fine a fire as you could wish, would be worth 800 golden scudi and an emerald of the same size and beauty would run to about 400, similarly a diamond would be worth 100 and no more while a sapphire would fetch about 10.' He goes on to describe how to set a fine ruby in a bezel, enhancing it with foils of which 'some should be of so deep a glow that they seem quite dark and others differing in intensity till they have scarce any red in them at all'. The goldsmith should experiment with all these shades of colour till 'his own good taste determines which foil will give most value to the stone'. Again, foiling was not universal, for the 'great Spinell' and a 'Faire rocke rubie sett in claws' in Queen Elizabeth's collection were both set in rings 'without a foyle'.

Cellini points out the importance of finding the right position for the stone, 'not setting it too deep so as to deprive it of its full value, nor too high to isolate it from the surrounding detail'. Solitaire settings vary from plain quatrefoils to the elaborate compositions of the school of Pierre Woeiriot. One such survives (D 2007). The high pyramidal bezel set with a cabochon ruby is garlanded with flowers tied with ribbons and flanked at the shoulders by goats' heads in the antique manner. A fine cluster from the grave of the Count Palatine Friedrich (1557–97) is set with one large point-cut and four small table-cut rubies in the centre and round the sides of the bezel, with four more on each shoulder; both the scrolled setting and the cartouche at the back are enamelled white, green, black and turquoise. This polychrome effect was unusual, for most ruby rings listed in documents are enamelled white only: of the twelve in the stock of the London jeweller John Mabbe in 1576 nine were white and only three in other colours.

The opening up of the New World by the Spaniards increased the supply of emeralds, hitherto mined only in Egypt and the Salzburg Alps. Cellini explained in his *Treatise* that, like the ruby, the emerald should be set with all the 'care, taste and delicacy of which an able man is master'. Both cut and uncut stones were mounted in designs 'wrought antique' with masks, grotesques and cornucopias, enamelled plain white, sometimes with contrasting touches of black and red. Besides solitaires in quatrefoils, round or box bezels, there were groupings of smaller stones formed into solid masses of colour. One such, a cruciform design with conical bezel set with nine emeralds amidst red and white scroll work, is flanked by shoulders each studded with four more stones, and the hoop terminates in a *fede* motif at the base (D 2008).

No longer esteemed as it had been in the Middle Ages, the sapphire is set in quatrefoil or box designs similar to those for emeralds and rubies, usually enamelled white rather than in bright colours, though occasionally mixtures are used. The turquoise ring worn by Thomas Cromwell in his portrait by Holbein (Frick Collection, New York) could be that 'gold ring with a turquoise like a heart' listed in his inventory of 1537; the more usual quatrefoil and hexafoil settings were enamelled black and white with touches of red, blue and green. Amethysts, opals, pearls, chrysolites, topazes, garnets, almandines, and aquamarines are also documented. They are usually found combined, for the contrast of stones of different tints is the essence of Renaissance design.

The rich red of rubies was set off by diamonds and opals in two of Queen Elizabeth's rings, a 'star of five little diamonds and little rubies on every side all being but sparckes'

p. 57
p. 64
p. 64

and a 'ring of gold with a faire Opall withoute a foyle enamelled under the same with a knott and fouer sparckes of rubies under it'. A rosette of eight rubies clustered around an emerald in the 1595 inventory of the Dame de Saint-Aulaire indicates a more Oriental taste for strong contrasts, as does a turquoise in a hexafoil bezel with black petals studded with garnets (O 277).

Substitutes for gems

Imitations of point- and table-cut diamonds were available in both crystal and paste. Coloured stones were similarly imitated in paste, skilfully foiled. The doublet technique, by which a slice of a ruby or emerald was sandwiched between layers of crystal, is described by Benvenuto Cellini. Set in silver, these doublets were made in Milan for sale to peasants 'when they wish to make presents at weddings, ceremonies and so forth, to their wives'. He complains that in the hands of unscrupulous jewellers the practice had been turned into a great evil, for when the doublet was beautifully set in a fine ring the fraud was difficult to detect, and might be sold for the price of a good or first-class stone.

Sculptural bezels

Sometimes instead of providing the setting for a gem or its substitute the bezel is wrought as a piece of sculpture conveying a message which is often enigmatic. Easy to identify are those illustrating the legend of the Wild Man and the Unicorn, Prometheus and the Vulture, and the classical river god reclining on an urn. For the sportsman there were miniature stags' heads and a hunter standing with hound. Others connected with love and remembrance are discussed below.

ENGRAVED GEMS AND SIGNET RINGS

Because it was indispensable for business the signet was always on the finger. The design might comprise a plain round or oval bezel containing a device framed in a beaded or cable border, supported by a smooth convex hoop widening at the shoulders; or it might be wrought with classical details such as masks, volutes and scrolls. Either way it had to be sturdy.

The culture of the Renaissance stimulated the revival of the art of engraving on hardstones and also the desire to collect those gems which had survived from antiquity. Cellini describes in his *Memoirs* some of the exquisite gems – an emerald dolphin, a topaz Minerva – dug up by the peasants in Roman vineyards and sold for a few coins. They were set in rings, as were both cameos and intaglios engraved by modern artists – busts of Roman emperors and empresses, Mars, Hercules, the Gorgon Medusa, scenes of sacrifice – which were cut on fine cornelians, sards, chalcedonies and precious sapphires and rubies.

There was also a demand for portraits of contemporary rulers, which were usually worn by favourites and officials. In Florence, Domenico di Polo engraved the portrait of Duke Alessandro de' Medici (1510–37), and the Milanese Jacopo da Trezzo succeeded

An Italian ring set with an onyx cameo head of Medusa. The stone is a superb example of the work of 16th-century Roman gem-engravers, and the setting, chased and enamelled with cartouches, masks and foliage, is fully worthy of it.

in engraving the portrait of Philip II of Spain on a diamond for a seal. Another famous gem was the ruby intaglio portrait of Henry VIII given to the King by Cardinal Wolsey and returned to him as a token in 1529. This has vanished, but another, a chalcedony depicting the King facing front wearing fur coat and flat cap, survives (OBR 46B). There is an impression from it on a deed signed in 1576 by Dorothy, wife of John Abington, cofferer to Queen Elizabeth.

Pride in the possession of engraved gems is reflected in the quality of the ring settings devised for them. One of the most remarkable, for a sard head of Lucilla, from the Bessborough/Marlborough collection, had torch-bearing nude figures in relief on the shoulders. C. W. King, who described it in the *Archaeological Journal* in October 1861, considered it worthy of Cellini himself. p. 62

The status symbol *par excellence* was a foiled crystal intaglio with the bearings of the coat of arms both engraved on the stone and depicted in colour on foil beneath. In this way impressions could be taken from the coat without exposing the colours to hot wax. A splendid French example has the achievement of Mary Queen of Scots carved on crystal with the colours on a blue ground below. The massive oval bezel is flanked by flowers and leaves at the shoulders and underneath is a cipher formed of the Greek letters for the names of Mary and her husband François II, surmounted by a crown. p. 71

 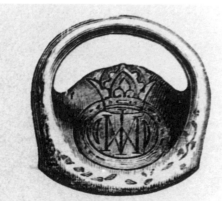 

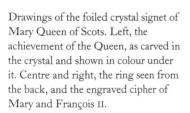

Drawings of the foiled crystal signet of Mary Queen of Scots. Left, the achievement of the Queen, as carved in the crystal and shown in colour under it. Centre and right, the ring seen from the back, and the engraved cipher of Mary and François II.

An interesting group of British provenance is associated with Sir Thomas Gresham, the celebrated Tudor businessman who built the Royal Exchange in London. His badge of the grasshopper is enamelled at the back of each of the five rings which have been identified. They bear the arms of Robert Taylor, Gabriel Goodman, Chaplain to Sir William Cecil (private collection), Jacques Wingfield (sold Christie's, London, 19 December 1977), Sir Richard Lee (O 486), and Sir William Fleetwood (D 319). A recent discovery is the foiled crystal signet of Sir William Feilding, ancestor of the Earls of Denbigh, knighted at the coronation of Anne Boleyn in 1533. p. 58 p. 58

Crests and coats of arms were also engraved on precious stones and on hardstones; Queen Elizabeth possessed a 'ring of Agatt with a seal of the arms of England'. Coral, so much softer, was used for signets too, in which case the entire ring was carved from the material, including figures at the shoulders: this type is represented by a ring bearing the arms of Duke Francesco de' Medici in the Museo degli Argenti, Florence.

Most signets are either of gold or silver, with the device engraved neatly and clearly onto the bezel. These devices are occasionally copies of classical imperial and military heads or composite creatures; but the majority are heraldic, like the Duchess of Somerset's 'little signet of gold with her Grace's own crest a castle therefrom issuant a demilyon crowned and holding in his arms a fireball'.

The mystique of these rings so symbolic of family pride and honour is illustrated by the history of the gold signet engraved with the family arms of the great soldier Stephen Báthory, King of Poland and Prince of Transylvania (d. 1586). He bequeathed it to his namesake, Stephen, whose will of 1603 designates the ring as an heirloom: confessing that he had never worn it himself because he did not deserve to, he in turn left it to his son Gabriel, 'who will pass it on to his heir and eventually someone will be worthy of it'.

p. 67 Signets with merchants' marks follow the pattern of other 16th-century rings, being either plain or embellished with motifs such as scrolls and volutes at the shoulders.

The initial signet used by all classes assumed a new form with two letters, representing the first name and the surname, linked by an elaborately tasselled Bowen knot, with flowers such as forget-me-nots in the field. On its own the single initial usually stood for the first name, as is indicated by the will of Anne Brickys: 'A signett of gold with an A and a raven's head'. The initials might be combined with an inscription from ancient philosophy, as on the signet of Nicholas Fenay of Yorkshire (d. 1617), mentioned in his will:

> having these letters NF for my name thereupon ingraven with this notable poesie about the same letters NOSCE TEIPSUM [*sic*; Know thyself] to the intent that my said son William Fenay in the often beholding and considering of that worthy poesye may be the better put in mynde of himselfe and of his estate knowing this that to know a man's selfe is the beginning of wisdom.

p. 67 Swivel signets with double bezels might combine two devices in one ring, such as a merchant's mark and a *memento mori* or the crests of two families.

LOVE AND MARRIAGE

> I gave my love a ring and made him swear
> Never to part with it.
>
> *The Merchant of Venice*

In 1518 when the infant Mary Tudor, daughter of Henry VIII, was married by proxy to the baby Dauphin of France, Cardinal Wolsey, who was officiating, put a diamond ring on her finger. This contract being annulled, she was again betrothed, at the age of six, in 1522 to her cousin the young Emperor Charles V who sent her a ring with his diamond

initial K surrounded by pearls and inscribed in Latin MARIA OPTIMAMUM PARTEM
ELEGIT QUE NON AUFERETUR AB EA (Mary hath chosen that good part which shall
not be taken from her; Luke 10.42). The symbolism of another diamond ring used at the
marriage of Marguerite of Angoulême to Henry II of Navarre in 1527 was explained by p. 60
Typotius: the round hoop signifying eternity and the diamond bezel signifying glory
represented a king and queen bound together by everlasting love, and twin cornucopias
meeting at the bezel were emblematic of the prosperity ensuing from the happiness of the
royal couple. Although Thomas Randolph told Queen Elizabeth that at the wedding of
Mary Queen of Scots with Lord Darnley at Holyrood in 1565 'the rings ... were three
the middle a rich diamond', it was the latter, in its red enamelled setting, that Queen
Mary regarded as her wedding ring, not the other two. In a will made before the birth of
their son (the future James VI and I) she left it to Darnley, recalling how he had put it on
her finger. Only one ring with such a history has survived: it is the diamond rosette made
for the wedding of Duke Albrecht of Bavaria in 1546. p. 66

Rings with the fede *and other symbols*

> A contract of eternal bond of love
> Confirm'd by mutual joinder of your hands
> Attested by the holy close of lips
> Strengthened by interchangement of your rings:
> And all the ceremony of this compact
> Seal'd in my function, by my testimony.
>
> *Twelfth Night*

Pierre Woeiriot designed two versions of the *fede* ring: in one the hands lie cradled one
within the other, and in the second they are firmly interlocked in a handclasp; both are
flanked by volutes supported by herms. Close to them is a ring in which the clasped
hands emerged from cuffed sleeves above cherub heads (Cologne 242). Further variants
have cuffs and sleeves wrought in relief above strapwork and volutes surmounting p. 62
masks, herms and caryatids. Sometimes there is a heart above the hands, as in a foiled
crystal ring dated 1585 at Grimsthorpe Castle associated with Peregrine Bertie, Lord
Willoughby d'Eresby. The most elaborate are combined with the gimmel ring, the twin
hoops terminating in hands which join together when the ring is closed up.

Hearts, resting on pine cones and flanked by twin Michelangelesque reclining
figures, occur on two rings of *c.* 1550 (Cologne 239, 240), with the Italian posies
SEMPRE W IL COR MIO (My heart W is yours for ever) and PER TUA BELTA (For your
beauty). A similar sculptural ring, with a *fede* at the base of the hoop, illustrates the power
of love with a ruby heart set between the figures of a young woman and a unicorn, tamed
by the spell of her beauty (Rijksmuseum, Amsterdam). Other symbols, usually wrought
in relief, include Cupid's head cameos, a faithful dog, and a wounded stag eating dittany p. 62

to ease the pains of love. The forget-me-not flower is common on German rings, with the letters VMN (*Vergiss mein nicht*); it was also adopted in England with the inscription FMN.

Gimmel rings

p. 63 The gimmel ring becomes more elaborate in the 16th century, with the shoulders strongly emphasized and the petals of the twin quatrefoil bezels chased and enamelled. The stones may contrast – emerald with ruby, garnet with chrysoprase – or match to form a square of solid colour. The hoops sometimes bear the names of the couple concerned, or an admonition such as MEMENTO PRAETERIT ET FUTURI TEMPORIS STET (Remember the past and that there is a future). Others are inscribed with a verse from the Bible asserting the permanence of the marriage vows: WHAT GOD HATH JOINED TOGETHER LET NOT MAN PUT ASUNDER (Matt. 19.6, Mark 10.9). This was the choice of Martin Luther, and also of Sir Thomas Gresham. The Gresham ring contained, hidden in cavities inside the bezel and invisible when closed, the *memento mori* symbols of an infant and a skeleton representing the beginning and the end of life. A p. 106 hundred years later similar rings were still being made.

The gimmel principle was extended to rings comprising more than two hoops. There was one in the Lauingen tomb of the Count Palatine Friedrich with three black and p. 116 white hoops and a *fede* bezel. More complex are 'puzzle rings' which might be composed of up to a dozen hoops, requiring a knack to fit them together into one single ring, with either a *fede* or gem-set bezel. Worn with several hoops dropped off the finger and the rest remaining on it, they served to remind the wearer of one or more things he had to do – hence their alternative name, 'memory rings'. They continued in use for several centuries and are still popular in Turkey.

Jewish rings

The Jewish betrothal ring with steeply sloping gabled roof on a broad gold band is well represented in public collections, although none has a provenance going back to the 16th century. They are individualized, with the type of architecture by no means uniform, some bezels being rectangular, others centralized, and one surviving example representing the canopy under which the couple stood during the ceremony. In some versions the p. 66 roof, imbricated to resemble tiles, is hinged and covers an inner compartment: the inscription MAZZAL TOV (Good luck) may be inside or else within the hoop which is covered with a line of filigree bosses enamelled green, black and blue with projecting rings between. In another design, similar hoops of varying width have the inscription but not the gabled-roof bezel. Although traditionally ascribed to Venice, according to modern research they are closer in style to the enamelled gold filigree work of 16th-century Transylvanian goldsmiths.

Posy rings

The gold hoop with which most women were married – left plain, or decorated with trails of running foliage, raised bosses, strapwork or lozenges – was inscribed with a short verse or posy in either roman capitals or italic script. In 1550 John Bowyer of Lincoln's Inn in London bought his bride, Elizabeth Draper, her wedding clothes and a ring weighing 'two angels and a duckett'. Inside was inscribed DEUS NOS IUNXIT (God joins us together) with their initials, JE BYR, the date of the marriage, 'at the hour of eight, the dominical letter F, the moon being in Leo with due regard to the aspects of the heavens'. (This unusually detailed description was published by W. Hone in *The Everyday Book*, 1826.) Other inscriptions, in French or English, declare affection, promise fidelity and pray for God's blessing. Anne of Cleves's choice for her ill-fated marriage to Henry VIII, GOD SEND ME WELE TO KEPE, alluded to the ring itself, meaning 'God grant that I [the ring] be faithfully preserved'.

Posy rings also commemorated other events besides marriages. Gabriel Goodman, chaplain to Sir William Cecil and Dean of Westminster, friend of Sir Thomas Gresham and owner of a grasshopper ring (and son of Edward Goodman who was painted with a pp. 68–69 *memento mori* ring on his finger), bequeathed numerous rings in his will. One of them marked the end of a family quarrel thanks to the efforts of Dean Goodman's mother Cecily, who succeeded in reconciling him and his brothers, and left each of them a ring inscribed CONCORDIA FRATRUM [Peace between brothers]   CG   4 JAN 1583 – her initials and date of death.

MEMENTO MORI

Memento mori symbols, admonishing the viewer to 'Remember that thou shalt die', met the eye everywhere, on the façades and interiors of houses, in paintings and in jewelry. Shakespeare's Falstaff begs Doll Tearsheet: 'Peace, good Doll, do not speak like a death's head, do not bid me remember mine end.' Most *memento mori* jewels were worn on the finger – as Biron indicates in *Love's Labour's Lost*, when he compares Holofernes to 'death's face in a ring'. They are often listed in wills, such as that of Agnes Hals who in 1554 bequeathed a gold ring with a weeping eye and another 'with a dead mane's head'.

Many people used these devices as seals. The signet of Martin Luther (Grünes Gewölbe, Dresden) bears his initials and the date 1538 cut on crystal over a white skull painted on a red ground. Around the side of the bezel are the inscriptions MORI SAEPE COGITA (Think often of death) and O MORS ERO MORS TUA (O death, I will be thy death), the latter from the antiphon before the first Psalm sung at Lauds on Holy Saturday. Most are engraved on the metal with the skull and sometimes a flowering plant accompanied by such mottoes as NOSSE TE IPSUM (Know thyself [and thou shalt know God]), COGITA (Think!) and MEMENTO MORI. Some were swivels. That used by one English merchant bore his mark on one face, and on the other a death's head encircled by p. 67 the inscription CREDE ET VICISTI (Believe and thou hast conquered); the sides of the bezel are inscribed MEMENTO MORI, and there is strapwork at the massive shoulders. The full-length skeleton offered an alternative to the death's head. An example in the British Museum, London, engraved on an oval gold bezel, holds an hour-glass and arrow and reminds the wearer QUOD FUI ERO QUOD SUM ERIS (What I was you are, what I am you will be).

Another type of *memento mori* ring appears in the portraits of both the Welshman Edward Goodman and the Scot Mark Kerr (SNPG, dated 1551). The flat hexagonal bezel is centred on a white skull, and bears an inscription such as BEHOLD THE EN, NOSSE TE IPSUM or DYE TO LIVE. The more massive examples bear further admonitions such as RATHER DEATH THAN FALSE OF FAITH inscribed round the edges of the bezel. There are also plain hoops without symbols, inscribed only MEMENTO MORI: one silver-gilt ring has a pyramidal bezel supported by a wide hoop of twelve transverse flutes each bearing a letter composing the inscription.

pp. 68–69

The theme is interpreted most dramatically by Pierre Woeiriot, who set a death's head upright on the bezel, supported by two full-length skeletons. This sculptural style is echoed by rings recorded in inventories such as that of John Mabbe (1576), where one was set with a carved ruby cameo skull, its eye sockets filled with diamonds. The most elaborate surviving ring has a locket bezel in the form of a book with toads and snakes crawling round the skull in the centre of the cover (cf. above, p. 24). Inside there is a recumbent figure allegorical of human life, resting on a skull beside an hour-glass, and two Latin inscriptions from the Bible. These translate 'Whether we live unto the Lord and whether we die unto the Lord' (Rom. 14.8) and 'Commit thy way unto the Lord, Trust also in Him and He shall bring it to pass' (Ps. 27.5). The shoulders are modelled in relief with two pairs of figures, the parents of mankind, Adam and Eve, before and after the Expulsion. Since there is a *fede* at the base of the hoop, the ring could have been made for a wedding or betrothal.

p. 69

DEVOTIONAL AND ECCLESIASTICAL RINGS

It was some time before the spirit of the Reformation changed attitudes to devotional jewelry in the Protestant countries of the North. The engagement ring of Martin Luther and Katharina von Bora, for instance, which is dated 13 June 1525, was set with a ruby amidst the Instruments of the Passion and Crucifixion. Many continued to wear rings bearing the Sacred Monogram: the Count Palatine Friedrich was buried with his at Lauingen in 1597.

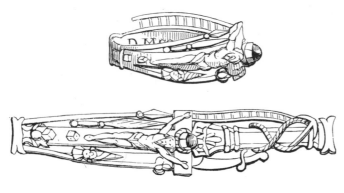

The engagement ring of Martin Luther and Katharina von Bora, as illustrated in the 19th century, when many copies were made. The original ring appears to be lost.

Pope Julius II, with three large rings on each hand, sat for his portrait by Raphael not long before his death in 1513 at the age of seventy.

Symbols – the Pelican in her piety, the head of St John the Baptist – and devotional images such as the Exposition of the Holy Shroud, carved in cameo or intaglio, have survived in ring settings. There are also enamelled reliefs, for instance the Nativity and the Annunciation inside a locket ring with ruby bezel in the Schatzkammer der Residenz, Munich.

'Decade' or 'paternoster' rings, with the Sacred Monogram, cross and nails on the bezel and ten projections round the hoop for saying the rosary, have been found on English sites. Since the use of the rosary was forbidden in England by a statute of 1571, most surviving examples, whether of gold, silver or bronze, are presumably Continental.

The six rings which Pope Julius II wears in his portrait by Raphael are each set with a large stone, for the pope was expected to have many rings, all splendid. The matchless settings made by Caradosso and by Benvenuto Cellini have all vanished and the records of the papal goldsmiths give few details. They do however mention the use of symbolic colours (for Faith, Hope and Charity) and commissions for the official 'Fisherman's Rings' (see above, pp. 19–20). A rare survival bears the name of Pope Gregory XIII, elected in 1573: attributed to Giacomo Anfossi, it is set with a jacinth cameo Cupid's head framed in a border set with pearls and blue, red and black strapwork (Bulgari Collection, Rome).

As in the Middle Ages, the pope gave each new cardinal a ring, identified by the papal arms on the back of the bezel, to mark his appointment at the consistory. The severely magnificent style of the mid-16th-century Roman goldsmiths is illustrated by a ring with table-cut sapphire, shoulders engraved with vine leaves, and at the back the papal tiara and arms of Paul III Farnese (1534–49).

p. 70

The episcopal ring of St Charles Borromeo (d. 1584) in the Treasury of Milan Cathedral is set with a sapphire in a plain pie-dish style bezel. Another, presented by Philip II to the Escorial, had an emerald in a setting of blue, red and white 'cartones y figuras al brutescos' (strapwork and grotesques). In England, in spite of pressure from extreme Protestants who wished to see the abolition of all symbolic ornaments, Matthew Parker, appointed Archbishop of Canterbury by Queen Elizabeth in 1559, maintained the traditional sign of his position and wore a sapphire ring.

MAGICAL AND SCIENTIFIC RINGS

Belief in the lore of the lapidaries listing the medicinal and magical powers of gems and incantations persisted. Philip II of Spain wore a ring set with a stone to prevent haemorrhages, and Sir Christopher Hatton gave Queen Elizabeth a ring 'which hath the virtue to expel infectious airs', and would protect her in time of epidemic. Sir Jerome Horsey, in Moscow in 1584, described how the Tsar, Ivan IV (the Terrible), was carried into his Treasury to look at the gems there and predicted his imminent death: 'I am poisoned with diseases, you see they shewe their virtue by the change of their pure culler and declare my death.'

Faith in the healing powers of gold and silver cramp rings hallowed by the kings of England remained strong too. Writing from Zaragoza in Spain in 1510, Lord Berners asked Cardinal Wolsey: 'If your Grace remember me with some crampe rynges ye shall do a thynge much looked for and I trust to bestow them well with Godd's grace who evermor preserve and encrease your most reverent estate.' In another letter Dr Thomas Magnus told the Cardinal that because of the number of miracles attributed to them there was a huge demand for cramp rings in Scotland. Henry VIII and his eldest children, Edward VI and Mary I, maintained the ceremony before it fell into disuse in Elizabeth's reign. There is a miniature of Mary I (d. 1558) engaged in this regal duty, kneeling before an altar on which stand candles and crucifix, with the rings in basins on either side of her prayer desk. (Westminster Cathedral Collection, London). A great jewelled bust of St George presented to the Chapel at Windsor by Henry VII, confiscated during the Reformation, was melted down by her orders so that the metal could be converted into gold rings to heal her 'gouty subjects'.

Rings which measured time reflected the growing command of the natural sciences. A signet owned by Philip II lifted up to show the hours engraved on a silver rim. Most coveted of all was a miniature watch, exemplified by a design by Pierre Woeiriot, with the round dial set in a bezel supported by rams' heads standing out at the shoulders. Two examples survive, both with royal provenances. The earliest is a fine black enamelled ring with watch inside and hour-striking mechanism, attributed to Jacob Weiss, *c.* 1590 (Schatzkammer der Residenz, Munich). The other is set with a large emerald engraved with the crowned imperial eagle and collar of the Golden Fleece above a tiny watch signed by Johan Butz of Augsburg (Kunsthistorisches Museum, Vienna). It was made for a Habsburg emperor – Rudolph II (d. 1612) or one of his successors, Mathias (d. 1619) or Ferdinand (d. 1637).

Less sophisticated timepieces such as shepherds' dials and armillary spheres which appear in the 16th century were also much used in the 17th century. Other curiosities include a ring with a lodestone or magnet, and a squirt ring with syringe attached to release water when required.

Sir Hugh Plat in *The Jewel House of Art and Nature* (1594) describes perspective rings used by French gamblers which being set with crystal cut and polished

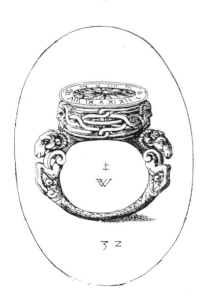

will give a lively representation to the eye of him that weareth it of all such cards as his companions that are next to him do hold in their hands especially if the owner thereof do take the upper end of the table and leaning now and then on his elbow or stretching out his arm do apply his ring aptly for the purpose.

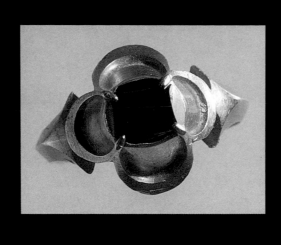

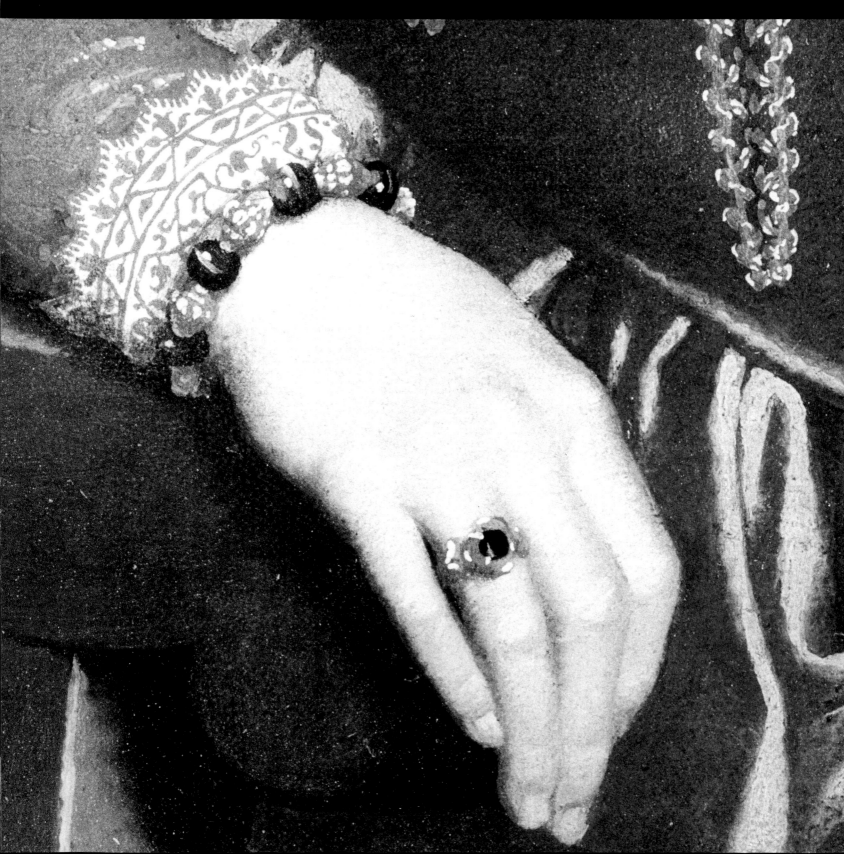

FOILED CRYSTAL SIGNETS

This page:
Signets with coats of arms cut on crystal, protecting the arms depicted in full colour on the foil below, were prized as status symbols (see p. 71). These two belonged to Elizabethan gentlemen: one to Sir William Feilding (*left*), and the other (*above*) to Robert Taylor, who received it as a gift in 1575 from Sir Thomas Gresham, founder of the Royal Exchange in London.

ROYAL DIAMONDS

Opposite page:
The exceptional quality of two surviving diamond rings is reflected in their provenances, for that shown in two views *below* bears the name of Queen Isabella of Hungary, and the one *above* was later given by Charles I of England to Sir Nicholas Kemeys. Both have elaborately scrolled and enamelled settings, and both combine different cuts of the stone: in the bezel, a point-cut is surrounded by four triangular-cut diamonds, and this is flanked by table-cuts at the shoulders.

Petrus Medices filius Magni Ducis Cosimi Hetrurie.

Mathias Hunniades, Rex Hungarie Bohe: Dalm: Crou: Sclau: et Bosnie

SEMPER

DVRAT · ET · LVCET

Joannes Cassimirus Comes Palatinus Rheni. Bauarie. Dux.

CONSTANTER ET SINCERE.

Margaretha Valesia Nauaroru Regina, uxor Henrici II.

SIMVL · ET · SEMPER

NOBLE SOLITAIRES AND MULTIPLE-DIAMOND RINGS

Renaissance rulers adopted the diamond solitaire as a symbol epitomizing the ideals of royalty and nobility. Their devices, or *imprese*, were published by Jacopo Typotius in his *Symbola Divina et Humana* (1603); five examples are shown here. *Top row, left,* the *impresa* of Piero de' Medici, with a ring gripped by a falcon and the motto 'Always'; *centre,* that of Mathias Corvinus, King of Hungary (1458–90), with a ring and a star and the motto 'Enduring and shining'; *right,* that of Cosimo I, Grand Duke of Tuscany (1569–74), with the motto 'I shall overcome' and three rings, representing fortitude, endurance and valour – qualities in which he, like the gem itself, excelled all others; *lower row, left,* that of the Count Palatine John Casimir (1583–92), 'Constant and sincere', with a *fede* motif and his coat of arms; *centre,* the ring used at the marriage in 1527 of Marguerite of Angoulême and Henry II of Navarre, where the diamond between cornucopias is emblematic of the prosperity of the royal couple and the motto means 'Always the same'. (See also pp. 43–44.)

In contrast to these solitaires are rings set with multiple diamonds. Pierre Woeiriot in *Le Livre d'Aneaux d'Orfèvrerie* of 1561 (*lower row, right*) proposes a double pyramidal bezel, cornucopia shoulders and hoop entirely studded with tiny point- and triangular-cuts. *Below left,* four triangular-cut diamonds are clustered together into one important rock-like bezel, flanked by scrolled shoulders and hoop studded with table-cuts. *Below,* five perfectly matched point-cuts are set like a star on a raised bezel.

LOVE AND MEDITATION

Left: This version of the ancient *fede* motif, of hands clasped in love and trust, has them cradled one within the other. The projecting shoulders are like cuffed wrists.

Below: The *fede* was not always on the bezel: here it appears at the base of the hoop of a finely wrought signet. (Compare the device of John Casimir, p. 60.) The bezel is set with an ancient Roman jasper intaglio of a lion with star, zodiacal sign for Leo.

Below left: A ring with a dog, symbol of fidelity, perched on the bezel, perhaps made for a widow to wear, alluding to her faithfulness to the memory of her husband.

Right: Interlocking gimmel rings (from *gemellus*, twin) were used at weddings, where their interdependence symbolized the marriage bond. They also served to conceal private messages. When closed, the one shown here looks like an important chased and enamelled ruby ring with scrolled and emerald-set shoulders; inside, however, is a Latin message that admonishes the wearer to 'Remember the past and that there is a future.'

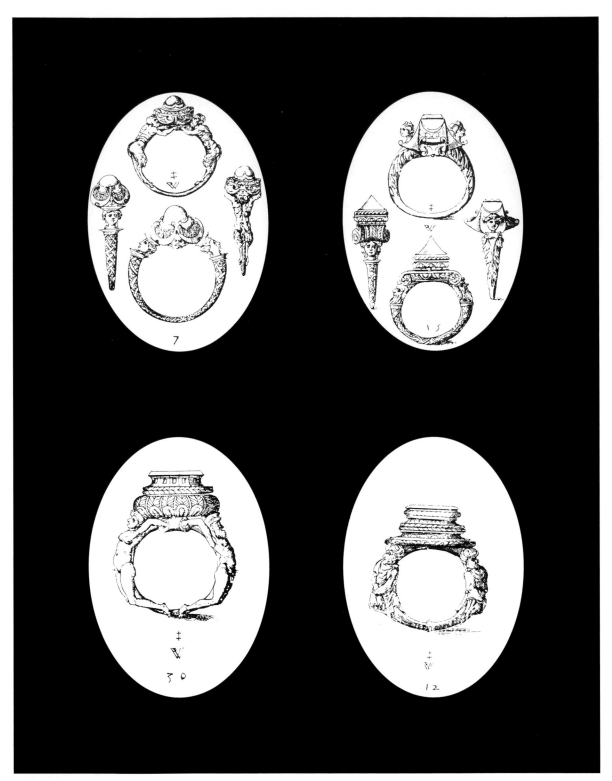

BALANCING THE ELEMENTS

The simpler form of 16-century design, in which the roles of stone and setting are perfectly balanced, appears in the ring at the *left*: the stone is a table-cut sapphire; the setting a square box bezel chased with double arches on a moulded base, with the shoulders emphasized by quatrefoils.

Opposite, above: Some of the most daring designs in Pierre Woeiriot's *Livre d'Aneaux d'Orfèvrerie* (1561) were inspired by the human figure. The bezel may be supported by women's heads, gripped by satyrs, held up by male and female acrobats, or carried by two turbanned Turks. In one unusual design (top right), tiny heads project from the petals of a quatrefoil bezel set with a table-cut gem.

Above: Hunting was the principal pastime of the goldsmiths' royal and noble patrons. The raised bezel of this ring is composed of two stags cradling an uncut emerald in their antlers. It is flanked by ruby-studded shoulders chased with volutes and bosses, and a crystal is set at the base of the hoop. The bright enamels are particularly well preserved at the back of the bezel.

WEDDING RINGS

Left: The wedding ring of Duke Albrecht of Bavaria, made in 1546, is set with sixteen lozenge-cut diamonds radiating outwards from a golden centre, in a cusped bezel supported by a wreathed and beaded hoop. Such diamond rosettes, first created in the late 15th century for the dukes of Burgundy, were prized as triumphs of cutting and setting.

Below left: Two views of a Jewish marriage ring. In contrast to Duke Albrecht's ring, with its huge intrinsic value, this broad hoop was striking at relatively little expense. The band is bordered by corded wire and ornamented with domed bosses alternating with blue flowers. This particular ring, unique among surviving examples, has a bezel in the form of an open canopy, pinned with pearls, supported on four twisted or Salomonic columns; reference is to the canopy under which the couple stood while making their vows. An inscription in Hebrew reads 'Mazzal tov' – Good luck.

IN THE MIDST OF LIFE

Right: An English merchant of the mid-16th century owned this swivel signet, which identified his property in this world and reminded him of the next. Around the sides of the bezel runs the inscription MEMENTO MORI (Remember that thou shalt die). One face of it is engraved with the merchant's mark in a cartouche; the other face has a white death's head framed by the words CREDE ET VICISTI (Believe and thou hast conquered). Similar swivel signets, variously showing initials, an armorial crest, or a merchant's mark, were made on the Continent.

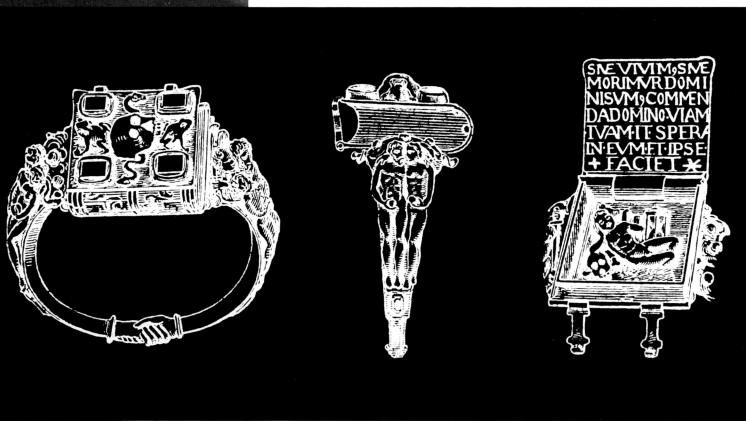

MEMENTO MORI

The Welsh lawyer Edward Goodman was portrayed *c.* 1550 displaying a *memento mori* ring with a white death's head enamelled on its hexagonal bezel. A surviving ring of similar design, though with more prominent shoulders (*far left*), has the inscription BEHOLD THE EN[D] surrounding the skull.

Above: The creation meticulously depicted in these three engravings is the most elaborate of all surviving *memento mori* rings. The book-shaped bezel has on the cover a ruby, sapphire, emerald and diamond framing a white skull surrounded by snakes and toads. Inside there is an infant reclining between a skull and an hour-glass, and on the lid Biblical quotations referring to death (see p. 53). Adam and Eve are represented on the shoulders. The *fede* at the base of the hoop suggests that, despite its macabre iconography, this could have been used for a betrothal or wedding.

ECCLESIASTICS' RINGS

The portrait of Bishop Nicholas à Spina by the Flemish artist Jakob Depunder, dated 1563, shows how the Church's tradition of splendour was interpreted in Northern Europe in the 16th century. Besides his jewelled mitre, ornate crozier and splendid vestments, he has wonderful rings. A secular grandee as well as a prince of the Church, he wears a foiled crystal signet (compare those on p. 58) and two table-cut gems in elaborately chased and enamelled bezels, displayed over tight-fitting embroidered liturgical gloves.

Opposite page:
Three views of a cardinal's ring presented by Pope Paul III (1534–49). It bears enamelled on the back of the bezel the papal tiara and crossed keys and the arms of Farnese; inside the shoulders is the pope's cipher, PIII. The stone is a table-cut sapphire, and the shoulders are engraved with trails of vine-leaves. Presented to a cardinal on his appointment at the consistory, it would have been a reminder of his commitment to the Church and his loyalty to the Papacy. Its sober magnificence illustrates the high standards demanded of a Roman goldsmith by a pope who was also the patron of Michelangelo and Titian.

71

PLEASURE IN DISPLAY

Above: Some wore rings over their gloves to display them; others took up a new fashion for slashed leather gloves, which not only accommodated but showed off the owner's rings. Lucas Cranach's portrait records the hands of a wealthy German lady around 1530; in Elizabethan England, similarly, a satirist noted that a man 'must cut his glove to show his pride, that his trim jewel might be better spy'd'.

Right: Mary Tudor, too, liked to see her fingers laden with rings (detail of a portrait by Anthonis Mor). Despite her austere appearance, the Venetian Ambassador to London reported that 'she seems to delight above all in arraying herself elegantly and magnificently . . . she makes great use of jewels and although she has plenty of them left by her predecessors yet were she better supplied with money than she is she would doubtless buy many more.'

3

The 17th century:
Baroque sobriety and splendour

By 1600 the great age of the goldsmith was over and his place had been taken by the stone setter. Pyramidal and box p. 98 bezels supported by eagles' claws and shoulders enamelled with *Schwarzornament* – flat patterns reserved in black enamel – lead the way to further simplification. In the next phase, the shoulders, if not cusped, are engraved with trails of leaves or embellished with small gems in raised collets. Characteristic of late 17th-century setting are indented and pp. 102, 107 saw-tooth collets. From the 1660s diamonds tend to be set in silver rather than gold, to avoid yellow reflections. Enamel – thick black, white and blue – highlighted with spots p. 99 of translucent colour is applied to the hoop, shoulders, sides and back of the bezel. Paris p. 92 was the creative centre, and designs for rings are included in the jewelry pattern books regularly published there. On a visit to Versailles in 1678 a French noblewoman married to the Roman Prince Orsini was obliged to have his family jewels reset, for although much admired in Italy they seemed absurdly old-fashioned to French eyes. On her return home these new settings were copied and Roman inventories from the late 1670s and 1680s mention jewels 'set in the French style'.

pp. 90–91 Many rings might be worn at once, and not only on the fingers but, as sometimes in the 16th century, on a string round the neck or cuffs. The fashion depicted in portraits by p. 89 which a ring was tied to a black string wound round the wrists and fingers may have evolved to prevent rings too large for the finger from falling off. Lady Northampton described how pleased her husband was to receive a ring from her mother: 'if it had been worth 1,000 guilders it could not have been more welcome to his Lordship and he hung it on the neckstring of his ruff and said "Look, your dear mother has sent me a love token".'

Designs for hoops in *Schwarzornament* with symmetrical strapwork and trails of peapod-style plants, 1619.

DECORATIVE GEM-SET RINGS
Diamond

Thanks to the enterprise of merchants such as the Englishman Sir Paul Pindar and the Frenchman Jean-Baptiste Tavernier, the supply of diamonds from India increased. Then in 1664 the English East India Company, who had maintained the monopoly for years, at last permitted outsiders to trade in precious stones. Members of the Portuguese–Jewish colony based in London took advantage of this opportunity and as a result of their gemmological and financial skills the City became the centre of the international market in uncut diamonds, which were forwarded to Amsterdam for faceting and polishing.

This coincided with rapid developments in all fields of science leading to the discovery of the laws of refraction and the introduction of analytical geometry, which resulted in great improvements in faceting. In the second half of the century the rose-cut, which had appeared late in the Renaissance period, was joined by the brilliant-cut. Robert de Berqhen, in *Les Merveilles des Indes Orientales* (1669), describes the dazzling effects now possible for a diamond, 'when worn on the finger and the sun shines, emitting as many rays of light as there are facets, each a different colour, like a fire opal, eclipsing all other precious stones'. The ways in which a stone could be shown off to advantage repeat 16th-century practice, black enamel being recommended as best for diamonds, and with very p. 98 few exceptions foiling, to disguise flaws and for additional brilliance.

A very fine stone such as the 'diamond cut with fawcettes [i.e., rose-cut] set in an open claw ring' which Anne of Denmark, wife of James VI of Scotland and I of England, bought from George Heriot in London was transparent set. Other solitaires in her collection were mounted in black box bezels; one is described as a 'Daissie ring set with a table diamond'.

Representative of the extravagant Versailles taste of the second half of the century is the collection which Princess Marie-Louise d'Orléans took to Madrid in 1681 as the bride of Charles II. For her state entry she wore on her finger 'the large diamond of the king's which is pretended to be the fairest in Europe'. Other solitaires – one of them a fancy coloured greenish-yellow diamond – were mounted in oval, hexagonal and octagonal silver bezels. The Duke of Marlborough also owned large diamond rings, given him by the Emperor of Austria and the King of Poland as a reward for his victories over the armies of Louis XIV.

The majority of diamond rings were not solitaires but vehicles for the display of small stones grouped into decorative patterns. Those supplied by George Heriot to Anne of pp. 94–96 Denmark in the decades before her death in 1618 include 'a frog all set with diamonds', a diamond leaf ring, a pansy – with a diamond in each of the five petals – and a 'ring sett all over with diamonds in the fashion of a lizard', as well as more formal fleur-de-lis, St Andrew's and Jerusalem crosses, and rosettes set with five, seven or eleven stones. Similar designs are recorded in later inventories too, for instance in those of Giovanni Giorgio Aldobrandini (1637) and his son-in-law, Prince Camillo Pamphilj (1653) – both in the

Doria–Pamphilj archives. In Rome the apprentice jeweller was required to make a ring 'alla Veneziana a rosette' as his 'prova' or trial-piece before admission to the guild.

p. 95
The 1689 inventory of Marie-Louise d'Orléans gives details of rosette and cluster rings, set with as many as twenty-four small diamonds, all foiled, mixing different cuts and mostly in silver collets. The table-cut was by no means obsolete, as is demonstrated by an exceptionally fine surviving ring with bezel paved with fifteen such stones, the sides and back enamelled black and white. All the rings illustrated in the ledgers of Sir Francis Child and still preserved at his bank in London, however, are set with rose-cut stones. The most popular designs are each set with seven diamonds – one version with three large and four small sparks between, another with a large central stone flanked by twin groups of three.

Coloured stones, pearls, and substitutes

pp. 90–91
The Cheapside Hoard, displayed in the Museum of London, shows the full range of gemstones available on the London market by the mid-century. It consists of a jeweller's stock hidden during the Commonwealth period (1649–60) and unearthed in 1912 during demolition work near St Paul's Cathedral; Cheapside was for centuries the centre of the local jewelry trade. The Hoard contains Colombian emeralds, topazes and Amazon stones from Brazil, chrysoberyls, spinels and iolites from Ceylon, Indian rubies, lapis lazuli from Afghanistan, turquoises from Persia, peridots from St John's Island in the Red Sea, and amethysts, garnets and opals from Bohemia and Hungary. The large stones are set in box bezels, the smaller in rosettes or aligned in rows, half-hoop style, in gold settings thick with white enamel tricked out with spots of colour.

 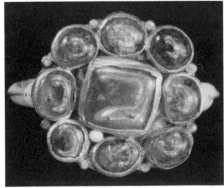

Two cluster rings from the Cheapside Hoard, set with faceted garnets (*far left*) and uncut emeralds (*left*). Both have white enamel on the hoop and the back of the bezel.

The ruby, according to Robert de Berqhen, was considered the most beautiful of all stones, and priced higher than the diamond. The colour was enhanced by the contrast with diamonds, set as borders or at the shoulders. This style, so often listed in the inventories of Marie-Louise d'Orléans and of her father, the Duc d'Orléans (d. 1701), was also the choice of William of Orange as a gift to his wife, the future Mary II of England, in 1677, three days after their marriage: that ruby is set in an octagonal bezel, flanked by diamonds at the shoulders, all in indented collets, the arcaded sides filled with black enamel (Portland Collection, Welbeck Abbey). The diamonds – rose-, table- or brilliant-cut – in such designs range in number from two to six according to size. Smaller rubies are set in rosette or cruciform patterns, centred on either a diamond or an opal; more colour may be introduced by turquoises between the rubies. Rubies also appear in seven-stone clusters similar to the design used for diamonds. p.98

Sapphires are used in a similar way, and again combined with diamonds. There were two in the inventory of the Duc d'Orléans: 'une autre bague d'un saphir d'Orient violet très beau avec deux diamants brilliants a costé' (a ring set with a fine violet Oriental sapphire between two brilliants) and 'une autre bague d'un petit saphir et 16 tous petits diamans autour' (another with a small sapphire set round with sixteen small diamonds).

Emeralds, Robert de Berqhen noticed, were usually small. Some of the best surviving examples have been salvaged over the past few years from the wrecks of Spanish galleons. Earliest is a ring with high box bezel resting on a moulded black base from the *Nuestra Señora de Atocha*, sunk off the Florida coast in 1622. Two others, from the *Nuestra Señora de las Maravillas*, wrecked in 1655, are designed as a nail-pierced horseshoe or circle, and p.99 as a rosette. Corresponding to the Louis XIV style illustrated in the *Livre des Ouvrages d'Orfèvrerie fait par Gilles L'Egaré, Orfèvre du Roi* (1663) is a ring set with a rectangular- p.92 cut emerald, the arcaded sides filled with pink, white and black ornament, and green pp.93, 99 acanthus scrollwork on the shoulders. In another of the same date the hoop is wrought into twin cornucopias, with flowers at the shoulders. Diamonds were incorporated into p.99 the 'bague d'esmeraude avec six diamants' in the 1663 inventory of Béatrix de Cusance, Duchess of Lorraine, and small table diamonds, all in indented gold collets, frame an oblong emerald in a ring with royal cipher on the back given by James II of England to his chaplain (B 32c).

In *A Lapidary or History of Precious Stones* (1659) the Cambridge don Thomas Nicols claimed that the turquoise was not only a delight to the eye but strengthened the sight and

A cluster made up of nineteen pearls threaded on wires. The ring was acquired by a 19th-century English collector in Milan.

reconciled man and wife. Most turquoise rings are combined with diamonds, set round the hoop, at the shoulders or bordering the bezel. A diamond lozenge-shaped ring set round with small diamonds and turquoises was the most expensive in Béatrix de Cusance's collection. The Duc d'Orléans owned one set with a 'turquoise de la vieille roche' – i.e., of the best quality – surrounded by eighteen diamonds.

A cluster consisting of a central table-cut diamond encircled by four rubies and four turquoises, within an outer ring of turquoises. This was acquired by the same collector at Lausanne in Switzerland.

Robert de Berqhen enthused over the amethyst which prevented drunkenness, and Thomas Nicols estimated that the very best stones could cost the same as diamonds of the same weight. The 1653 inventory of Prince Camillo Pamphilj includes 'un anello smaltato di nero, con un rosa di 9 amatisti' (a ring enamelled black set with nine amethysts in a rosette) and a solitaire, 'un anello smaltato di bianco turchino et nero con amatista' (an amethyst ring enamelled white, black and turquoise). The rich velvety colour, which de Berqhen compared to that of a violet, a pansy or a columbine, was much enhanced by diamonds: Marie-Louise d'Orléans possessed a ring consisting of a central amethyst set with fifteen small diamonds in enamelled gold.

Cornelian, lapis lazuli, catseye and opal were set in these styles too, epitomized by the carbuncle listed in the 1679 inventory of the Duchess of Savoy: 'Un scarbonchio in anello d'oro ligato a griffe di 2 carrati circa attorniato dett'anello di 14 piccoli diamante a facette' (a two-carat carbuncle claw-set in a gold ring set round with fourteen little rose-cut diamonds).

Pearls were set in rings for the finger as well as worn in the ears and at the neck and wrists. In surviving rings a large baroque specimen is mounted in a substantial gold bezel supported by a baluster hoop, while smaller pearls, secured by claws, are set in concentric rows in round bezels, forming multiple clusters. Pearls may also be combined with diamonds.

Substitutes continued to be devised: crystal was point-, rose- and table-cut in imitation of diamonds for setting in rings, and there were also good imitations of coloured stones.

Monsieur d'Arre in his premises near the Temple at Paris was so successful at counterfeiting 'les diamants, esmeraudes, topazes et rubis' that by 1657 he had made a fortune. Then in 1699 H. Blancourt in *The Art of Glass* published his formula for making imitations of natural gems to be set in rings. He claimed that once worked, polished, foiled and set by a good goldsmith his imitations of emerald, garnet, ruby, turquoise, chrysolite and sapphire 'can scarce be distinguished from fine ones except by a very nice discerner'.

LOCKET RINGS

Locket rings with hinged bezels opening up to reveal cavities, with or without figures, were made by George Heriot for Anne of Denmark. There was one with a frog bezel, another shaped as a scallop shell, and third set with five diamonds 'opening on the head with the king's picture in that'. A diamond signet engraved with the double-headed eagle of the imperial Habsburg house associated with Rudolph II (see below) is also hinged and contains a small compartment. Whereas there are several surviving examples containing skeletons, skulls and other symbols of mortality, non-*memento mori* themes are much rarer. A ring with 'figurines' inside is recorded in the 1653 Pamphilj inventory; it was perhaps similar to a surviving example where a gardener holding a flower and a piece of rope is hidden inside a diamond cluster bezel. pp. 110–11

SIGNETS AND PORTRAITS

Signet rings become rarer in the 17th century, since many now preferred seals in ornamental mounts worn on a chain close to the watch. Those that have survived are engraved with coats of arms, crests and initials or with classical themes.

Sovereigns with a taste for luxury commissioned diamond signets. Rudolph II owned one with the imperial double-headed eagle in a hinged square box bezel with hoop and sides enamelled in *Schwarzornament* (Kunsthistorisches Museum, Vienna). Three others were made for James I, his son the future Charles I, and Charles's queen Henrietta Maria. James's ring has vanished, but the other two survive in their original enamelled settings. p. 104

Francis I, Duke of West Pomerania and Szczecin (1577–1620), was buried with his signet consisting of an octagonal ruby bearing his arms; his name is inscribed within the hoop (National Museum, Szczecin). As hard to engrave as the ruby was the sapphire. One was used by Mary II, set in a heavy gold mount, the shoulders enamelled with dynastic Tudor roses on long stems. The seal of her father, James II, is an octagonal topaz engraved with the royal arms and motto DIEU ET MON DROIT; at the back of the scrolled green, blue and white setting is his cipher JR (D 651). Others whose arms were engraved on less expensive hardstones include the diarist John Evelyn, who when robbed by highwaymen in 1652 'begged for my onyx and told them it being engraved with my arms would betray them'. p. 104

Of the rings with arms, crests and initials engraved on a metal rather than a hardstone bezel the most remarkable survival is the steel and gold signet of Charles II. The Stuart p. 105

royal arms are on the oval bezel and the royal motto is inscribed on cartouches round the sides; there are steel heraldic supporters – a lion and a unicorn – at the shoulders, and the hoop is in the peculiarly fleshy 'auricular' style of ornament associated with the Flemish silversmith Adam van Vianen (1570–1627).

Non-armorial intaglios vary in quality. among the finest is a superb sapphire Medusa head cut by an Imperial Roman artist of the 1st century AD, set *c.* 1620 in a ring of fine proportions enamelled with *Schwarzornament* (O 306). Of the same date is a swivel ring p. 100 with two intaglios, one on each face, mounted in a medallion engraved and enamelled on the sides with hunting scenes, and with green, white and blue flowers on the black hoop and shoulders. Made for a man who combined sporting interests with classical tastes, it is probably South German. P. J. Mariette in his *Traité des Pierres Gravées* (1750) attributed the outstanding quality of these 17th-century enamelled settings to the value their owners placed on the gems themselves, suggesting that the collectors of those days were 'plus sincèrement curieux' (truer connoisseurs). Much more modest are two rings from the Cheapside Hoard set with ancient paste intaglios: these were made for the middle market *c.* 1650. At the end of the century gems are mounted in indented collets, sometimes flanked by diamonds (e.g., D 659).

A rare group of signets represent portraits of rulers. Two bloodstone intaglio busts of Louis XIII and of his mother Marie de Médicis are mounted in substantial gold rings p. 97 enamelled with trails of lilac-coloured plants, dating from shortly after his accession in 1610, and portraits of James II, on a topaz and on an emerald, were also set in rings (Harari Collection 154).

A few cameo portraits were commissioned for setting in rings. A black jasper bust of Charles I remains in the original setting of *c.* 1640, the back enamelled with a formalized flower (D. 1368). The veiled profile of Madame de Maintenon, carved on a ruby, appears in a ring with fleurs-de-lis below the pierced shoulders which point the way to 18th-century designs. The Cheapside Hoard includes two cameos, a chalcedony toad and an opal St George, set in bezels shaped to follow the contours of the stones and with arcaded sides filled with enamel.

A ruby cameo of Madame de Maintenon, mounted in an enamelled setting. Louis XIV had married her in 1684.

LOVE AND MARRIAGE

During the Commonwealth in England after 1649 the Puritans, who detested the bishops and the ritual laid down in the Prayer Book, tried to have the wedding ring abolished, but so strong was the feeling for it that they failed to carry public opinion with them. In 1655 the Anglican cleric Jeremy Taylor summed up its appeal: 'the Marriage ring ties two hearts by an eternal band: it is like the Cherubim's flaming sword, set for the guard of Paradise.' The wedding ring was a woman's most treasured possession: Sir John Bramston described how his stepmother lost hers riding over the sands by the sea and refused to advance any further until she had found it again, 'it being the most unfortunate thing that could befall anyone to lose the wedding ring'. Treasured as they were, these rings passed from mother to daughter or to daughter-in-law. Lady Fanshawe's wedding to the diplomat Sir Richard Fanshawe took place 'in the presence of my father who by my mother's grace gave me her wedding ring with which I was married'.

A ring with a gem was still the choice of those with money. Christian, Countess of Devonshire, was married in 1608 with a diamond in a black enamel – presumably *Schwarzornament* – setting. In 1660 Samuel Pepys commented on his aunt, 'mighty proud she is of her wedding ring being lately set with diamonds'. When in 1673 Mary of Modena was married by proxy to the future James II, a diamond ring was put on her finger by the Earl of Peterborough. (She kept it and forty-six years later her son James, pretender to the throne of England, married Clementina Sobieska at Montefiascone with the very same ring.) When Mary arrived in England there was a second ceremony and this time the ring was a gold chain studded with five faceted rubies, like a miniature p. 102 bracelet. This she always considered the real 'pledge' between herself and her husband. After her death her son gave it to the Convent of the Visitation at Chaillot outside Paris, near the home she made in exile after 1688, and eventually it was acquired by the Duke of Norfolk.

Without a provenance, it is impossible to know that a gem-set ring was used for a wedding unless it is also inscribed. Thus only the posy LOVE FOR LOVE on the back of the bezel of a gold ring set with seven diamonds in a double trefoil indicates that it played a role in courtship and marriage as well as serving a decorative purpose (O 671). In Denmark, Charlotte-Amélie, Countess of Aldenburg, described how Monsieur von Guldenlowe came to a masquerade disguised as a French peasant and presented her with a ring set with a large diamond, bearing his name on the back, to mark their engagement. She immediately showed it to the Queen, who gave her another to give her future bridegroom in return.

For the majority the wedding ring was a broad gold band, plain, or with the outside pearled, garlanded with roses, imbricated, chequered, or patterned with lozenges or stars in relief, and bright with enamels. Alternatively, there were hoops of jet or tortoiseshell lined with silver. Inscribed within was a posy chosen from published collections such as *The Mysteries of Love or the Arts of Wooing* (1658) or composed specially for the couple concerned. Much thought was given to them, and on 3 February 1660 the family of the diarist Samuel Pepys spent several hours collaborating on a suitable posy for Roger Pepys's marriage while their lamb was roasting. The posies, which usually ask God's blessing or promise fidelity, were sometimes combined with symbols such as clasped hands, hearts, lovers' knots, and a death's head, a reminder of the vow to KEPE FAYTH TILL DETHE.

The passion of the time for heraldry is reflected in a hoop ring without a posy commemorating the marriage of Elizabeth Chibnall and Sir Antony Haselwood, which is enamelled on the outside with the letters EC and AH separated by four hearts. Inside, the shields of the arms of the two families and those of the mothers of the bride and groom are enamelled on the white ground (OBR 60A). In another version there is a shield flanked by the letters A and G on the outside and the posy WEE JOYNE OUR HEARTS IN GOD PRL (D 1317).

p. 107

The heart, pierced by arrows, clasped in two hands, crowned and amidst forget-me-nots, is the centrepiece of a very broad hoop all enamelled and studded with gems in plain box collets, inscribed within in Dutch WAT GODT THO SAMENDE FOEGET SCHAL NEEN MEN SCHE SCHEIDEN 1610 (What God hath joined together ...). Another of similar design exists, with no inscription inside (British Museum, London, Waddesdon

p. 107

Bequest 8). Hearts were a popular subject for rings. Heart-shaped diamonds, rubies, emeralds and turquoises appear on their own, crowned, winged, aflame, pierced by arrows, encircled by snakes emblematic of eternity, or held by hands. The inventory of Marie de Médicis mentions several such rings: 'deux autres diamens en cueur, taillez a facettes, esmaillez de noir, donnez par le Roy et gaignez au jeu' (two rose-cut heart-shaped diamonds in gold enamelled black, gifts from the King won at cards), 'ung rubis cabochon en forme de cueur dont l'anneau est esmaillé de noir' (an uncut heart-shaped ruby in a black enamelled ring), and 'deux petites bagues en façon de serpens couverte de force petit diamens' (two little snake rings paved with tiny diamonds). In Rome, the Aldobrandini inventory of 1637 includes 'un anello con un Core di Diamanti a faccetta' (a rose-cut heart-shaped diamond ring). King Gustavus Adolphus of Sweden (1594–1632) gave his beloved Ebba Brahe a ruby heart ring mounted obliquely amidst diamonds, not of the best quality. Thereafter the engagement rings of the countesses Brahe were always of this type.

The motif of the *fede*, or two hands clasped together in mutual consent to an agreed contract, continued in use. As in the 16th century the rings may be enamelled and inscribed inside the hoop with a posy, such as LET VERTUE BE THY GUIDE. The motif itself, instead of being wrought from gold, is sometimes carved from hardstone. There were 'deux bagues de foy de rubis entournez chacune de petitz rubis non esmaillé' (two ruby cameo *fede* rings each set round with small rubies, no enamel) in the collection of Marie de Médicis, and another in the Aldobrandini inventory of 1637 was supported by a diamond-studded hoop. A surviving ring of the same date which has a Roman provenance has an emerald cameo *fede* bordered with rubies (D 2032). The *fede* may also be combined with hearts and with another traditional type, the gimmel. Gimmel rings are inscribed inside the hoops with the names of the couple, their initials, and the Biblical QUOD DEUS CONIUNVIT HOMO NON SEPARET (What God hath joined together . . .). This inscription is found again on a ring of conservative design dated 1631 that recalls Sir Thomas Gresham's wedding ring (above, p. 51), made some ninety years earlier: it combines the motifs of hearts and hands with the *memento mori* symbols of a skeleton and an infant hidden within cavities under the double bezel, which is set with a ruby and a diamond. p. 106

The popularity of the blackamoor motif in the 1690s is mirrored in two gimmel type rings of Mediterranean origin. The triple hoops of one bear an esoteric inscription in Spanish, MENDRE CANPO TESAVO SI SCIAVO MEAI GATENATO P.C. (private collection, Barcelona); on the twin hoops of the other we read, TAL QUAL MI MIRI IO FUI SEMPRE PER TE (As you see me, so I have always been for you). These inscriptions look forward to the more lighthearted love rings of the next period. p. 112

Jewish rings
According to De Gaya's *Cérémonies Nuptiales de Toutes les Nations*, published in Paris in 1681, the Jewish custom was still for the bridegroom to hand the rabbi a gold ring without a gem which witnesses then had to verify was of the required standard. (Glückel of Hamburg remembered in her Memoirs, 'my husband wedded me with a costly ring weighing an ounce of gold'.) Then having placed it on the bride's second finger the rabbi proceeded to read out the marriage contract. Some rings take the architectural form that we saw in the 16th century, above a broad filigree band inscribed with good wishes in Hebrew (Jewish Museum, London). There are also Jewish versions of the posy ring: one, with a plain band, has a Hebrew inscription translating 'Good luck Joshua and Judith Tsarfathi: May their Rock and their Redeemer guard them' (D 1330). p. 66

MEMENTO MORI AND MEMORIAL RINGS
Memento mori emblems and inscriptions maintained their hold, particularly in Germany, devastated by the Thirty Years War, and in England during the great plague of 1665. Jeremy Taylor advised Christians to be ready for death:

> It is a great art to die well and to be learnt by men in health: he that prepares not for death before his last sickness is like him that begins to study philosophy when he is going to dispute publicly in the faculty. Learning duties requires study and skill, time and understanding in the way of godliness. Place your coffin in your own eye: dig your own grave.

It was in this mood that John Evelyn had his portrait by Robert Walker show him holding a copy of Seneca's *De Brevitate Vitae* beside a skull, and that so many jewels bore *memento mori* devices. Thus, Gilles Légaré's designs for rings of 1663 incorporate skulls, crossbones, skeletons, winged hour-glasses, and the gravedigger's pick and spade. He p. 92

p. 92 sets a stone above four skulls – two wreathed with laurel, two with bats' wings – supported on a hoop on which the funerary tools are wrought in relief.

p. 109 Most rings display the skull only, engraved on the back or front of the bezel or else wrought in relief, enamelled white and embellished with rose-cut diamonds in the eye sockets and jaw. Some skulls rest on crossbones or snakes – the creeping things of Ecclesiastes – and there are locket types inscribed MEMENTO MORI within. In spite of their stern purpose they were by no means austere. There was an emerald cameo death's head with diamonds studding the eyes and shoulders in the collection of Marie-Louise d'Orléans, and others were carved from amethyst and agate. Double-faced skulls – one showing a golden-haired woman in the full vigour of life and beauty, the other ghastly in death – reminded the wearer of the *vanitas* passage in Ecclesiastes, that beauty ends in decay and putrefaction. The skull is not invariably placed on the bezel: in some versions it is depicted resting on crossbones on the shoulders, flanking a gem-set bezel. In one dramatic design two skeletons grasp a coffin-shaped bezel which opens to reveal another skeleton inside (D 1453).

Signets are engraved with *memento mori* devices. That of the evangelist John Bunyan (1628–88), found on the site of Bedford jail, bore a skull, his initials and the words MEMENTO MORI (cf. D 821). Another type shows a skeleton holding a dart and an hour-glass with two flowers in the field (D 823).

From the mid-century *memento mori* rings were given a more personal stamp by the
p. 103 addition of names (usually in the form of initials), dates, and even coats of arms, transforming them from exhortations to virtuous living into memorials of individuals. Some were distributed at funerals, others bequeathed in wills. The type is recorded in the Pamphilj inventory of 1653: 'un ricordo smaltato di nero con tre diamantini' (a memorial ring enamelled black set with three small diamonds); and 'one black mourning ring' appears in the 1685 will of Elizabeth Page, a London spinster. Like medieval reliquaries, some contained curls of the person commemorated. Thus after the death of his daughter Anna Maria at the age of four, Ralph Verney promised his brother Henry: 'you shall herewithal receive a ring filled with my deare girl's hair – she was fond of you therefore I send this to keep for her sake.' The hair might be enclosed in a hollow hoop, as in a ring inscribed SAMUEL NICOLETS OBIJT 17 JULY 1661 CHRIST IS MY PORTION and enamelled with two skulls and two shields of arms (OBR 94A). More usually, the hair is placed in an oval, round or octagonal bezel with indented edges over a piece of corded silk with the cipher of the deceased worked in gold wire and covered with a slab of faceted rock crystal. The designs were not uniform; Rear Admiral Sir John Chicheley (d. 1691) instructed his executor to 'give to Lord George a mourning ring according to the new fashion with my hair and cypher and two small diamonds on each side somewhat better than ordinary'. Coffin-shaped bezels were adopted for this purpose by the end of the century, some with white skeletons which could be seen under the glass cover, and with the name of the deceased inscribed within the hoop. A type associated with royalty was bequeathed in the will of the Countess of Aldenburg (d. 1695): 'la bague de cheveux de la

feue Reine de Dannemark ou il y a un diamant en coeur et trois plus petits avec le nom de Sa Majesté' (a heart-shaped diamond with three smaller set in a ring with the hair of the late Queen of Denmark and inscribed with her name). It might of course have been a ring given as a keepsake during the Queen's lifetime.

Portrait rings of Gustavus Adolphus, with his bust carved from hardstone as a cameo (Bayerisches Nationalmuseum, Munich), in relief like a miniature medallion (D 1388), and enamelled under crystal (O 785) were worn in his memory by the German Protestants on whose behalf he fought and died at the battle of Lutzen. Similarly, after the execution of Charles I in 1649 the English Royalists wore rings with his painted or enamelled miniature set under glass in oval or heart-shaped bezels with his cipher, the date of his death and symbols of mortality on the back. The most individual surviving example is set with a cornelian intaglio portrait, which swivels round to another cornelian p. 102 engraved with symbols of sovereignty, the bezel with indented sides above black arcading and the openwork hoop studded with rose-cut diamonds. During their lifetime all the descendants of Charles I – his sons Charles II and James II, and his granddaughters Mary II and Queen Anne and the former's husband, William III – gave portrait rings to supporters of their particular cause, and these might be converted to memorial rings with the addition of appropriate inscriptions, dates and symbols. The hardstone intaglios and cameos which were so demanding of time and skill were always very rare, but miniatures, whether painted or enamelled, were more easily commissioned. A mid-century French swivel ring is set with miniatures of Anne of Austria (the Queen Mother) and her son, the young Louis XIV.

A miniature of Louis XIV as a child, set in a swivel ring. On the other side is a portrait of his mother, Anne of Austria. He succeeded to the throne in 1643, at the age of five; she acted as regent until 1654. The hoop is enamelled with coloured flowers on a white ground.

ENAMELLED HOOPS

There were six enamelled hoop rings in the collection of Anne of Denmark, and two others in the 1652 inventory of the Earl of Eglinton. They are echoed by the 'Due cerchietti uno smaltato di torchino l'altro di verde' (two enamelled hoops, turquoise blue and green) in the Pamphilj inventory of 1653. Developments in the techniques of enamelling made it possible to use a wide hoop both inside and outside as a canvas to illustrate scenes from the Bible and from contemporary life. Abraham and the angels, Hagar and Ishmael, the sacrifice of Isaac, and Lot and his daughters appear enamelled on a white ground in a continuous frieze on the broad hoop of a ring which gives no indication of place of origin. Another, which shows groups of merchants in contemporary dress beneath arcades, is inscribed in English RL TO T and T TO KL, confirming that whether or not such rings were manufactured in Britain they were worn there (OBR 94C).

pp. 100–101

DEVOTIONAL AND ECCLESIASTICAL RINGS

p. 108

Some religious images, such as the Crucifixion and the Virgin and Child, were painted on the bezels and covered by glass and framed in garnets or other stones. Marie-Louise d'Orléans owned a ring which was like a locket, the hinged lid set with diamonds in the form of a rose, and inside a miniature of the Virgin of the Immaculate Conception. There were cameos of Christ: the Roman goldsmith Domenico Ostili made 'un anello con un Cristo' (a ring with a figure of Christ) as his 'prova' to pass into the guild in 1665. A coral ring carved with the figures of the founders of the Church, Peter and Paul, on the shoulders bears the portrait of the reigning pope, Urban VIII (1623–44), on the bezel. More usually the pontiff distributed rings with a medallic portrait under glass; that bearing the head of Innocent XI (1676–89) in a round silver-gilt bezel is studded with garnets at the shoulders (O 788).

pp. 102–3

The letters IHS of the Sacred Monogram, enclosed in a heart with the three nails of the Crucifixion below, appear in relief on rosary and other devotional rings, including signets. These signets with religious imagery were not exclusive to Roman Catholics: the poet John Donne (d. 1631), Dean of St Paul's in London, left rings set with heliotrope intaglios of Christ crucified on an anchor-style cross for his friends to wear in his memory. Crosses were formed of gems as well as engraved and enamelled for rings. Special to Spain was the dark chiastolith, or cross-stone, quarried near Santiago de Compostella, which was set in rings: one such was recovered from the wreck of the *Nuestra Señora de Esperanza* which sank off the Cuban coast in 1658. Spanish devotion was also demonstrated by rebus rings with the letter S pierced by a nail (*clavo*), composing the word *esclavo*; richly studded with emeralds, these were worn by the 'slaves' or members of religious confraternities.

The day of the reliquary ring had by no means passed. In 1672 the Duc d'Orléans was allowed to remove a fragment from the relic of the True Cross preserved in the Sainte Chapelle in Paris: it was set in a diamond ring, recorded in his inventory of 1701.

Religious sentiment in Protestant England was chiefly expressed through posies inscribed on rings rather than by devotional imagery. The 1642 will of the Dowager Countess of Devonshire records bequests to her sons of diamond rings, each inscribed FEARE GOD, which she recommended as the best guiding principle for living. Other posies affirm a strong faith: FRIENDS FAIL BUT GOD NEVER, and AS GOD HAS PRESERVED ME SO I TRUST HE WILL REWARD ME.

The higher clergy took great pride in the robes and insignia of office. When the French Court went into mourning in 1674 on the death of Anne of Austria, Madame de Sévigné observed in a letter to Bussy Rabutin that the cardinals were as resplendent as ever. Licetus quotes the will of Cardinal Francesco Guido, who exhorts his heirs never to part with his cardinalitial ring nor 'the fine diamond ring with facets the loved present of her Most Serene Majesty Mary de Medicis the Queen of France and which I leave for the ecclesiastics of my family to inculcate them to virtue'. The large sapphire ring on the finger of the Archbishop of Naples, Cardinal Ascanio Filomarino, in his portrait by p. 108 Domenichino illustrates the type of these cardinalitial rings, a speciality of the Roman goldsmiths. Either square or octagonal, they bore the arms of the reigning pope. The sapphire might also be framed in table- or rose-cut diamonds, the shoulders engraved and enamelled with black and white acanthus. One such ring, worn by the archpriest at ceremonies at Monza Cathedral in northern Italy, was drawn by Giuseppe Grisoni in 1719: the octagonal aquamarine in an arcaded bezel is supported by a hoop engraved with scrolling acanthus and enamelled black (British Museum, London, Department of Prints and Drawings). Ecclesiastical signets engraved with the arms of the see, which were also permitted in the Protestant dioceses, follow the same simplified styles as those of the laity.

MAGICAL RINGS

Belief in the healing powers of stones was challenged by only a few. According to Archbishop Tenison, the Duke of Monmouth (1649–85) was convinced that a charm which lay under the stone in his ring would save him from danger and defeat in battle. (He was wrong.) Thomas Nicols in his *Lapidary* of 1656 gives an uncritical account of their properties, quoting from Pliny and later writers including Albertus Magnus. Twenty years later, Robert Boyle, one of the founders of the Royal Society in England, while admitting that 'he never saw any great feats performed by these hard and costly stones that were worn in rings', did not entirely reject the possibility that they might have some medicinal value. Toadstones in particular were set in both silver and gold rings, as were other substances such as ass's hoof and wolves' teeth, the latter set in pairs for engagement rings and believed to ensure good luck.

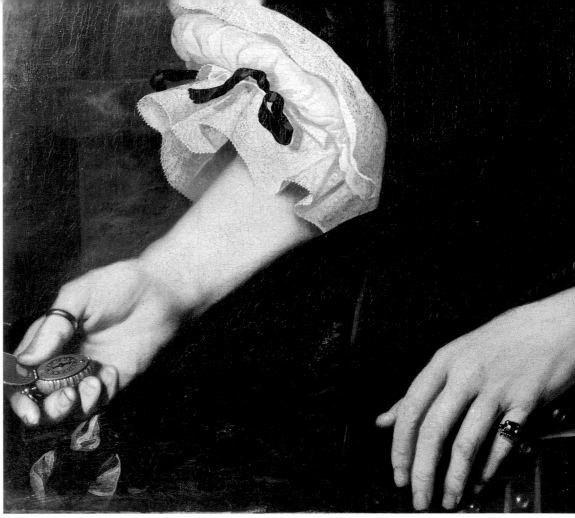

THE CHEAPSIDE HOARD

Some time during the Commonwealth (1649–60), a London jeweller hid his stock for safekeeping; he never returned for it, and it lay hidden for almost three hundred years before it was found, in Cheapside, near St Paul's Cathedral. Among the rings, the five gem-set examples shown here illustrate the simplified styles popular at the time, with solitaires in plain square and rounded bezels, and smaller stones in rows across the width of the finger. They are supported by plain hoops with almost no emphasis at the shoulders, decorated with a thick layer of white enamel.

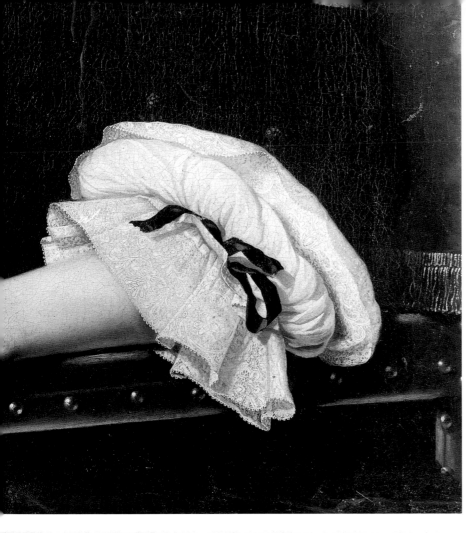

MORE THAN ONE WAY TO WEAR A RING

Far left: On the index finger; detail of a portrait of a young man by the Dutch artist Hendrik Bloemaert (1601–72).

Left: Wedding hoop on the thumb and jewelled ring on the little finger; from a portrait of an elderly Dutch lady by Pieter Nason (*c.* 1612–90).

Below left: A diamond in a box bezel nestling amid the pleats of a ruff; from a portrait of Lady Emily Howard, *c.* 1610.

Below: On the little finger, and threaded through a ribbon on the wrist; detail of Van Dyck's portrait of Thomas Killigrew, 1638.

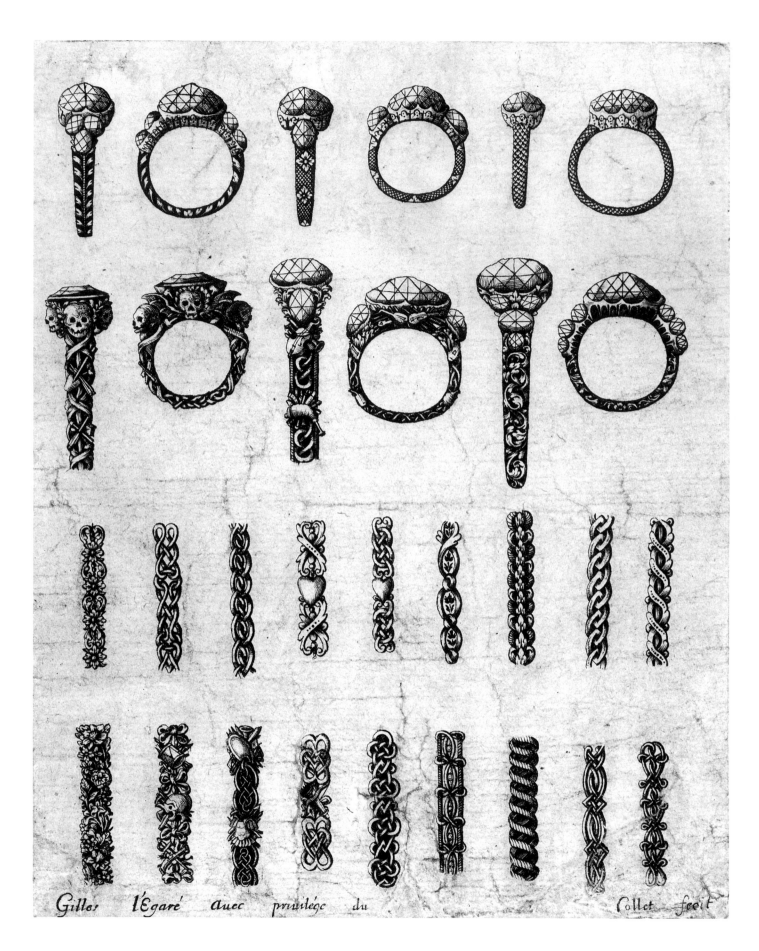

Gilles l'Egaré auec priuilége du   Collet fecit

THE STYLE OF GILLES LEGARE

Gilles Légaré, goldsmith to Louis XIV, published a set of Baroque designs in 1663. The rings are large, and there is a choice of intricate hoops. The diamonds are now all rose-cut. A *memento mori* ring (second row, left), set with a coloured stone, has gravedigger's equipment in relief.

Views of three solitaires in the Louis XIV manner. The ring on the left is set with a sapphire intaglio, that on the right with an emerald, and that in the centre with a peridot. The sapphire and emerald rings have bezels decorated with acanthus leaves and foliage trails on the hoops, all picked out in coloured enamels. The peridot ring is ornamented with botanical enamelling – a full-blown flower at the back of the bezel, more flowers tied with ribbons round the hoop, and a marguerite on each shoulder.

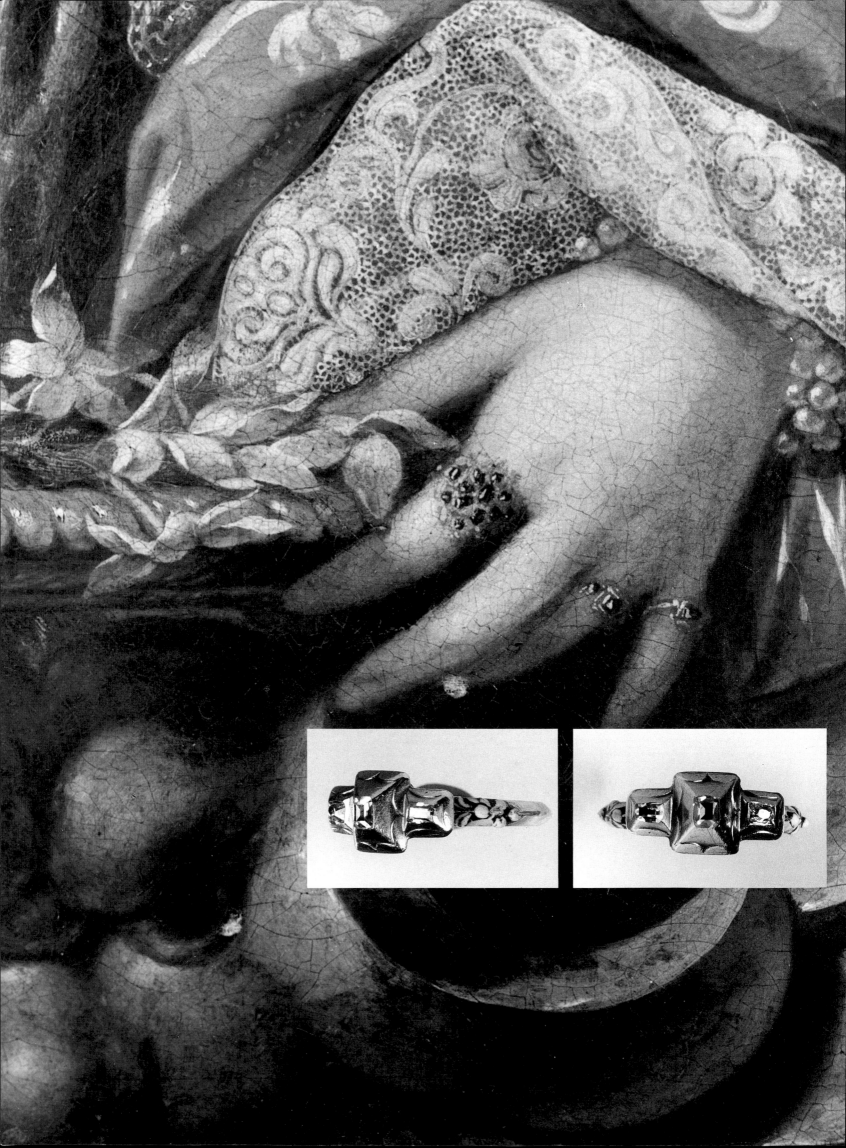

CLUSTERS AND MULTIPLE BEZELS

Baroque taste for the grand and splendid
required rings that made a great impression
even when seen from a distance. Large
stones for solitaires were at a premium:
while the less rare gems could be easily
obtained, this was not the case with
diamonds, rubies, sapphires and emeralds.
The jeweller therefore combined groups of
small precious stones into showy clusters,
like that shown on the finger of a Spanish
lady in a portrait of *c*. 1660. Other designs
incorporated table-cut diamonds, probably
removed from old-fashioned jewels. In the
ring *inset*, three table-cut diamonds are set
in gold indented collets across the top; the
sides and shoulders are enamelled with
black-and-white acanthus ornament. Much
more ambitious is the large ring, *left*, set
with fifteen table-cut stones in a wide
mosaic pattern, backed with a black-and-
white enamelled rosette.

Whereas solitaires of importance were
remodelled in the 18th century, these
composite rings set with old cut stones
survived because the intrinsic value of the
stones was so small.

95

Three designs utilizing small diamonds – both table- and rose-cut –
occur more frequently than any others. The most characteristic
(*below*) has seven table-cuts in square collets set cornerwise in two
groups of three on each side of a larger stone in the centre; the
arcaded sides of the bezel here are filled with black enamel spotted
with white. Another design is based on the emblem of the Virgin
Mary, adopted by the Bourbons of France as a symbol, the fleur-de-
lis (*left*). Rosettes, often mentioned in inventories, were the most
difficult to achieve: a rare survival (*below left*) set with rose-cut stones
is enamelled in bright colours at the back.

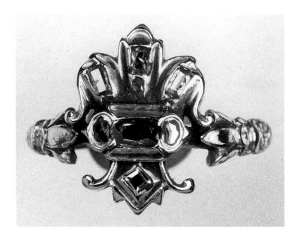

SOLITAIRES AND SETTINGS

Opposite page:
Among the 'vanities' of this world depicted by the Dutch artist
Paulus Moreelse (1571–1638) in his painting *Girl with a Mirror* are
three grand solitaires – table- and point-cut stones, and a large pearl
– sheltered in an elegant black lacquer ring box. Point-cuts were not
superseded as diamond faceting improved, but their settings
changed: a relatively small stone could be given greater importance
by one of the new arcaded box bezels (*above*), flanked by shoulders
engraved with foliage. Alternatively, exquisite enamelling could give
grandeur to the simplest of settings: two early 17th-century French
signets (*inset*), of Louis XIII and his mother, Marie de Médicis,
have strong shapes decorated with lilac-coloured trails of leaves.

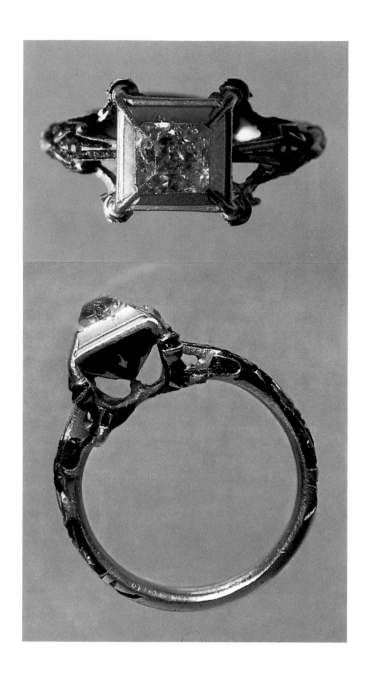

SOBER MAGNIFICENCE

Left: Two views of an early 17th-century table-cut diamond ring, decorated with the chaste black patterning known as *Schwarzornament*. The pyramidal bezel is held by eagles' claws that terminate the cusped shoulders.

Below: Seven rubies grouped to make an effect, a larger central stone flanked by smaller gems in a standard 17th-century manner (see pp. 95, 96). The engraved hoop displays black trails of leaves.

Opposite page:
Above: French jewellers applied enamels in a wide variety of colours to great effect – in cornucopias on the hoop and shoulders of an emerald ring (top), and in acanthus ornament filling the arcaded sides of two other rectangular bezels set with a sapphire and an emerald. The style is that of Gilles Légaré, who worked for Louis XIV.

Below: The mines of Colombia yielded the emeralds which gave Spanish jewelry its special character. These rings, a cruciform cluster and a nail-pierced horseshoe, were salvaged from the wreck of the galleon *Nuestra Señora de las Maravillas*, which sank off the Bahamas in 1655.

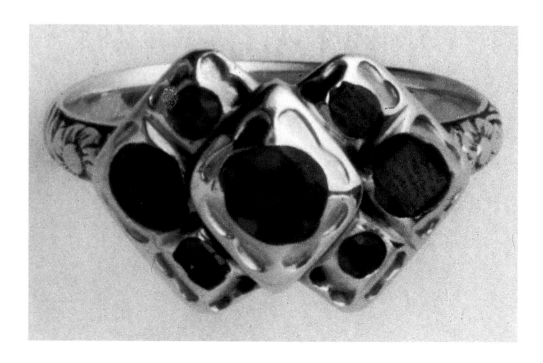

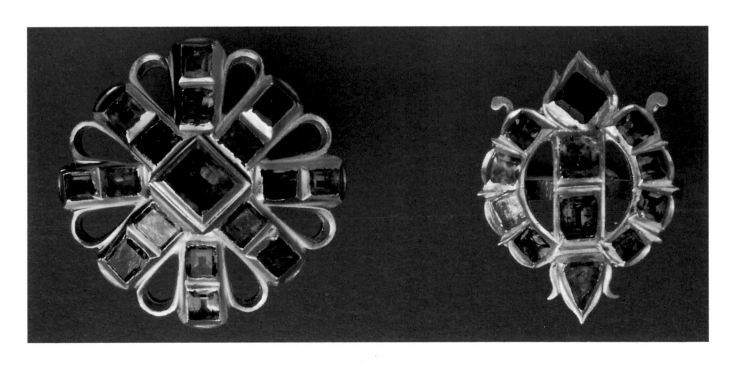

NARRATIVES IN MINIATURE

Developments in enamel techniques meant that rings could now tell stories, like paintings. The origin of this type of enamelled hoop ring is uncertain; one showing groups of merchants has an inscription in English, indicating that they were at least worn in Britain.

Above: A sporting scene with huntsman and hounds in pursuit of a stag and a boar is depicted round the sides of a swivel bezel set with two intaglios.

Above right: A hoop ring enamelled inside and out with scenes of everyday life.

Below: Five views of a ring illustrating episodes from the Bible relating to Abraham and his friend Lot. *Upper row, left and centre:* Abraham entertains the angels and learns that he and his wife Sarah, both of them old, are to have a child; she listens in the doorway, incredulous. *Bottom row, left*: Part of a scene of an angel appearing to Hagar, mother of Abraham's first son, who had been cast out into the wilderness for despising the barren Sarah. *Bottom row, right*: Abraham prepares to sacrifice Isaac, his son by Sarah. *Upper row, right*: Lot and his daughters; after the destruction of Sodom, believing themselves to be the only survivors, the daughters made their father drunk and slept with him to perpetuate humankind.

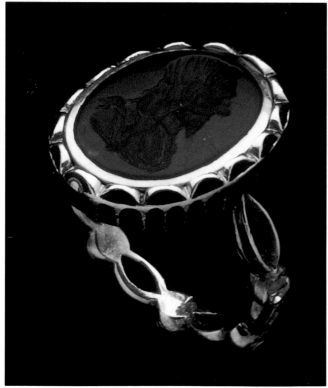

DEVOTIONAL, WEDDING AND MEMORIAL RINGS

Left: Two views of a carved coral ring bearing the portrait of Pope Urban VIII (1624–44). The shoulders are formed by figures of the two founders of the Church – St Paul with a sword, and St Peter with a key, both holding Bibles. A ring of this importance would have been given by the Pope to a distinguished pilgrim or prelate as a souvenir of an audience. It was also an amulet, protecting from the snares of the devil.

Far left: After the execution of King Charles I in 1649 British Royalists regarded him as a martyr and wore rings with his portrait. Most are painted or enamelled miniatures, but there is also this cornelian intaglio, which swivels round to a second face engraved with symbols of sovereignty. The arcaded sides of the indented bezel are filled with black enamel, and rose diamonds stud the openwork hoop.

Below, far left: The wedding ring of Mary of Modena, who married Charles I's younger son, the future James II, in 1673. It is in the form of an intricate gold chain studded with five rubies, like a miniature bracelet.

Below left: In the second half of the century individualized memorial rings appeared, reminding the wearer not of his or her own death but of a lost relative or friend. Such rings are easy to identify: they have oval or octagonal box bezels set with a faceted crystal over the cipher of the deceased, which is worked in gold thread and overlies a lock of hair or fragment of a shroud. In this example the cipher, in a double wire border, is framed by ten crystals.

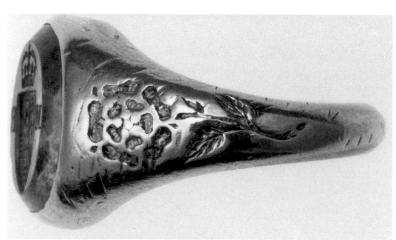

A remarkable set of signets survives made for members of the house of Stuart, from the future Charles I, who became Prince of Wales in 1616, to Mary II, who came to the throne in 1688 with her husband, William of Orange.

Left: Two views of Charles's ring. It is a shield-shaped diamond, engraved with the device and motto of the Prince of Wales (three ostrich feathers and ICH DIEN) and the cipher CP. The back of the bezel is enamelled with a bow and quiver.

Below left: The diamond signet of Queen Henrietta Maria, with her arms and cipher. Charles, by then king, paid the engraver Francis Walwyn £267 for his work in 1628. It is set in a gold ring ornamented with the rose and thistle, perhaps made by a Dutch jeweller in the employ of Charles I.

Below, far left: The Stuart taste for luxury was inherited by Charles's granddaughter, Mary II, whose signet (seen in two views) is a sapphire with crowned coat of arms and cipher. The Tudor rose is enamelled at the shoulders.

Right and below: Most unusual is the signet of Charles II (1660–85), which combines steel with gold. The arms and cipher are engraved on a steel plaque set in an oval gold bezel, whose sides bear scrolled cartouches with the motto DIEU ET MON DROIT. At the shoulders, terminating the gold hoop, are the royal lion and unicorn cut in steel. The ornament is in the swirling, knobbly 'auricular' style, introduced into England from Holland in the mid-17th century.

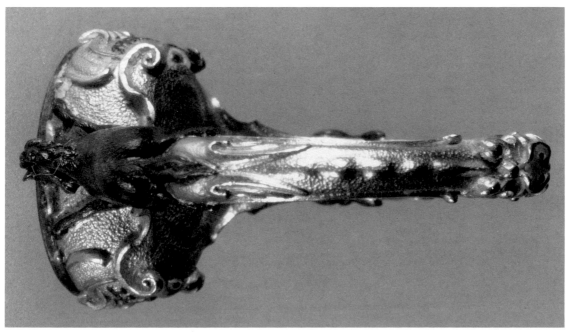

LOVE AND MARRIAGE

In the 17th century great variety was still permissible in both the forms and the iconography of rings used to mark betrothals and weddings.

Right, below: The earliest of the three rings shown on these two pages served for a wedding in 1610; that date is inscribed inside the hoop, along with the Biblical injunction from the marriage service, 'What God hath joined together let not man put asunder', in Dutch. The broad hoop, studded with rubies and emeralds, displays a pair of hands clasping a heart wounded by arrows, flanked by enamelled forget-me-knots. The top and bottom bands terminate in monster heads each swallowing a pearl.

Left: Two views of a gimmel ring dated 1631, also used at a wedding. This elaborate example has a double bezel set with a ruby and a diamond, held up by hands each clasping a heart. When open, two hidden cavities are revealed: they contain figures of a baby and a skeleton, symbolic of the cycle of human life. The same scheme had been used nearly a hundred years earlier, in a gimmel ring belonging to the English financier Sir Thomas Gresham. The hoops are inscribed in Latin with the same Biblical phrase ('What God hath joined . . .') as on the earlier wedding ring.

Right, above: Hands with cuffed wrists emerge from a black-enamelled hoop to hold a flaming heart set with rose-cut diamonds.

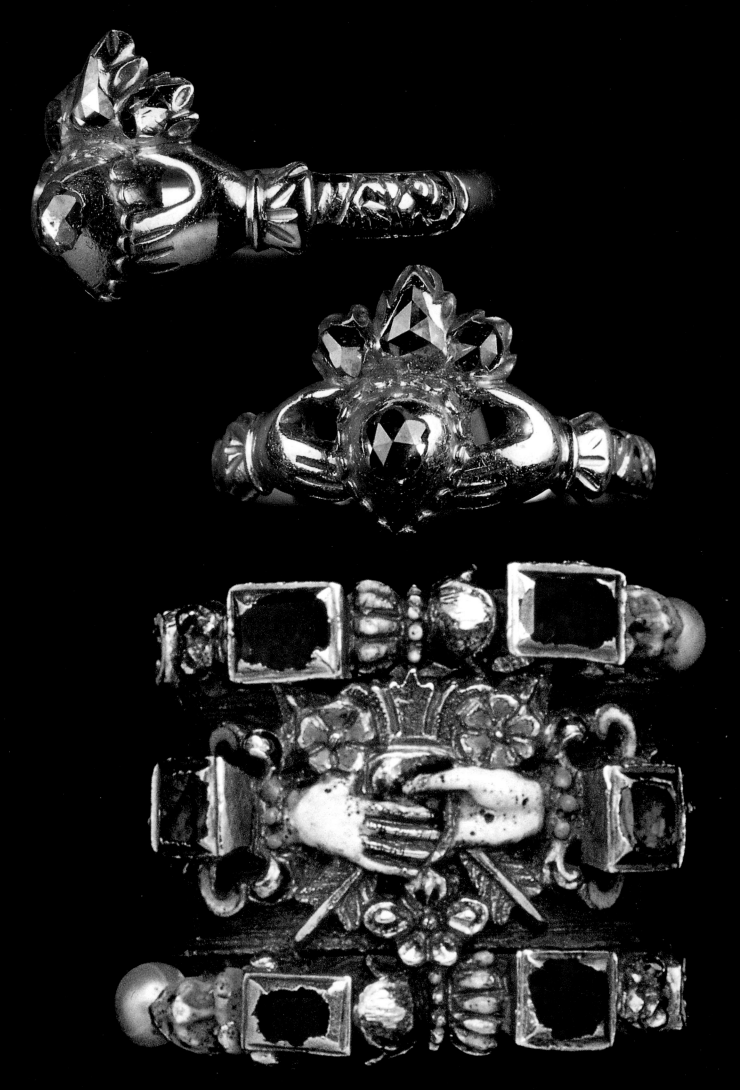

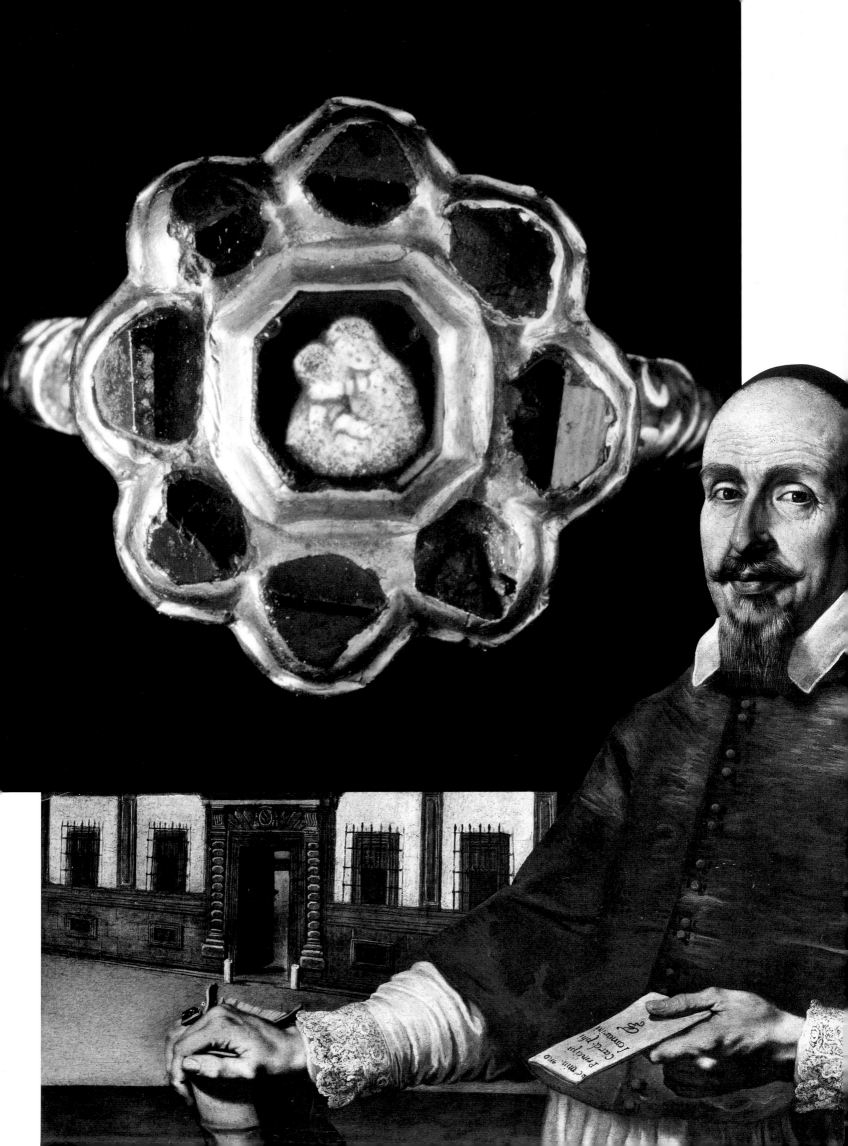

FAITH AND DEATH

Opposite page:

A ring painted with the Virgin and Child, framed by eight garnets, continues the Roman Catholic devotional tradition for a private individual.

The important sapphire ring worn by Cardinal Filomarino, Archbishop of Naples, in his portrait by Domenichino proclaims his high status in the hierarchy of the Church; it is probably the ring he received when appointed cardinal by Urban VIII in 1641.

This page:

Memento mori rings reached a peak of richness and elaboration. The example in the centre, with a grimacing skull looking up from crossbones, glitters with diamonds. The surrounding ring has for its bezel a skull that rests disconcertingly upright on crossbones; on the shoulders, picked out in white enamel, are more symbols – pierced hearts, a scythe and hour-glass, and an open and closed book. Inside is engraved the reminder, MEMENTO MORI.

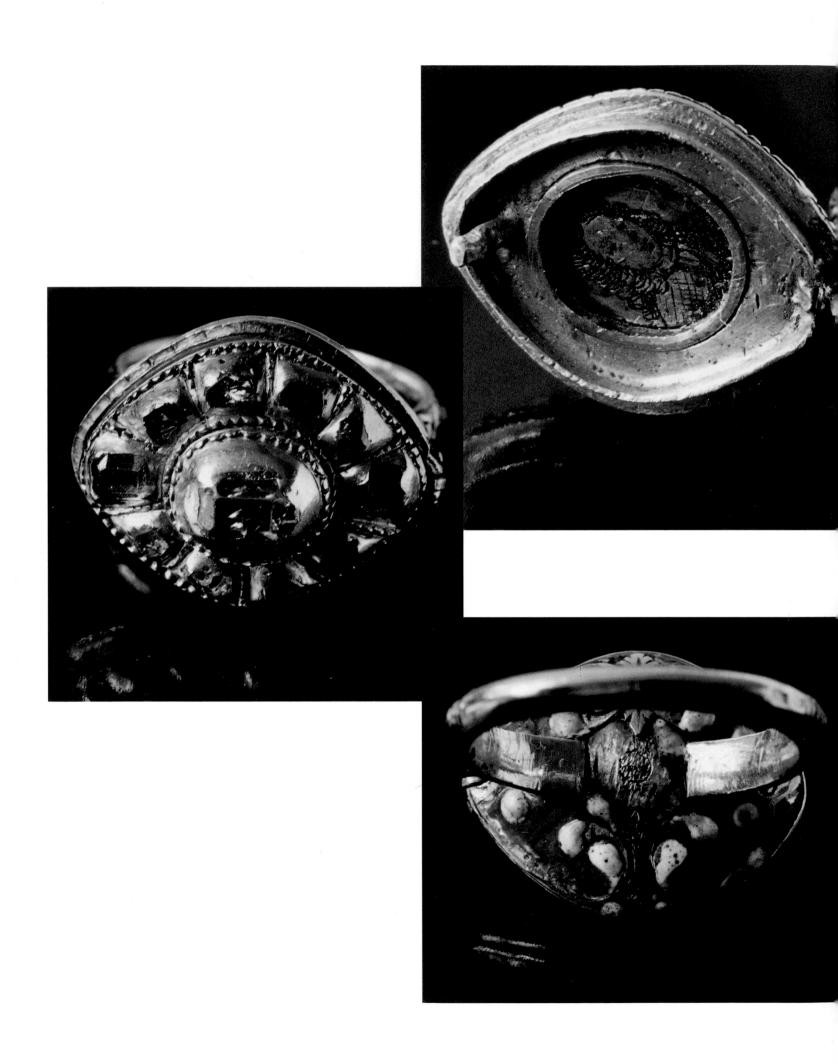

A MYSTERIOUS LOCKET

Whereas most locket rings contain *memento mori* symbols or portraits of proscribed political leaders, this one hides the full-length figure of a man in workman's clothes, with a piece of rope and a flower – probably a gardener. Inside the cover is the portrait of a gentleman. Like a gimmel ring, when this is closed no-one would suspect it contained a surprise. The oval bezel is set with a cluster of table-cut diamonds, and the back is enamelled in blue with spots of white and pink.

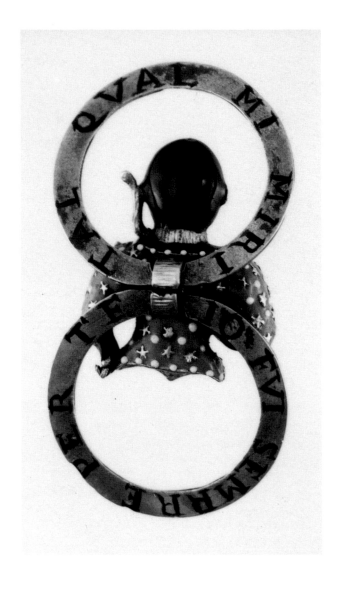

A CARNIVAL GIMMEL RING

The bust of a blackamoor, enamelled black, blue and white and set with table-cut diamonds, rubies and paillons, crowns the hinge of this gimmel ring. Inside, the hoops bear an inscription in Italian: TAL QUAL MI MIRI / IO FUI SEMPRE PER TE – literally, 'As you see me, so I have always been for you'. Might one imagine that it was a gift from a suitor, telling his beloved that he had always been her slave?

4

The 18th century:
Rococo and Neo-Classical elegance

When required to serve 18th-century 'douceur de vivre' the decorative arts attained new levels of perfection, rarely equalled since. Jewellers rose to the prevailing high standards and adapted to the light-hearted and delicate styles which were now preferred to the massively splendid. The impulse continued to come from Paris, where every fashion-conscious woman traveller paused to have her jewels reset. Styles changed so quickly that remodelling was necessary every two or three years. French standards were diffused abroad by the Huguenots who settled in the Protestant countries of the north and by the eminent jewellers who went from Paris to appointments at the courts of St Petersburg, Madrid and Copenhagen.

The Rococo style which developed in the first part of the century is epitomized by a number of published designs: those of the Venetian identified only as 'D.M.T.' who published a set of twenty-two plates in 1741; Christian Taute's, of c. 1750; and J. H. Pouget's *Traité des pierres précieuses* (1762 and 1764). Since relatively few rings have survived and they are rarely shown in portraits, these designs are an invaluable record of the variety of models available. The bezel becomes much lighter, with openwork motifs echoing themes familiar in textiles, ceramics and furniture. Emphasis is given to the shoulders by ribbing, by the application of volutes, by studding with small gems, and by bifurcating the hoop and filling the empty space with a leaf or a flower. The convex or flat hoop can be broken up into sections of scrolling curves or wrought into a leafy branch. Plain gold symmetrical and asymmetrical patterns or a single flower stand out in relief at the back of the bezel, which is no longer enamelled. There is a new role for enamel in the design of fancy and love rings. Because of the improvements in faceting and foiling stones looked more beautiful than ever, especially by candlelight, when the most important social events took place. Sparkling beneath the wide taffeta and lace sleeves, rings added the final touch of elegance to the toilette and showed a woman's white hand to advantage. Madame de Pompadour (1721–64), who set the standard of taste and fashion for her generation, had a collection of over forty rings; her lover, Louis XV, did not like to see her wearing them, so she put them on as soon as he left her company and removed them when he came back. Every man of consequence wore rings too, and the Italian adventurer Giovanni Jacopo Casanova (1725–98) recalled in his *Memoirs* how it was his snuff box, diamond and ruby watch chain, and rings that made him seem 'un personnage imposant'.

pp. 132–33

pp. 130, 136–37

pp. 134–35

DECORATIVE RINGS

A large brilliant- or rose-cut diamond on the little finger was the mark of the grandest men and women. On his death in 1729 the 2nd Duke of Devonshire bequeathed to his daughter, Lady Betty Lowther, 'the yellow diamond ring I often wear'. These fancy coloured stones, usually improved by foiling and tinting, were highly prized. There were three such – pink, violet and blue, and straw-coloured – in the large collection of Queen

Maria Amalia, daughter of Frederick Augustus of Saxony, who married Charles III of Spain in 1759. Madame de Pompadour, whose most splendid parure was designed as ribbons studded with pale pink, soft green and canary yellow diamonds, wore other tinted diamonds set in rings. The best, a large aquamarine-coloured solitaire, she left in her will to the Duc de Choiseul; his brother-in-law, the Duc de Gontaut, received a cluster of pink and white diamonds tied with a knot of green tinted rose-cut stones. Another important diamond, which was olive-shaped, was crowned with a garland of flowers mounted with smaller stones combining all the colours of the rainbow.

This passion for colour accounts for the large number of rings in Madame de Pompadour's inventory that are set with semi-precious as well as precious stones – malachite, moonstone, carbuncle, topaz, square-cut emeralds and sapphires, violet and cherry red rubies, and two catseyes, one foiled red, the other green. They were mounted in gold, and their colour was further enhanced by borders of white or tinted rose- or brilliant-cut diamonds, set in silver collets, which were sometimes placed on the shoulders as well, and also carried round the hoop. The trend was always towards lightness: the solid cruciform ring was transformed into an openwork cross formed of small stones linked together by curved scrolls usually framing a large stone of contrasting colour.

Fancy rings
Very small and inexpensive stones were mounted into the new category of 'fantaisie' or 'fancy' rings reflecting the love of nature and the amusements of society – chiefly music,

p. 134–35 cards, sports and the masquerade.

The counterparts to the graceful bouquets of flowers patterning the silk dress and

p. 130–33 painted on the porcelain dish were the openwork *giardinetti* (literally, 'little garden') rings which imitated nature with bright coloured stones in gold highlighted by rose diamonds

pp. 130, 136–37 in silver collets. Pouget puts flowers in a cornucopia, arranges them in baskets, and ties them up with ribbons. As an added touch of realism he lets a butterfly or a bee hover above them. These are not the only themes inspired by nature, for he also illustrates bezels with fruit, a sheaf of wheat and a peacock in its pride.

For the sporting enthusiast Pouget offered a ring with horn and quiver bezel, and for the musical, trophies of a lyre and trumpet and the rustic bagpipe and shepherd's pipe.

p. 134 Rings with two or three playing cards displayed between tiny stones and sometimes carried round the hoop might recall the winning hand at the gaming table. The excitement

p. 135 of the masquerade was evoked by carnival masks, cheeks spotted with patches which had a language of their own used to signal flirtatious messages. Blackamoor masks mirror society's fascination with the exotic features and satin-black skin of the negro boy pages who as the 'êtres chéris' or pets of fashionable women were allowed the freedom of the drawing room and boudoir. Some rings have hinged locket bezels containing secrets usually of a sentimental nature – a heart inscribed A VOUS SEULE (Yours alone) inside a carnival mask, an infant with an inscription in Danish translating 'In love' concealed in a *giardinetti* ring (Schmuckmuseum, Pforzheim).

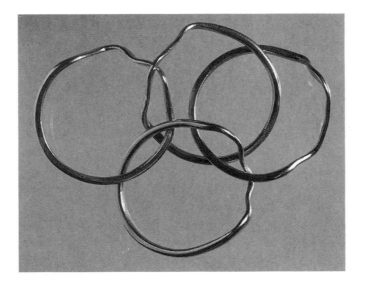

Two gold puzzle rings – one closed, made up of seven hoops; the other open, of four.

Multiple-hoop or puzzle rings continued to be made to amuse the clever and baffle the slow-witted. Cornelia Knight remembered in her *Autobiography* how the famous bluestocking Mrs Elizabeth Montagu (1720–1800) called her a stupid child because 'I did not find out the puzzle of a gold ring she wore.'

Much valued as curiosities were moss agates, that is stones with inclusions adventitiously representing trees, figures, heraldry and landscapes. The famous Parisian luxury goods dealer Lazare Duvaux sold some to Madame de Pompadour who mounted them in rings. Each was framed like a picture by a line of brilliants and the hoops were paved with rose diamonds. Landscapes were also rendered in hairwork or painting on ivory: these cheaper versions were bordered by amethyst- and emerald-coloured pastes. p. 146 p. 146

Paste of excellent quality could be obtained in Paris, where G. F. Strass perfected the formula for transparent glass which resembled diamonds when cut, and his rival, Chéron, successfully imitated rubies, emeralds, topazes and sapphires. Another source was Venice, where a turquoise paste was made, considered by some more beautiful than the stone itself.

LOVE AND MARRIAGE

Rings given as love tokens adapt to the taste for the light and graceful. This is Cupid's domain and he appears in person running away with a stolen heart in an enamelled gold ring inscribed STOP THIEF (O 698). More usually he is represented by his attributes of bow and quiver, which Pouget garlands with flowers or flanks with turtledoves (sacred to p. 130 Venus) who also stand guard over a nestful of eggs. The happy association of love and music is celebrated in a trophy combining the bow and quiver with bagpipe, trumpet and flowers.

pp. 134–35, 137 Hearts, transfixed by Cupid's arrows, twinned, winged, crowned and bound together by lovers' knots, are usually set with rubies and diamonds. Madame de Pompadour, who led and never followed fashion, owned two heart rings. The most valuable was certainly unique, for it was set with a diamond intaglio of two crowned hearts in a border of small green-tinted brilliants. The other, a heart-shaped opal surmounted by a diamond crown, was framed in green enamel ribbons. For the general public there were delightful trifles, such as an enamelled tulip enclosed in an openwork heart inscribed DOUX ET SINCERE (Sweet and sincere), which conveyed the same sentiments but at lower prices (B 34B).

Discussing the various talismans which could console lovers when absent from one another, *The Spectator* in 1711 dismissed them all and declared: 'I never found so much benefit from any as from a ring in which my mistress's hair is plaited together very artificially in a kind of true lover's knot.' The Duchess of Marlborough told her jeweller how to set hair into a heart ring: 'you must set the ring with this ruby heart and a crystal heart of the same size by it with this hair put loose into it without being wove. The hoop must be light blue enamel with [a] motto round it in gold letters and the two hearts must be crowned with these other diamonds.' Marie-Josèphe de Saxe, the daughter-in-law of Louis XV, wore a ring with the hair of her husband, the Dauphin, identified by a diamond cipher. Cheaper versions were studded with marcasite or enamelled. Pouget's designs combine ciphers with Cupid's bow and quiver within a jewelled border or a symbolic crown of evergreen myrtle.

The miniature set in a ring also provided a reminder of a beloved individual. Some were covered by a crystal or even by a picture diamond so that all could see them, but others were discreetly hidden. One such, which belonged to Madame du Châtelet, was removed from her finger on her deathbed. Voltaire, whose mistress she had been, asked the valet to bring him the ring, thinking that it concealed his picture – only to discover that he had been replaced by her last lover.

French asserted itself as the language of love in a number of stock phrases: AMOUR POUR AMOUR (Love for love), VOTRE AMOUR FAIT MA FELICITE (Your love makes my happiness), NOS DEUX COEURS SONT UNIS (Our two hearts are united), and, on billing turtledove rings, AIMONS COMME EUX (Let us love as they do). Special commis- p. 148 sions, too, were in French; the hoop of a cameo ring, for instance, is inscribed SI VOUS SOUHAITEZ MON REPOS VOUS AUREZ SOIN DE VOTRE SANTE (If you care for my peace of mind you will look after yourself). There was one notable contribution from

A German 'Treu' ring, with a black-enamelled figure 3 surrounded by three rubies.

p. 151

Germany: the figure 3 (in German, *Drei*) could be a rebus for the word *Treu* (trust), for when pronounced in Saxon the two words sound alike. One ring shows a '3' enamelled black amidst three rubies, tied with a lover's knot. The fashionable enthusiasms appear in love rings. An angora rabbit, for many years treated as a favourite pet, crouches amidst jewelled foliage: the hoop is inscribed TOUJOURS CRAIGNETTE (Ever shy). The affection of a negro servant inspired another enamelled ring (sold Christie's London, 3 October 1990) on which a dusky-skinned turbanned slave of love kneels before a diamond sun, supported by a hoop inscribed J'ADORE CE QUI ME BRULE (I worship that which burns me).

The wedding ring itself might be ornamented with symbols such as burning hymeneal torches amidst flowers. A couple whose ring is inscribed DUDLEY AND KATHERINE UNITED 26 MARCH 1706 chose the symbol of hands holding a crowned rose diamond heart (O 697). *The Tatler* in 1710 recorded a ring in which the posy WHILE LIFE DOES LAST I'LL HOLD THEE FAST was illustrated by the 'hand in hand graved upon it'. Posies were still the essential feature of the wedding or love ring, and according to *The Tatler* the poetical lover went to the trouble of obtaining the exact dimension of the marriage finger in order to make sure that the posy could fit.

Whether the wedding ring was set with an expensive stone or just a plain gold band with posy inscribed, it was usually protected by a keeper, and all who could afford them chose diamond hoops for this purpose.

ENGRAVED GEMS

According to Mariette's *Traité des Pierres Gravées* (1750) most engraved gems were set in rings, notwithstanding the fashion for mounting seals bearing coats of arms, crests and ciphers to hang from the waist. He observed that designs were generally plain: 'aujourd'hui on est assez dans le gout de n'introduire aucun ornement dans leur monture & d'imiter les anneaux antiques, qui etoient presque toujours fort unis et fort simples' (taste today is sufficiently in tune with that of the ancients to refrain from elaborate settings and instead imitate the simplicity of classical rings). The owners were usually connoisseurs. The Regent of France, Philippe, Duc d'Orléans (1674–1723), constantly wore a signet set with a gem chosen from the magnificent family collection (now in the Hermitage

Museum, St Petersburg). It is an intaglio head of Bacchus, radiant with youth, wild locks crowned with ivy. In contrast, the most important English collector, the 2nd Duke of Devonshire, preferred the calm dignity of the Roman Empress Sabina, whose aquamarine intaglio portrait he had mounted in a gold signet bearing his cipher crowned with ducal coronet. Device and setting correspond in a ring from the collection of the 4th Earl of Carlisle, which is set with a cornelian intaglio head of Jupiter with his attributes, thunderbolts, on the shoulders. These noblemen did not have the exclusive right to such signets. There was the famous Italian contralto Vittoria Tesi who sealed with a portrait of herself, posed theatrically with her long hair tied at the nape of the neck. Casanova was pleased, when dining out in London, that his ring with a portrait of Louis XV was noticed and passed round the table while the company agreed that the likeness was striking.

p. 139

A remarkable group of cameo and intaglio portraits of Louis XV was commissioned by Madame de Pompadour from Jacques Guay (1715–93). Guay taught her engraving and one portrait, set in a gold ring, is signed POMPADOUR F[ECIT]. His first task was to record the victory of Fontenoy in 1745 when the King revived tradition and led his troops into battle accompanied by the Dauphin, his heir. The cornelian intaglio depicted father and son in Roman dress in a chariot drawn by four horses, crowned by Victory; it was set in a ring for the Marquise to wear. Other engraved gems in her collection mounted as rings were a ruby intaglio of Henri IV (founder of the Bourbon dynasty), her spaniel Mimi, and two classical female heads. She bequeathed an intaglio of 'La Fidelle Amitié' in her will to the Prince de Soubise in remembrance of their long friendship. Her own portrait, engraved by Guay on a white cornelian, is set in an elegant but large plain ring, thought to have been worn by the King (Cabinet des Médailles, Bibliothèque Nationale, Paris).

p. 138

Another Frenchman, Louis Siriès, was commissioned by the Empress of Austria, Maria Theresa, to engrave gems. His *Catalogue des Pierres Gravées par Louis Siriès Orfèvre du Roi de France Présentement Directeur des Ouvrages en Pierres Dures de la Galerie de Sa Majesté Imperiale à Florence* (1757) illustrates a suite of sixty-eight gems. His technique, following Renaissance precedent, consisted in carving the stone in such a way that the design – intaglio or cameo – is contained within a reserved border. The resulting gems were then set in gold rings of solid and classical style enriched with neat banding and finely polished cornices.

A famous cameo ring which belonged to Prince Eugene of Savoy is set with a moss agate leopard, crouched ready to spring: the setting acts as a platform, flanked by shells and brilliant-cut diamonds at the shoulders and supported on an openwork chain hoop. Monkeys, which inspired Rococo decorators, were also a favourite theme for cameos; they were considered best rendered in a shimmering stone such as chrysoberyl, and usually bordered with rose diamonds. An enemy who resented the inordinate influence of Madame de Pompadour over the King commissioned her portrait caricatured as a monkey, 'habillée' with diamond jewelry and mounted to wear in a ring.

p. 150

p. 138

POLITICAL THEMES

Rings enclosing portraits – in the form of painted or enamelled miniatures, medals, p. 139 cameos or intaglios – accompanied by crowned ciphers, sometimes with a lock or hair, were given by monarchs as gestures of favour and friendship. In 1749, for instance, Marie Leczinska, daughter of the King of Poland and wife of Louis XV, had the portraits of her daughters Henriette and the Infanta of Spain painted by Drouais and mounted in a swivel ring by Jacques Guay as a present for the Duchesse de Brissac. Rondé, the court jeweller, made a diamond setting for the miniature of another daughter, Madame Louise.

Occasionally, rings commemorating political struggles might be called the jewelry of treason. In Britain they are associated with the Stuart cause, which was rekindled in 1745 by the romantic adventure of the Young Pretender, Prince Charles Edward (1720–88), who landed in Scotland without arms or money and went on to win sufficient support to lead an army as far south as Derby before being defeated at Culloden. Some of his Jacobite followers wore rings with portraits of his forebears – his father the Old Pretender, grandfather James II, Charles I and Mary Queen of Scots. Others wore the portrait of the Prince himself, in the form of a miniature, a medal or a paste gem, flanked by the emblems of the white rose and thistle and inscribed with the motto DUM SPIRAT SPERO (While he breathes I hope). One particular surviving ring commemorates the spate of executions that followed the failure of the rebellion: the names of four peers beheaded on Tower Hill in 1746 – Lovat, Balmerino, Derwentwater and Kilmarnock – and those of the seventeen executed officers, accompanied by coronets and dates, are ingeniously inscribed together with the axe, rose and thistle on bezel, shoulders and twin hoop (D 1417).

MEMORIAL RINGS

Rings commemorative of political events are closely linked with those distributed in memory of private individuals. Clarissa Harlowe, the heroine of Samuel Richardson's novel (1747–48), lists in her will the names of friends to be given 'each an enamelled ring with cipher Cl. H. with my hair in crystal'. Most memorial rings are of standard design: the bezel is set with a gem or crystal which may or may not enclose hair, and the hoop is divided into five scrolls enamelled black for the married, white for the unmarried, and inscribed with name, age and date of death. Some enclose hair in coffin- or urn-shaped p. 141 bezels. Austere hoop styles enamelled on the outside with the funerary emblems of skel- p. 140 etons, hour-glass, pick and shovel are inscribed with the name and dates of the deceased inside, close to the finger.

ECCLESIASTICAL AND DEVOTIONAL RINGS

Resplendent in violet or rose-coloured moiré silks, lace, jewelled crosses and insignia hanging from wide ribbons, cardinals and bishops wore rings of comparable elegance. The type is exemplified by the ring of the Italian diplomat Giorgio Doria, Cardinal of

The Cardinal-Archbishop of Salzburg, Count Hieronymus von Colloredo. Mozart's haughty patron, who became Archbishop in 1772, wears an elaborately jewelled ring and pectoral cross, displayed against ermine, silk and lace.

San Lorenzo in Panisperna (1743–59): the long octagonal bezel is set with a foiled sapphire and has the arms of Pope Benedict XIV enamelled on the back; the hoop is chased and divides at the shoulders (O 782).

As a princess of the house of Poland and Saxony, Marie-Josèphe de Saxe shared the family devotion to the Jesuit missionary St Francis Xavier, whose portrait she wore in a ring, set about with diamonds, listed in her posthumous inventory of 1767. It was in a ring of this kind with a picture of St Catherine in the bezel that Casanova concealed a miniature of himself to be worn by his mistress, resident in a convent. At the touch of a spring the saint vanished and in her place came the portrait of Casanova himself, 'une figure divine qui n'a pas du tout l'air d'un saint' – divine but quite unsaintly.

Around 1770 there was a reaction against the light-hearted Rococo style and under Neo-Classical influence rings became more formal, 'chaste' and serious. This coincided with a change in dress: the women who rejected hoops and crinolines stiff with gold and silver for softer draperies chose to wear rings emphasizing culture and sentiment as well as wealth. Men still wore as many rings as ever: in Rome both Don Luigi Braschi and his bride Costanza Falconieri received numerous gifts of rings as presents for their marriage in 1781.

The austere yet elegant designs reflect the return to classical principles of order and symmetry. The new geometric, lozenge, octagonal, round, pointed oval (navette or marquise) and shield shapes are supported by hoops which broaden out and fork at the shoulders. They covered the finger right up to the knuckle, a change of scale commented p. 149 on by L. S. Mercier in *Le Tableau de Paris* (1788): 'on porte actuellement des bagues énormes' (today's rings are huge). The sharply defined bezels are bordered by minute gold beads like pearls, by bright-cut ornament and by bands of husk or laurel. Enamel is not only used to outline these shapes and to highlight details but is also applied, in celestial blue, green and red, on the surface of bezels engine-turned to glisten like moiré pp. 142–43 silk. Paste of better quality than ever was also available in many colours to provide a background for motifs worked in seed pearls or rose diamonds (small rose-cut stones of indifferent quality). The range of materials used includes marcasite, cut steel, ivory and ceramics, especially Wedgwood.

DECORATIVE GEM-SET RINGS

Although the ostentatious display of riches was out of tune with the philosophy fashionable at the time, men and women indulged in the pleasure of showing off a valuable gem on the finger. Mercier inveighed like Seneca against 'la vanité des femmes qui portoient un ou deux patrimoines à leurs doigts' (the vanity of women who display several family fortunes on their fingers). The various styles were described in the *Cabinet des Modes* of 15 July 1786: large stones are set on a coloured ground – usually paste – either as a solitaire or framed within pearls or rose diamonds, with others outlining the geometric shape of the bezel. A smaller stone is mounted in a group between two others at each end of the bezel. The very smallest diamonds are arranged as stars twinkling across the entire surface like the sky at night: these, the commonest design, were called 'bagues au firmament'. Another type of ring, 'à l'enfantement', alludes to the birth of the Dauphin in 1785. Again, the *Cabinet des Modes* explains: 'au lieu de pierres blanches au milieu du chaton, on met des pierres de couleur en observant d'unir comme il faut la pierre de composition du chaton avec la pierre enchassée' (the bezel is mounted with coloured instead of white stones, chosen to harmonize with the colour of the paste ground). These styles were diffused internationally from Paris but there were also some regional designs, of which the most distinctive is the golden white chrysolite ring popular in Spain and Portugal. The stones are massed onto the pointed oval bezels edged with minute gold beads; sometimes an extra line of beading divides the rows of stones clustered round the centre.

Hoop rings, studded with pearls, diamonds and coloured stones either in harlequin mixtures or a single colour, are increasingly popular.

Fancy rings

In the Neo-Classical version of the *giardinetti* ring the coloured stone, diamond or seed pearl sprig or bouquet – now stylized – is set against an enamel or paste ground within an octagonal or pointed oval bezel. Nature is also the theme of pastoral rings, with a seed pearl trophy of a shepherdess's hat, horn and crook (D 2160) or a miniature of a young woman tending her flock in a rural landscape.

The excitement of watching the ascent of the balloon invented by the Montgolfier brothers in 1783 is recorded in rings with balloon-shaped bezels, studded with rose diamonds. Another ascent, which took place from the Tuileries Gardens in Paris, was painted by Van Blarenberghe and set in a ring with a diamond border. Other miniatures by this artist, of harbour scenes, village life, Commedia dell'Arte actors, and elegant ladies and gentlemen arriving in sedan chairs at a masked ball are similarly mounted in rings. (All are in the collection at Waddesdon Manor.) A miniature showing the interior of a palatial mansion in the Blarenberghe manner is set in a large ring for a gentleman, presumably the owner, who could thus continue to enjoy the sight of his possessions even when away from home. Views including ships at sea, genre scenes, and people walking in a palace garden are also found minutely rendered in ivory; like the miniatures, they are covered by glass and set in plain gold or diamond rings.

p. 147

Cipher and name rings

Most rings individualized in this way bear initials only, wrought in seed pearls or rose diamonds on red, blue or green grounds, filling rectangular or oval bezels worn across or following the length of the finger. They were often commissioned as wedding presents for a bride about to change her name. The Roman jeweller Filippo Pentini made one in 1773, 'con cifra di brillianti destinato a Donna Ottavia Bracciano futura sposa dell' exc.mo Don Giuseppe Rospigliosi' (with cipher of brilliants for Donna O.B., future wife of H.E. Don G.R.). Rings inscribed with the names ALBA and GOYA are worn by the Duchess of Alba in her portrait by Goya of 1797; two others in her collection bore the name of her husband.

LOVE AND MARRIAGE

Love rings are adapted to the enlongated geometric bezels and the symbols themselves are classicized. Tableaux of amorous themes are painted in miniature on vellum, or made from an ivory-like composition which stands out in relief against coloured grounds. The devotion of the rejected lover – SANS ESPOIR MAIS FIDELE (Faithful though without hope) is illustrated by Cupid, quiver hanging abandoned on a tree, kneeling beside a faithful hound, the whole carved in wood by Giuseppe Maria Bonzanigo who specialized in miniature sculpture for jewelry (British Museum, London, Hull Grundy Collection

226). Another symbol of fidelity, the clinging evergreen ivy leaf, often with the motto JE NE CHANGE QU'EN MOURANT (Only death can change me), is added to the vocabulary of love: it appeared on the ring which the adolescent Prince of Wales, the future George IV, gave his first love, the actress Mrs 'Perdita' Robinson.

The message THE FARTHER I FLY THE FASTER WE TYE, meaning that absence makes the heart grow fonder, is conveyed by two turtle doves joined by a long string tied with a lover's knot. The misery of separation is expressed by rings with miniatures of a woman gazing out wistfully to sea, writing a love letter or admiring the portrait of a gentleman. A more cheerful note is struck by a ring consisting of a clock face bezel with a heart substituted for the figure 12 and the hoop inscribed LE TEMS NOUS JOINDRA (Time will bring us together). p. 145 p. 145

Nymphs in Greek costume make sacrifices and kindle flaming hearts at altars of love in classical temples or out of doors. Short mottoes are inscribed on the plinth, longer messages round the pointed oval bezel. Inscriptions, addressed as they are to heart and mind rather than to the eyes, can be the sole ornament, replacing symbols. These mottoes are almost always in French, the traditional language of love. Sometimes the message was conveyed by letters alone. Two rings thus inscribed were acquired by the Prince of Wales from the jeweller Thomas Gray in 1786: one spelt in pearls M MOI (*Aimes moi* – Love me), the other JM, for *J'aime* (I love). Another much more elaborate version must have been a special commission, with its wide hoop composed of four gold panels engraved with the four letters LACD, for *Elle a cédé* (She has yielded). The large bezels offered the space for rebus or riddle rings with pictures as well as words whose sense has to be puzzled over: again most are in French. p. 144

Hair is sometimes enclosed in the bezel, arranged into a lover's knot or bouquet; or it may be woven into a wide loop with moulded border. These rings are distinguished from their memorial counterparts by symbols – doves, lovers' crowns, arrows, flaming hearts – and by amorous mottoes such as DU BIEN AIME (From the beloved). pp. 142–43

As before, miniatures in enamel or painted on ivory or vellum were set under glass for rings, with or without a lock of hair. They are usually bust-length likenesses, but around 1785 it became fashionable to represent the eye alone, which was considered wonderfully expressive. The feelings evoked by miniatures were expressed by Tysoe Paul Hancock in his will of 1774: he left his daughter Betsy 'a miniature of her mother painted by Smart and set in a ring with diamonds round it which I request she will never part with as I intend it to remind her of her mother's virtues as well as her person'.

Silhouettes, available from the 1770s, provided a cheap and popular alternative to the miniature. The stark black profiles stand out against the pale ivory grounds and the best artists, such as John Miers, succeeded in capturing good likenesses. Most are framed in neat, crisp bright-cut borders with a cipher at the back of the pointed oval or rectangular bezel: only those of the grandest people were bordered by brilliants. In one ring the silhouette of an elegant woman, enclosed in a black border, is inscribed with the heartfelt declaration JE CHERIS JUSQU'A SON OMBRE (I even love her shadow).

A ring set with a silhouette under glass.

The wedding ring

p. 144 The ring with which the Prince of Wales wed Mrs Fitzherbert at their morganatic marriage in 1785 was a gimmel inscribed with his names, GEORGE AUGUSTUS FREDERICK, on one hoop, and hers, MARIA ANNE, on the other. Jewelled rings continued in use: one in the 1780 inventory of the Colonna family in Rome is described as 'un anello a mariage brillianti e rubini' (a ruby and diamond wedding ring). The Protestant clergy recommended single gold bands – 'plain, precious, pure, as best becomes the wife', in the words of Dr Denman (*Collection of Poems*, Dublin 1801). Whether the intrinsic value was great or small, the wedding ring was so prized that it was usually safeguarded by an enamelled or jewelled keeper. This respect was voiced by a writer advising on 'how to promote and secure happiness in the married state' in the *Lady's Monthly Museum* (1799): 'Always wear your wedding ring for therein lies more virtue than is usually imagined – if you are ruffled unawares, assaulted with improper thoughts, or tempted in any kind against your duty cast your eye upon it and call to mind who gave it to you, where it was received and what passed at that solemn time.'

Souvenirs of weddings sometimes took the form of rings with the initials of the bride and groom: John Marling, guest at the marriage of the Duke of York with Princess Frederica of Prussia in 1791, received one with two Ys interlaced on the oval blue bezel and the hoop inscribed SOYEZ HEUREUX (Be happy; O 794). Ladies present at the wedding of the future Louis XVI with the Archduchess Marie-Antoinette in 1770 were given rings with their miniature portraits as keepsakes.

MEMORIAL RINGS

The ritual of mourning was carried out to the letter. It was more than just an expression of regret for the death of a respected and beloved individual: it was the homage paid to the institutions on which society was founded, the family and the monarchy. Widows wore black for a year, mirrors were covered up, seals were stamped on black and not red wax, and church memorials provided sculptors with important commissions. The classical severity of these monuments is echoed in rings worn in remembrance of the dead. Symbols – the broken column, the obelisk and urn – were derived from antiquity. The pp. 142–43 funerary urn was the most widely used, painted on ivory or vellum, enamelled, highlighted with rose diamonds, the name of the deceased either on the plinth or at the back of the bezel. It is sometimes romanticized by the presence of a faithful dog or weeping willow. Paintings by Angelica Kauffmann and Benjamin West exalting the devoted widow Agrippina bringing home the ashes of Germanicus and Andromache mourning Hector inspired miniatures of women in classical drapery sorrowing over funerary urns and consoled by inscriptions. Many memorial rings contain locks of hair which are pp. 142–43 identified by cipher and date, the hair accompanied by or arranged into appropriate symbols – weeping willow, cypress, or sheaves of wheat, alluding to the Biblical text: 'Those who went sowing in tears ... came back singing, carrying their sheaves' (Ps. 126.5–6).

Rank was always respected. Thus on a ring for a member of the aristocracy the appropriate coronet – of a viscount, baron, earl, marquis or duke – surmounts the urn which is individualized by a cipher. On the death of a monarch there was always a large demand for commemorative rings, often with portraits. Some of those issued on the death of Frederick the Great of Prussia incorporated not only his portrait, with the inscription SEIN ANDENKEN IST UNVERGESLICH GES 1786 (His memory is unforgettable; died 1786), but that of his successor, Frederick William II, both in gold relief under crystal. One of these is in the Victoria and Albert Museum, London.

Contrasting with portrait and symbolic memorial rings is the much simpler category of plain metal or plaited hair dog-collar hoop wide enough to bear the name of the deceased and date of death only. Two bands are intertwined when two persons are com- p. 143 memorated.

ENGRAVED GEMS

Interest in the art of antiquity, intensified by the thrill of the discoveries at Herculaneum and Pompeii, brought the passion for engraved gems to a peak. The modern school of pp. 148–49 engraving, led by Giovanni Pichler, was centred on Rome, but elsewhere in Europe talented artists flourished under royal and aristocratic patronage. Each connoisseur had his own cabinet, and competition for the best gems, both ancient and modern, raised prices to very high levels. The possession of a ring set with a cameo or intaglio thus established the wearer as a man of means as well as of taste. The great majority of cameos were portraits: those who wore them on their fingers could thus demonstrate their admiration for a great philosopher, dramatist, monarch, man of action or celebrated beauty, past or present. Carved in onyx, the top white layer polished like marble and standing out in relief against the dark ground, they are the miniature counterparts of contemporary monumental sculpture.

Intaglios, more austere than cameos, were also worn in rings. Whether they were versions of ancient sculpture or Renaissance paintings, the modern gems were the right scale for the large bezels now fashionable. Those who had to make do with the smaller ancient intaglios might group several together into one long oval or rectangular setting. Not all were engraved with classical themes: the Prince of Wales bought cornelians engraved with the twelve signs of the zodiac as talismans to bring good luck for his friends. Religious and devotional subjects were also commissioned: for the Hon. Mrs Onslow in London Edward Burch engraved a chalcedony intaglio of the woman healed of the issue of blood, inscribed WHO TOUCHES LIVES, after a model by the sculptor John Bacon.

Whereas each hardstone intaglio or cameo was a unique work of art, imitations were available in glass or ceramics for setting in seals, rings and other jewels that brought the fashion within the reach of those of modest means. James Tassie's *Catalogue of Engraved Gems* (1791) lists 15,000 copies of ancient and modern gems made in glass from moulds taken from the most celebrated collections. Tassie specialized, too, in paste cameo

p. 149 portraits of famous contemporaries. Josiah Wedgwood also succeeded in mass-producing gems for jewelry, but using ceramics as his medium. His pure white figures stand out against glossy or matt jasperware grounds tinted in a variety of beautiful colours. Other cheap versions of famous gems were made by stamping the image in gold p. 149 and then applying the relief to a slab of hardstone such as lapis lazuli. These were usually mounted in rings with plain channelled gold rims supported by round hoops broadening out at the shoulders, a style known as Roman settings, being derived from the solid type worn in ancient Rome.

POLITICAL THEMES AND PORTRAITS

Rings held pictures of friends and lovers, as we have seen; they also served to show allegiance to a social group, such as the Freemasons or the Prince of Wales's Je Ne Scais Quoi Club. In addition, all the political issues of the period and leading personalities are mirrored in rings. In Sweden Gustavus III gave those who supported his attempt to restore his royal prerogative against an oligarchy of the nobility a ring with his monogram GIII and crown in rose diamonds on a blue enamel ground, inscribed on the back DEN 19 AUGUSTI 1772.

Meeting the distinguished woman President of the Russian Academy, Princess Dashkov, in 1774 Gustavus took the portrait ring surrounded with diamonds from his finger and presented it as a mark of his regard. These portrait rings might be miniatures, or carved from hardstones or ivory. The most extravagant of all was a portrait of Louis XVI in relief, paved all over with minute rose diamonds (Hope Collection). At the other extreme there were glass copies of gems by Tassie, Wedgwood's jasperware, and stamped gold medallions. By this means far more than a privileged few could show support for a cause and admiration for a personality. So many admirers bought gold medallions of Benjamin Franklin that towards the end of his stay in Paris he wrote to his daughter: 'Your father's face is now as well known as that of the moon.'

In England those loyal to the Hanoverians wore rings set with portraits of George II, p. 149 George III and their families. Others, who hoped for the restoration of the Stuarts, displayed a profile of Prince Charles Edward at the time of his 'accession' as 'Charles III' in 1766. The cause did not entirely fade out with his death in 1788, to judge by Tassie's *Catalogue*, which includes several portraits of him. Political affiliations could also be indicated by classical ringstones. Upholders of the established order wore rings with a portrait of Julius Caesar, while those such as Sylas Neville, who detested the Hanoverians and the Stuarts equally, displayed the head of Brutus (who struck the first blow against p. 152 Caesar) with the dagger and Cap of Liberty. In his *Diary* in 1768 Neville recorded his pleasure when the enigmatic Frenchman, the Chevalier d'Eon, 'admired his ring and noticed his principles of Liberty'.

The storm of fury which swept the country after the Whig demagogue John Wilkes was accused of libel in 1768 and after the government overruled his election to Parlia- p. 152 ment in 1769 is recalled by rings with his portrait, worn by adherents to the cause of

Portrait of an English lady, *c.* 1740, and
detail showing her openwork cluster ring
worn above a gold hoop.

'Wilkes and Liberty'. Wits and Whigs – Wilkes among them – liked to meet at the Beefsteak Club in London, which had been founded for convivial enjoyment in 1735. The
members or 'Steaks' wore rings enamelled with a gridiron surrounded by the slogan p.152
BEEF AND LIBERTY.

The events leading up to and following the French Revolution can all be traced
through rings. The Bastille, seized by the people on 14 July 1789, became a quarry from
which metal and stones were removed for conversion into iron rings bearing such symbols as a bird in an open cage, and inscribed SACRE A LA LIBERTE (Consecrated to freedom) or LIBERTE FRANÇAISE 14 JUILLET and BASTILLE. Next came portraits of
eminent politicians such as C.-J.-M. Barbaroux (1767–94), the symbol of the Cap of
Liberty, and miniatures of nymphs clad in tricolour tunics placing wreaths on the altar of
patriotism. According to the Parisian *Journal de la Mode* for June 1790, 'alliances
civiques' made their appearance: these were like gimmel rings, seemingly single when
closed but opening to show the inner side of the hoops enamelled red, white and blue and
inscribed with the slogan LA NATION LA LOI LE ROY. Next came the 'alliances nationales', with the revolutionary inscription LIBERTE EGALITE FRATERNITE. The assassin-
ations of Marat and Le Peletier de Saint-Fargeau in 1793 were marked by rings with p.152
their stamped portraits. Variants bear those two heads with that of a third martyr to
liberty, Joseph Chalier, guillotined in 1793.

Rings served to declare devotion to the monarchy too. In 1791 little tortoiseshell rings
inscribed in gold piqué with the prayer DOMINE SALVUM FAC REGEM (God save the
King) were put on sale. Then after the executions of the royal family in 1793 came reliquary rings enclosing hair identified by the symbol of the Bourbon lily. Plain mourning
rings were made for English friends, such as Countess Spencer; hers is inscribed in black
enamel on the outside MARIE ANTOINETTE LOUIS XVI IMMOLES EN FRANCE
PLEURES EN ANGLETERRE (. . . immolated in France, mourned in England), and
inside '21 JAN 16 OCT 1793' (private collection). According to Henri Vever, the historian of French 19th-century jewelry, when Talleyrand was in America between January
1793 and November 1795 a number of people decided to copy the signet on his finger,
which bore three lilies lying on the ground, with the words ILS SE RELEVERONT UN
JOUR (One day they will rise again).

In 1798 Helen Mary Williams contributed 'An account of the Present State of Paris'
to the *Lady's Magazine*, and in it she describes the women, 'dressed à la sauvage or à la
Grecque' with classical elegance,

> lamenting most pathetically the subversion of the ancien régime, declaiming against
> the new order to which they owed their elevation. They held fans sparkling with
> spangled fleurs de lys, rings bearing the insignia of royalty and bore about in a
> triumphal manner bonbonnieres with sliding lids displaying the forbidden images
> of regal greatness.

ROCOCO FANCY RINGS

In the 18th century a new type of ring appeared, using small, inexpensive stones in gay designs of no profound significance. This style was diffused through pattern-books, such as the Parisian jeweller J. H. Pouget's *Traité des Pierres Précieuses* of 1762 (*below*). This detail shows designs on the theme of flowers (ribbon-tied and in a basket), love (birds in their nests), and rustic music (panpipes and bagpipes). The central illustration is for the shoulder of a ring, where the split hoop leaves space for a cornucopia filled with flowers.

Rococo *giardinetti* ('little garden') rings – *left* and *opposite* – have openwork shapes that contrast with the massive and sober rings of the Baroque period. Coloured stones are set in gold, diamonds in silver. The pomegranate ring (*left*) belonged to the Scottish heiress Charlotte Strange, who married the 3rd Duke of Atholl in 1753.

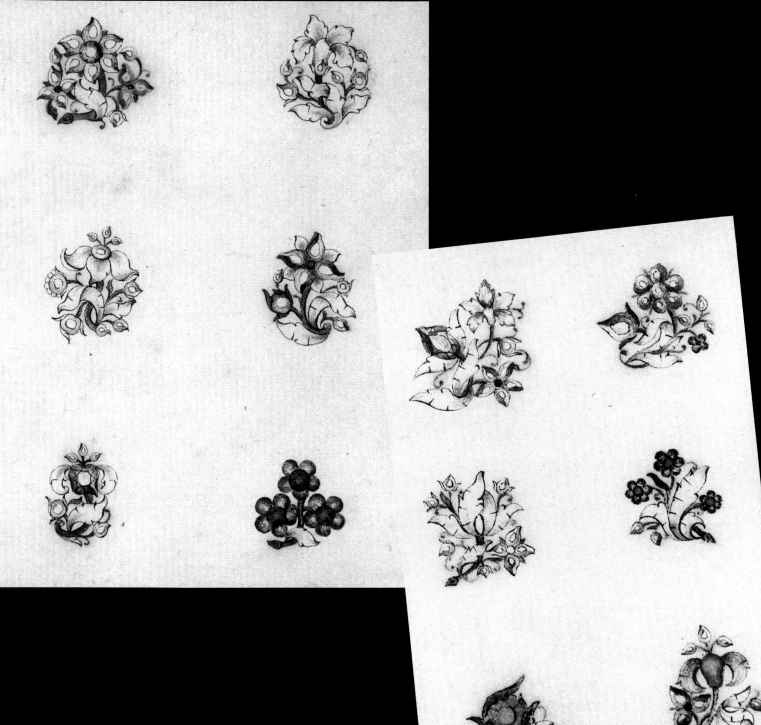

FLOWERS FOR THE FINGER

Designs for the bezels of *giardinetti* rings,
published by Christian Taute, a jeweller working
in London *c*. 1750. Quintessentially Rococo in
spirit, light, delicate and asymmetrical, set with
coloured stones and sparkling diamonds, this style
of ring echoes the floral and fruit patterns of
contemporary silk dresses. Nature poetry was
coming into fashion; soon high-born ladies would
play at being dairymaids and shepherdesses.

LOVE, CARDS AND THE MASQUERADE

Flirting, gaming and masquerading provided other themes for 'fancy' rings in the mid-18th century. Hearts, of rubies and diamonds, may be interlaced or crowned – either as a plump single cabochon or paired. A winning hand at cards is immortalized in enamel, with a diamond in the middle and emeralds round the edges (*below left*). And a face wearing a carnival domino, painted in black and white enamels and with rose diamond eyes, is fixed between delicate split shoulders (*below*).

HEARTS
AND FLOWERS

In 1764 J. H. Pouget published
a further collection of designs.
In addition to *giardinetti* designs
– flowers in baskets, sprays and
little flowerpots – the motifs
include a peacock in its pride,
and love rings with a symbolic
knot, united hearts wreathed in
flowers and ribbons, and
turtledoves guarding Cupid's
bow and quiver.

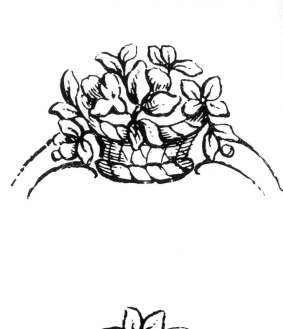

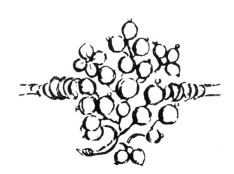

THE PORTRAIT RING

On your finger you might wear the image of your ruler, a famous Greek or Roman, a personal hero, a beloved individual, or even an enemy, depicted satirically.

This page:
Right: Gem-engraving became one of Madame de Pompadour's chief interests, and taught by Jacques Guay she succeeded in carving a cameo portrait of her lover, Louis XV.

Below: Someone who disliked Madame de Pompadour commissioned this chrysoberyl cameo caricature of her with monkey features, wearing elegant diamond jewelry.

Opposite page:
Above: The signets of connoisseurs were set with their favourite gems. William Cavendish, 2nd Duke of Devonshire, who succeeded his father in 1707 and whose magnificent collection of gems is still at Chatsworth, chose an aquamarine intaglio of the Roman Empress Sabina, which he had mounted in a ring bearing his enamelled cipher and coronet at the back.

Below: The most popular form of picture for a portrait ring was the miniature. This one, of Augustus the Strong, Elector of Saxony and King of Poland (1696–1763), is covered by crystal and framed in a brilliant-cut paste border. At the back is a box for hair.

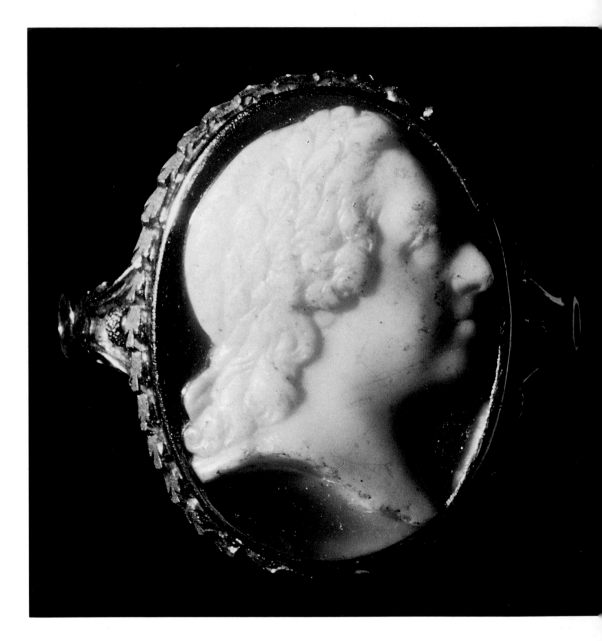

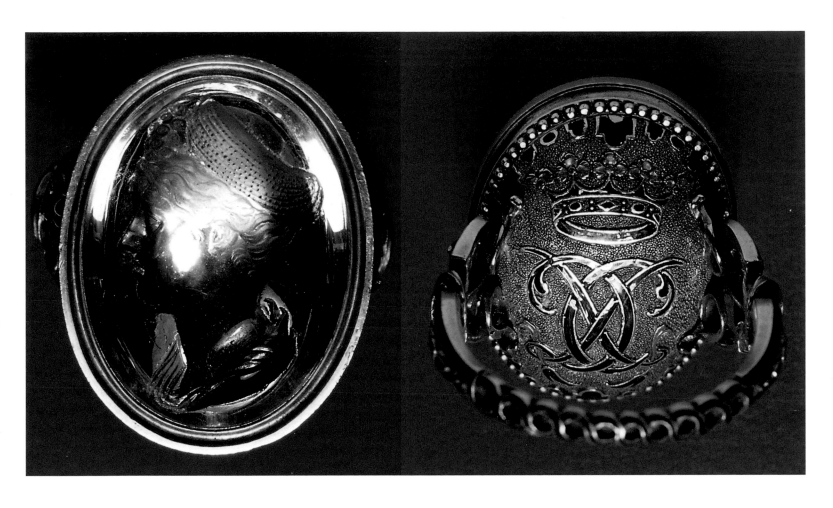

DEATH AND DECAY

Right: A *vanitas* painting dated 1769, inscribed in Latin 'Remember, man, what thou art, and what thou shalt be.' Among the 'vanities' is the lady's jewel-box, which contains rings of lively *giardinetti* shape.

Below: Two hoop rings, with skeletons and gravedigger's tools, of a type popular in the first half of the century. The lower one is inscribed NOT LOST BUT GONE BEFORE.

Far right, above: A locket ring containing hair. The bezel, coffin-shaped, bears a diamond and white enamel memorial urn, outlined in amethysts. The white-enamelled hoop is inscribed AB OB MAY 19 1755 IF I FORGET THEE.

Far right, below: A memorial to George II, who died in 1760 at the age of 77, this sober design sets a pyramid in front of a trophy of arms. The commemorative inscription on the pyramid is carried around the black-enamelled hoop.

With the exception of the dog-collar hoop, these have the austere elongated shape characteristic of the later 18th century, designed to cover the finger up to the knuckle. Diamonds or half-pearls outline the bezel, framing a crystal which protects locks of hair or a symbolic urn or obelisk. Also new is the use of transparent coloured enamel over an engine-turned ground, which gives a shimmering effect. The most expensive here (*second from the left*), inscribed LEONORA LYTTON OBT 13TH MARCH 1790 AET. 67, commemorates the heiress who was the ancestress of the earls of Lytton at Knebworth.

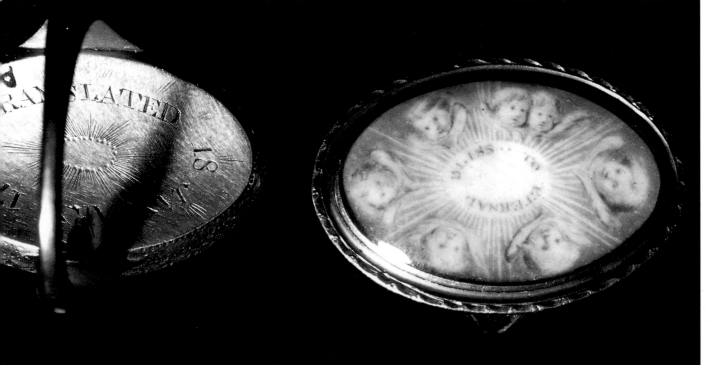

Far left: A pair of rings commemorating two infants. The back is engraved TRANSLATED 18 JANUARY 1782; on the front, protected by a glass, is a miniature of cherub heads surrounding the words TO ETERNAL BLISS.

Left: A new form of hair ring was this plaited dog-collar with a beaded border. The oval disc bears the initials of the deceased, CFS, identified by an inscription inside the hoop as C. F. STEVENS OBT. 31 MAY 1799 AET. 21.

143

Above left: United hearts burn on an altar in a Temple of Love made of hardstones.

Left: The message SOUVENIR, spelt out in rose diamonds, is enclosed in a wide dog-collar ring with an emerald bezel.

Below left: The gimmel ring survived, but much simplified. The one chosen by the Prince Regent (the future George IV) for his marriage to Mrs Fitzherbert in 1785 bears their names – GEORGE AUGUSTUS · FREDERICK on one hoop, MARIA ANNE on the other – and no more.

The new large elongated shapes gave scope for poetic fancy in miniature scenes set under glass and framed by enamel, bright-cut decoration, stones or paste. Those shown here allude to absence from the beloved. In one, a girl in a romantic landscape composes a letter, using a column as a desk (her pose recalling Scheemakers' famous monument to Shakespeare in Westminster Abbey). In the other, two doves – one stationary, one flying away – are linked by a thread tied in a lover's knot; the reassuring message is THE FARTHER I FLY THE FASTER WE TYE.

PICTURES ON THE FINGER

This page:
Above: A tiny scene of a church beside a bridge with trees worked in hair, framed in garnet pastes. The back is inscribed with the name ALICE KEAY.

Below: A polished moss agate, with inclusions suggesting misty trees by a river. This ring belonged to the painter Thomas Gainsborough.

Opposite page:
Above: A splendid Parisian interior, complete with books, portrait, and bust on a Louis XVI console table; a smaller bust stands on the chimneypiece under a glass cover. Through the doorway we glimpse an elegant couple. A little white dog, no doubt the lady's pet, stands near the fireplace. The coloured miniature, under glass, is set in a large ring for a gentleman.

Centre: A pensive shepherdess. The miniature, painted in black, is (like the Parisian interior) covered with glass and set in the simplest of bezels.

Below: An exquisite scene carved of ivory, laid on a background and protected by glass framed in diamonds. Christ and the Woman of Samaria are seen by the well at the moment when He says to her: 'Whosoever drinketh of this water shall thirst again: But whosoever drinketh of the water that I shall give him shall be in him a well of water springing up into everlasting life.' They are watched by two of the disciples, surprised to see Jesus, a Jew, speaking with a Samaritan.

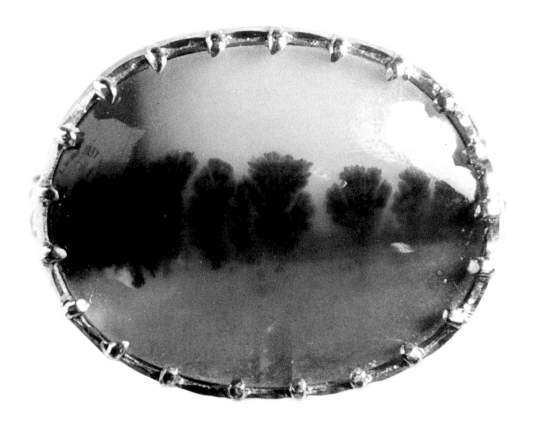

CAMEOS AND INTAGLIOS

The discoveries made at Herculaneum and Pompei from the 1730s on intensified interest in the antique world, and with it the passion for engraved gems. At first, small ancient gems were set in rings; then, as rings grew in size, larger stones were called for. Modern engravers, making copies or new designs, satisfied both fashions. Finally, Tassie's glass-paste gems brought the genre within reach of a wide circle.

This page:
Left: Two views of a ring set with a chalcedony cameo of the infant Hercules, arm raised to strangle a snake sent to kill him. The hoop is inscribed SI VOUS SOUHAITEZ MON REPOS VOUS AUREZ SOIN DE VOTRE SANTE (If you care for my peace of mind you will look after yourself); the back is inset with a heart.

Above: An 18th-century cameo by the Florentine engraver Santarelli showing Omphale, Hercules's wife, parading in his lion skin and carrying his club: beauty triumphs over strength.

Opposite page:
Above left: Detail of a portrait of an Italian gentleman by G. F. Briglia, 1768; he wears a cameo portrait ring.

Above right: A paste cameo of Frederick, Duke of York, mass-produced by Tassie for presentation as a souvenir.

Below left: Detail of the portrait of John Smith, M.P. for Pontefract, painted in Rome by Pompeo Batoni in 1773; he wears a cornelian intaglio in a Roman setting.

Below right: Beryl intaglio of Demosthenes, copied in the 18th century from a Roman original by Dioscourides. The great Athenian orator would have appealed as a subject to a politician such as John Smith.

BEASTS BOTH GREAT AND SMALL

Opposite: A moss agate cameo leopard, crouched ready to spring. This great gem was a gift to Prince Eugene of Savoy, one of the most outstanding generals of his age, from Cardinal Alessandro Albani, himself a celebrated collector. The mount, made for the Prince *c.* 1720, has a chainwork hoop and split shoulders studded with diamonds, extending out to terminate in shells. Described by the antiquary A. F. Gori as 'unico al mondo', this was one of the most admired rings of the 18th century.

Above: A white enamelled rabbit hiding amidst leaves and flowers, mounted on a hoop inscribed TOUJOURS CRAIGNETTE (Ever shy). Presumably it was intended to tease a well-brought-up young lady

HEROES AND ALLEGIANCES

In a political age, rings could proclaim your principles. For
English Whigs there was the portrait of the controversial
politician John Wilkes (*above*), enemy of the Tory Government
from the 1760s on, and champion of parliamentary reform,
freedom of the press, and the rights of North American colonists.
Whigs and wits might also be members of the Sublime Society of
Beefsteaks, a dining club founded in 1735, and wear its ring
(*above right*) with a gridiron surrounded by the motto BEEF AND
LIBERTY. French Revolutionaries, not yet disillusioned by the
Terror, could display rings such as the one *centre right*, of iron,
with stamped gold busts of the 'martyrs' Marat and Le Peletier
de Saint-Fargeau, both assassinated in 1793. All lovers of liberty
not afraid of taking direct action saw Brutus, the assassin of
Julius Caesar, as a hero. An onyx intaglio of *c.* 1760 (*right, below*)
depicts his head in profile, together with his daggers and the Cap
of Liberty.

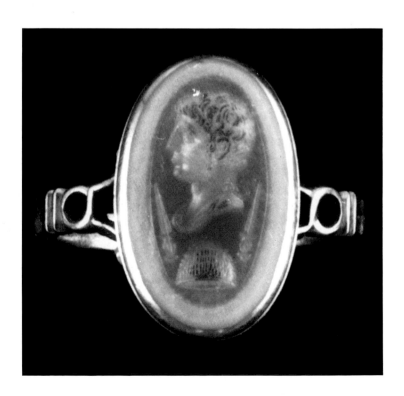

5

The 19th century:
Romanticism and riches

The course of design during the first half of the 19th century was determined by two major influences. The first was the rich Neo-Classicism devised in France by the painter David and the architects Percier p. 159 and Fontaine for the Napoleonic Empire. It was interpreted by the court jeweller Marie-Etienne Nitot in fabulous parures of diamonds and pearls worn with rings set with stones of such importance that none appears to have survived in original condition. This grandiose style did not vanish with the defeat of Napoleon in 1815 but was adopted throughout Europe, not only by the restored Bourbon monarchy but by the other courts of Europe as a means of asserting authority and of commanding respect. The second influence was Romanticism, which also found expression in rings, but of less expensive materials and designed to match the ideas and sentiments of that particular time. Inspiration for designs came from history and legend as vividly evoked by the novels of Sir Walter Scott. Not only writers but architects and artists turned away from classicism to the more recent past. The theme was taken up by jewellers: according to the *World of Fashion*, published in London in 1839, 'the forms of our bijoux are now entirely borrowed from the Middle Ages'; a man-about-town complained that every time he kissed a woman's hand he was bruised by a knight in armour, a page or a greyhound on her fingers.

Drawing of the central motif of a ring in Troubadour style, showing a knight in armour with his weapons and shield (set with nine tiny diamonds encircling a ruby). The sculptural design – here modelled and then cast in gold – is similar to those of F. D. Froment-Meurice.

p. 161 These, and Neo-Renaissance mermaids and cherub heads, were associated with the Parisian jewellers Jean-Paul Robin and François-Desiré Froment-Meurice, the latter hailed by Victor Hugo as the Benvenuto Cellini of Romanticism. Every jeweller kept stock patterns, and family rings were sometimes copied. In London the famous firm of Rundell, Bridge and Rundell sold George IV 'an elegant diamond and ruby ring William of Wykeham pattern' presumably derived from the cruciform ring on the funeral effigy of the Bishop of Winchester (d. 1404) at New College, Oxford. Inscriptions in Gothic lettering, the revival of heraldry for signets, and the return to religious symbolism all echo medieval and Renaissance culture. Jewellers also went to the Baroque and Rococo periods for ideas.

p. 169   It was smart to wear not one large but many smaller, even, hoop rings as *The Lady's Magazine* commented in 1822: 'numerous rings are worn and these form the principal ornaments of value except in grand costume.' Then, of course, one wonderful ring might be worn, set with an important coloured stone framed in a row of diamonds. Men were equally attached to their rings. In 1811, the diarist Henry Crabbe Robinson met 'Incledon the singer on the coach and found him just the man I expected. Seven rings on his finger and five seals on his watch ribbon.' Balzac was inspired by the ring which his beloved Madame Hanska gave him: 'While I work I have it on the index finger of my left hand which is holding the paper and it makes me feel I have you beside me, so that instead of searching in the air for the right word and thought I just ask my lovely ring.'

DECORATIVE GEM- AND PEARL-SET RINGS

The late 18th-century octagon, lozenge and marquise shapes did not go completely out of fashion but overlapped with the new broader, more compact squares and ovals sup- p.170
ported by wide shoulders on substantial hoops. These hoops are often wrought with flowers and leaves in relief or studded with gemstones. Steel and iron make their appear- p.171
ance, especially for Renaissance Revival designs: the ledgers of the Parisian jeweller Fossin for 1842 record the sale to Auguste Thuret of 'une bague corps en acier forme antique' (a steel ring after the antique). Filigree, twisted and curled into scrolls or outlining motifs such as the lyre and studded with bright coloured stones, is introduced p.189
around 1830.

Only the very rich could afford large solitaires such as those sold in 1842 by Fossin to the bankers Colonel Thorn and Baron Schickler. Both were brilliant-cut, mounted in gold; that of Colonel Thorn in an octagonal bezel enamelled black with chased hoop, and that of Baron Schickler in a round bezel supported by twin hoops bound together by a diamond ribbon. Most clients settled for smaller stones in clusters, or in rows, single, double or triple, across the bezel.

Coloured stones are often set in clusters too. A large one may be bordered by a single row of diamonds, enclosed within an outer frame of small stones echoing the colour of that in the centre. The shoulders are emphasized by scrolls, shells, Neo-Renaissance strapwork and mermaids, sometimes embellished by diamonds. Dog collars, jewelled p.186
and enamelled, were the height of fashion with as many as five hoops being worn on one finger. Lady Fitzhenry, the bride in Lady Charlotte Bury's novel *A Marriage in High Life* (1828), happily admires the 'circles of diamonds, rubies – presents of doting parents and perhaps envious friends' above her wedding band. The stones might be uniform in colour or in harlequin mixtures such as that given by George IV to Lord Albert Conyngham (son of his favourite, the Marchioness Conyngham), with the hoop set round with groups of diamond, emerald, sapphire and ruby repeated thrice round the circumference.

Colour is also supplied by opals, garnets, chrysoprases, peridots, malachite, turquoises, aquamarines and other semi-precious stones. Being large and relatively inexpensive, these were often set as solitaires in chased enamelled gold bezels, as well as in single or double clusters. In 1842 Fossin set a turquoise in an exotic design with chased gold hoop terminating at the shoulders with two Indian-style dragon heads.

Whereas most pearls were set in plain hoops or half-hoops, occasionally the finest specimens were mounted as solitaires. Various designs for them are recorded in the Fossin ledgers during the 1840s. One pearl was secured by four lions' claws and supported by a turquoise blue and rose diamond hoop. Others were inspired by the past, with Gothic-style cusped bezels, Celliniesque damascened steel and gold hoops, and Rococo ribbons and bows. Both black and white pearls were set amidst diamonds which either encircle the bezel or are mounted at the shoulders.

Fancy rings

Insect and flower rings in the 18th-century taste remained in fashion for some time. Seed pearl and rose diamond bouquets of flowers set in marquise or octagonal bezels enamelled blue in the Neo-Classical style were still made in the 1840s. The cipher ring was adapted to Romanticism by the use of angular Gothic letters: this type was chosen by Louis Philippe, king of France 1830–48, for presentation. His crowned cipher LP is set against an oval royal blue bezel framed in white paste leaves (B 43D).

The range now available made it possible to convey names, messages and dates in all languages using the initial letters of stones. According to Etienne de Jouy, in *L'Hermite de la Chaussée d'Antin* (1811), the Parisian jeweller Mellerio was the first to use stones in this way. Thus a ring for someone called Rose would be set with a *r*uby, *o*pal, *s*apphire and *e*merald. Others, studded with stones spelling out the days of the week, were called 'Semaines' when introduced in 1827. The long-established puzzle ring was brought up-to-date with the multiple hoops – chased, ribbed, cable twist or plain – each set with a stone combining into a message or motto such as REGARD when closed up to support a bezel.

p.180

Enamelling was used to depict motifs which might reflect personal interests, such as squirrels, hounds, fox masks, blackamoors, carnival dominoes, open and closed books, or purses. More popular than any of these novelties was the cassolette, or container for perfume or camphor sniffed in the hope of avoiding infections, which was hung from a chain attached to the finger ring.

p.188

LOVE AND MARRIAGE

The heroine of Mrs Gore's novel *The Debutante* (1846) looks down with pleasure on the 'small ruby ring that sparkled on her finger, the first pledge of love from Lord Mortayne which brought back all the pride of conquest to her heart'. It had no other meaning; on the other hand, the ring which Prince Albert gave Queen Victoria when their engagement was announced in 1839 was an emerald-studded snake, symbolic of eternity.

Snakes – coils twisted round the finger, once, twice or more, head studded with a precious stone, ruby eyes gleaming wickedly – were made of gold, chased to simulate scales and sometimes enamelled royal or pale blue. This symbol was combined with a butterfly, emblematic of Psyche, Cupid's beloved, in a ring sold by Rundell, Bridge and Rundell to George IV in 1823. Filigree butterflies set with diamonds and coloured stones also

p.179

appear on their own, or hover over pansies (symbolizing thought), their petals composed of stones of contrasting colour, such as amethyst with turquoise or tawny gold topaz. *The Lady's Magazine* in 1822 described 'ingenious kinds of rings given as remembrances from one friend to another with little forget-me-nots formed of turquoise stones with a p. 179 diminutive diamond or topaz in the centre of the flower to imitate the natural appearance of this little interesting hedge blossom'. Evergreen ivy, which clings tenaciously wherever it grows, was another symbol of fidelity, used by Fossin for brooches and bracelets but especially for rings, the trails of leaves standing out on bright red hoops.

Succinct compliments – REGARD, AMORE, SOUVENIR – are conveyed by hieroglyphs of stones (see above, p. 157). Longer messages such as GAGE DE FIDELITE (Pledge of fidelity) and JE VOUS AIME (I love you) are inscribed in seed pearls or in rose diamonds. The more individual posies were hidden inside the hoop. In her novel *Glenarvon* (1816), Lady Caroline Lamb tells how Alice's lover had given her an emerald ring inscribed ETERNA FEDE (Ever faithful) in token of his fidelity; 'time had worn off and defaced the first impression' and in its place she had it re-engraved ETERNO DOLOR (Eternal sorrow), 'thus telling in a few words the whole history of love – the immensity of its promises – the cruelty of its disappointment'.

Single and twinned coloured stone hearts continue another long tradition. A single p. 181 heart ring may be hinged like a locket, the inside enamelled with a symbolic pansy or a forget-me-not. Some were highly personal, like that of Ortia, former favourite of Queen Maria Luisa of Spain, which according to Lady Holland contained 'secret springs and devices which I was given to understand were not to be examined'. The *fede* ring with clasped hands carved from onyx, malachite or coral, wrought in gold, paved in turquoises, highlighted with diamonds or rubies, was equally in demand. Lady Hamilton wore hers – a gift from Lord Nelson – as a keeper to her wedding band. Hearts and hands terminate not only single but also gimmel hoops inscribed with the names of the pp. 180–81 couple and date of the marriage. The wedding ring, whether a twin jewelled hoop or plain single gold band, was accorded immense respect, summed up in a poem, 'The Moral Influence of the Wedding-Ring', published in *The Lady's Monthly Museum* for May 1828, which concludes:

> this round of gold
> Safe, though unwatched, can wildest beauty hold,
> And proves that virtue by one pledge controls
> Our island goddesses and free-born souls.

The *fede* ring given by Nelson to Emma Hamilton.

HAIR AND MEMORIAL RINGS

The Empress Marie-Louise wore a ring containing the hair of her husband, Napoleon, and of their son, because it made her feel they were closer to her. The hair, hidden beneath glass, a stone or a miniature, is identified by initials and sometimes accompanied by a motto or prayer such as VEILLE SUR CE QUE J'AIME (May God watch over my pp. 186–87 beloved). Some firms made hair jewelry exclusively. The rings were usually made of plaited hair strengthened by a metal hoop supporting a bezel with love and friendship symbols and plaques with initials in Gothic letters or the name, or FATHER, MOTHER, BROTHER, SISTER, inscribed. In the more elaborate models the hair is fitted into a Greek key pattern or worked into oblique bands alternating with strips of gold. These patterns can easily be distinguished from 18th-century rings for they are solid rather than elegant, wide rather than elongated. Keepers, enamelled and embellished with pearls, kept the hair rings safe on the finger.

Memorial rings – thickly enamelled black or white – worn in remembrance of the dead nearly always contained hair too, enclosed in square or round bezels supported by broad hoops with the name of the deceased inscribed within the hoop or at the back or front of the bezel. Besides the obvious funerary motifs, such as urns and weeping wil-p. 179 lows, some of the same features are found as on love rings. Pansies, forget-me-nots and snakes were considered equally appropriate in a memorial context, signifying as they did either faithful remembrance or a love enduring beyond the limits of human life. Crests and coronets, diamonds and pearls proclaimed the worldly importance of the royal and noble, while ordinary folk made do with no more than a name and date inscribed round black or white dog-collar-style hoops.

Celebrated individuals such as Sir Walter Scott were recorded by small stamped gold medallions set under glass or by Tassie-style paste imitations of cameo and intaglio portraits. Silhouettes by John Field were used for some of the rings worn in memory of p. 185 Jeremy Bentham, propounder of the theory of Utilitarianism (d. 1832): that given to the Guatemalan politician José Cecilio del Valle is proudly displayed in his portrait, in token of his staunch Benthamite principles.

POLITICAL THEMES

The battles for national independence, the struggle for more liberal government, and the careers of political leaders are all recorded in rings. Napoleon asserted his authority with gifts of rings bearing his symbol, the imperial eagle, or his cipher N crowned by the laurel branches of victory. Those closest to him received his portrait painted in miniature by J. B. Isabey or engraved on hardstone, like a Roman emperor. For wider distribution there were stamped gold or paste portraits: two such rings were among the jewels of the actress Mademoiselle Mars stolen in 1827. Other gold medallions were hidden in the locket rings given to the six officers who assisted in Napoleon's escape from Elba in 1814, beneath lids enamelled with bunches of the symbolic 'immortelle' or everlasting flower. During the years of the Emperor's exile at St Helena optimistic loyalists wore

A Napoleonic memorial ring. On the gold bezel (which conceals a glazed locket compartment for hair) is the crowned N of the Emperor, between laurel sprays; on the shoulders are the imperial eagles. The ring is inscribed with the name of Charlotte Bonaparte, Napoleon's niece.

rings with sailing ships inscribed IL REVIENDRA (He will return). Then after 1821 came the memorial rings. In the most dramatic a coffin-shaped bezel contains an enamelled figure of the Emperor which springs up when the lid opens. Further commemorative jewelry was made in 1841 when the remains of Napoleon were returned to France. For Mrs Bingham, wife of an American banker living in Paris, Fossin made a coffin-shaped ring with the cipher N engraved on rock crystal flanked on each side by the imperial bee in black enamel.

p. 182

The British public, in gratitude to the statesman William Pitt, Admiral Lord Nelson and the Duke of Wellington, who had saved the country from invasion by the French, wore their portraits in rings. One, a signet set with a jasper intaglio of Nelson inscribed with the famous Trafalgar signal, ENGLAND EXPECTS EVERY MAN TO DO HIS DUTY, has maritime motifs of anchor chains at the shoulders. Another ring set with a classicizing cameo head of the Emperor Otho flanked by crocodiles, emblematic of the Nile, could also allude to Nelson's defeat of Napoleon in Egyptian waters.

p. 184

p. 172

In Prussia citizens gave their gold jewelry to finance the wars of liberation from the armies of Napoleon. In return they received jewelry made by the Berlin iron foundries, including rings. Some reproduce the portraits of Marshal Blücher and King William III in relief, like cameos; others bear patriotic inscriptions. The Iron Cross, established in 1813 to honour those who had distinguished themselves in the campaign and therefore symbolic of national pride, appears in rings too.

p. 184

The restoration of the French monarchy in 1814 allowed free expression of regret for the deaths of Louis XVI and Marie-Antoinette. That mood, and the reign of Louis XVIII, the fall of Charles X in 1830, and the hopes for the eventual accession of the Bourbon Pretender, the Comte de Chambord, known to his supporters as Henri V (1820–83), are reflected in rings in the form of portraits, the symbolic fleur-de-lis, and mottoes. The latter include MON DIEU MON ROI ET MA DAME (My God, my king and my lady), evocative of feudal chivalry, and MADAME VOTRE FILS EST MON ROI (Madam your son is my king), deriving from a phrase used by the statesman Chateaubriand in a letter to the Duchesse de Berri, mother of the Comte de Chambord.

p. 187

p. 182

Supporters of the cause of Greek independence signalled their involvement with rings of tortoiseshell inlaid with gold Greek crosses, designed by the jeweller Lormeau in Paris. In Ireland, patriots disappointed by the failure of the British Government to emancipate the Catholic Church after the Act of Union in 1800 wore rings with the national symbols of the harp and the shamrock.

DEVOTIONAL AND ECCLESIASTICAL RINGS

A return to religion followed the atheistic excesses of the French Revolution. In Paris old churches were restored and new ones built to make room for the crowds who wanted to hear famous preachers such as the Dominican father Lacordaire. Fashionable women carried missals mounted in gold and bound in velvet, hung crosses round their necks, and carried medallions of patron saints in the centrepieces of bracelets and on their p.192 fingers. Rosary rings were a speciality of Parma in Italy: in 1816 the ex-Empress Marie-Louise sent one to her friend the Comtesse de Crenneville, asking her to use it to say prayers for her 'as I so much need'. Although the Holy Office ruled in 1836 that rosary rings were not granted indulgences, Fossin's clients went on buying them. That made for the Comtesse de Saint-Cloud bore a rose diamond cross on the bezel supported by a hoop studded with a decade of rubies. Other rings alluded to the Christian virtues, with the cross of Faith, the anchor of Hope and the torch of Charity, engraved, enamelled, or set with the emblematic diamond, emerald and ruby. The two powerful symbols of Faith and Wisdom were combined in rings made by Fossin during the 1840s: a blue enamel p.192 snake with diamond studded head, alluding to the Biblical injunction, 'Be ye wise as serpents', is entwined round a small diamond cross mounted in gold.

The German custom of giving a ring as a memento of confirmation originated in the early 19th century. In a novel set in the winter of 1812–13, Theodor Fontane's *Before the Storm* (1878), one of the characters declares that since the ring was a symbol of eternal and inviolable loyalty no solemn occasion, least of all an ecclesiastical one, was complete without it. For a confirmation the Biblical quotation BE FAITHFUL UNTO DEATH (Rev. 2.10) was recommended.

The Roman jewellers continued to supply popes with the intaglio of the Fisherman casting his net for the papal seal, the traditional cameo portraits for presentation, and the usual sapphire and amethyst rings for cardinals and bishops. The superb cameo ring of p.183 Pope Pius VII (1801–23) given to Cardinal Caleppi for his exemplary loyalty during the Napoleonic period echoes the legendary commissions of the Renaissance. It is mounted on a swivel; the top face bears the portrait, habille in gold and diamond vestments, while on the other side his device, a processional cross, and the word PAX stand out on the paved diamond ground. The space between the forked shoulders is filled by cameo heads of blindfolded blackamoors, also taken from the Pope's Chiaramonti family arms.

SIGNETS

Essential to the appearance of the well-dressed gentleman was a signet bearing his crest or coat of arms which might show a family tree going back to the Crusades. Most settings were inspired by Renaissance designs. The massive gold ring of the 6th Duke of Devonshire is set with a light green chrysoprase intaglio of his cipher D surmounted by a ducal coronet and framed in the collar of the Order of the Garter. The more figurative styles were revived by Froment-Meurice; a ring ordered by the Duchesse d'Orléans from Fossin in 1843, described as having two putti holding a bezel set with a jasper seal surmounted by a gold princely coronet, was clearly close to his sculptural manner.

A silver-gilt signet in the style of Froment-Meurice, bought in Paris in 1852 by Lord Londesborough.

The second half of the 19th century was a time of unprecedented economic expansion in Europe and America, enriching both the old aristocracy and the new business class who spent fortunes on luxury goods. It was therefore a golden age for jewellers: the established firms such as Tiffany in New York and Garrard in London prospered more than ever, and two newcomers, Cartier and Boucheron, emerged in Paris. There was a demand for the formal grandeur of tiaras, necklaces and stomachers; rings, though somewhat overshadowed by so much splendour, echoed the great display of wealth on head and bosom.

The supply of precious stones increased. The British annexation of Burma in 1886 meant more rubies and sapphires were available, and after the discovery of mines in South Africa the market was flooded with diamonds. Fine natural Oriental pearls, both white and coloured, were more prized than ever before. Designs now emphasized scale. The enamelled gold rings worn by day derived from Japanese and Russian art as well as from the Western tradition. The English journal *Queen* reported in 1870 that 'the novelty is cloisonné enamel applied to gold and made into beautiful brooches and rings ... the grounds are lapis lazuli blue, dark yellow or dusky olive, almost covered with brilliant floral decorations in the Russian style.'

The various styles can be followed through the pages of albums preserved in the Cartier Archives, recording rings made from the founding of the firm in 1847. They reflect the eclecticism current in all the arts. The opening of the Suez Canal in 1861 stimulated the revival of motifs derived from ancient Egypt, already part of the French and English traditions since the Napoleonic campaigns. *Queen* in 1870 described a ring made by the London jewellers Howell and James which was 'reproduced from the ancient Egyptian: four large oriental pearls with a diamond centre form the main arrangement of the ring while extending from this central arrangement are golden plates or escutcheons on which groups of papyrus are richly enamelled.' Jacques-Emile Blanche remembered the aesthete Oscar Wilde in 1889 walking about Paris 'with a sun-flower in his button hole and with his famous sphinx ring on his finger'. The papyrus motif appears on the shoulders of a ring sold by Cartier in 1897 and on three other designs – one of them, by Paul Robin, p. 191 combining it with Pharaonic heads. Scarabs, which were found everywhere in the ruins of ancient Egypt, were often brought home after a tour there and set in rings.

Even stronger was the influence of Greek and Roman jewelry, now reinterpreted with far more archaeological accuracy than in the Empire period. There were three austere Roman-style rings in the casket of classicizing gold jewelry made by Castellani of Rome p. 173 and presented to Princess Maria Pia of Savoy, daughter of Victor Emmanuel II of Italy, on her marriage to the King of Portugal in 1862. The acquisition of the Campana collection of antiquities by Napoleon III for the Louvre brought beautiful models to the attention of Parisian jewellers: according to *Queen* (1863), 'the Campana museum has obviously had a great influence on the designs and tastes of working jewellers and some of the most exquisite things to be seen in the rue de la Paix are reproductions on a very improved scale of some of the filigree and gold ornaments forming part of it.' Jules Wièse made rings set with large uncut coloured stones in bezels gripped by snakes, copied from

p. 173 a model found at Pompeii.

Gothic-style rings are much rarer. There were two in the parure which the Gothic Revival architect A. W. N. Pugin showed at the Great Exhibition of 1851 in London, and thereafter the principal English exponent of medievalizing jewelry was William Burges, also an architect.

p. 176
pp. 174–75 The richer Neo-Renaissance ring was much more in tune with fashionable taste during the second half of the century. Jules Wièse proved a master of the type, reproducing rings with box bezels, chased sides and projecting shoulders, all brightly enamelled. The figurative style introduced by Froment-Meurice and Jean-Paul Robin in the 1840s then became a speciality of the latter's son, Paul Robin, who supplied Fossin and his successors, Morel and Chaumet. In London, the Neapolitan jeweller Carlo Giuliano, a protégé of Castellani, made his reputation by adapting the enamelled designs of the Renaissance and Baroque periods to the Victorian desire for the ample and solid.

p. 177 The affinity of the Empress Eugénie for Queen Marie-Antoinette encouraged the revival of Neo-Classical rings, particularly in the form of the oblong and marquise bezels filled with glass paste and ornamented with diamond sprigs or ciphers made by Frédéric Philippi from the 1850s. Ciphers remained in fashion: a version by Frédéric
p. 177 Boucheron, with the interlaced initials set with rose diamonds, dates from 1887.

DECORATIVE GEM- AND PEARL-SET RINGS

pp. 190–91 Settings for gems and pearls were inspired principally by 18th-century Rococo and Neo-Classical styles. Cartier's ledgers for 1873 illustrate diamonds set in clusters, or closely paved onto marquise bezels, and two large pear-shaped brilliants tied with a ribbon. In
p. 191 1897 a brilliant appears framed in rose diamonds tied with a bow in the 18th-century style. Silver was polished bright so as not to detract from the white brilliance of the stones. Platinum was now coming into use too, knurled into millegrain or tiny beaded edges sparkling with myriad points of light. Another new development was the Tiffany setting, introduced in 1887, which lifted the stone away from the mount so that the light could flood in from all sides and be reflected back again from the facets revealing the brilliant-cut to fullest advantage. In contrast, the gipsy setting, introduced at the same time,
pp. 171,
190 sunk one or three stones deep into the metal so that the top surface of the stone was flush with the mount. Then came the increasingly popular twist and cross-over styles, the
p. 171 stones set at the extremities of the hoop so they lay across the finger.

The most unusual designs came from the workshop of Paul Robin. Some were for diamonds, but most seem to have been for coloured stones. The style is naturalistic, with the stones gripped by reptiles, held in leopards' paws, swallowed by monsters, set in the breasts of eagles, nestling amidst waterlilies, bullrushes, vine leaves and peapods, supported by elephant heads or hoops of interlaced branches. Two nymphs hold up a sapphire; twin mermaids, their tails running down the hoop, frame a ruby. This Neo-Renaissance style is also represented by an 1897 Cartier drawing of an emerald flanked

The classic Tiffany setting, introduced in 1887.

by monsters. Another unusual design, but one that owes nothing to the past, was made for Cartier by Alphonse Fouquet in 1879: a drop-shaped sapphire is set in a diadem bezel outlined in rose diamonds, placed at right angles to the hoop.

p. 190

Cartier's ledgers also show pearl settings typical of the later 19th century: large specimen pearls, pure white or coloured – pink or bronze – were mounted between diamonds or encircled by brilliants in a cluster, and pearls of contrasting tints – pink, grey and white – might be grouped into trefoils, sometimes outlined in rose diamonds. A novelty was reported in *Queen* in 1865: 'a quaint little ring consisting of the device of a pearl in an oyster'. Most popular of all the semi-precious stones used was the turquoise, followed by the opal and then the catseye.

Mrs Florence Fenwick Miller, columnist of the *Illustrated London News*, complained in 1887 that most designs were banal and regretted seeing 'fine stones set in straight rows with as much notion of beauty and originality in their arrangement as in an old fashioned box edging to a garden. Anybody else's diamond ring is just like anybody else's diamond bangle. The beauty of the stones is quite sufficient: ladies do not want attention drawn from that by any peculiarity of the setting'. This accounts for the standardization of the majority of rings, which are no more than half- or full hoops set with stones, sometimes uniform in colour but often with the coloured stones alternating with diamonds or pearls. A refinement illustrated by Cartier in 1874 and 1881 consists of five very thin bands of diamonds highlighted with rubies, sapphires, and emeralds, joined into one wide dog collar. An innovation was noticed in *Queen* in 1887: 'Aluminium band rings set with rubies and diamonds are just introduced. They are already popular as being uncommon and wonderfully light in weight.' Until a cheap method of producing it commercially was developed in the early 20th century, aluminium remained an exotic and sought-after material.

pp. 170–71

p. 190

LOVE, MARRIAGE AND FRIENDSHIP

Immediately after the engagement was announced the fiancé bought the most expensive ring he could afford. For a few years pearls were fashionable: *Queen* informed its readers in 1876, 'engagement rings are usually pearls. Last year the pattern was two medium sized pearls but separated by small diamonds, this year it is a single pearl of great size and without diamonds.'

Symbolic *fede* rings with clasped hands, and hearts – twinned, crowned, flaming – retained their hold over the popular imagination, especially in rural districts. The betrothal rings of the Bolzano region in South Tyrol are particularly distinctive, being made of silver-gilt and set in patterns of coloured pastes alternating with blackberries. The *fede* motif is at the base of the hoop. The people of West Connemara in Ireland used *claddagh* rings with hands holding a crowned heart, and similar designs were given in France by the peasants of Vendée, Normandy and Brittany. Expensive versions were made by the great jewellers. For her marriage in 1888 with the Marquis d'Eyrangues, Henriette de Montesquiou Fezenzac chose, according to *Queen*, an 'engagement ring, une bague normande, like those used by the people of Normandy in the shape of two

p. 178

hearts, one a ruby set with diamonds, the other a diamond set in rubies.' These heart-shaped gem rings, or *bagues coeurs*, were made by Cartier and by Robin, and were also advertised in the trade catalogues of the London jewellers. In a version by Castellani the ruby heart is offered by a gold hand. Such rings were not reserved exclusively for pledges of engagement. Close friends exchanged them as keepsakes, and at the wedding of Louisa Wilkinson with the Viscount Maidstone in 1887 each bridesmaid wore a heart-shaped pearl and diamond ring as a memento of the occasion.

p. 181

The wedding ring itself was usually a massive gold band, narrowing down in the 1890s. Continental husbands as well as wives wore wedding rings, but few Englishmen followed the example of Prince Albert in this respect. Exceptions included the Prince of Wales, the future Edward VII, and his son the Duke of York. It was still customary to inscribe the ring with the initials, date of the marriage, and sometimes a motto. Keeper rings varied from chased gold bands and the popular buckled strap design to the more expensive jewelled hoops. For Princess Alexandra in 1863 the Prince of Wales ordered a keeper from Garrard set with stones spelling out his familiar name, Bertie, by means of *b*eryl, *e*merald, *r*uby, *t*urquoise, *j*acinth and *e*merald.

Rings exchanged by friends and lovers bore appropriate symbols and inscriptions. The snake, coiled several times round the finger, with date and initials inscribed within, and the ivy leaf of fidelity remained favourites.

For those facing separation there were rings inscribed MIZPAH, recalling the Biblical phrase, 'the Lord watch between me and thee when we are absent from one another' (Gen. 31.49). The Greek AEI (Always) was also popular. It was inscribed on a small gold ring which Isabella Blagden gave in 1857 to the poet Elizabeth Barrett Browning, who thanked her in a letter 'for this exquisite little ring – shall I not keep it for ever as a memorial of what must last as long, my true love for you, dear?'

Close friendships between young men were also marked by gifts of rings. The painter John Everett Millais, just before the departure of his brother Pre-Raphaelite William Holman Hunt to the Holy Land in 1854, wrote:

> I don't think I shall have the strength to say good bye – scarcely a night passes but what I cry like an infant over the thought that I may not see you again – I wish I had something to remember you by and I desire that you should go to Hunt and Roskell and get yourself a signet ring which you must always wear ... get a good one and have your initials engraved thereon.

This signet, with the two men's initials engraved on a pink and white sardonyx, was worn by Hunt for the rest of his life and has remained in his family. The gold buckled strap which Oscar Wilde and Reginald Harding gave their fellow undergraduate William Ward when he went down from Oxford in 1876 commemorates the bond between them. It has their initials inside and on the outside a Greek inscription translating 'A memento of friendship from two friends to a third' (Magdalen College Library, Oxford).

MEMORIAL RINGS

Since the conventions of mourning were most strictly respected, memorial rings – now large, stark and simple – were much in evidence. In *Great Expectations* (1861) Charles Dickens describes the good-hearted Mr Wemmick, who 'appeared to have sustained many bereavements for he wore at least four mourning rings . . . I noticed too that several rings and seals hung from his watch chain.' Trade catalogues advertise stock types, with braided hair enclosed in metal bands enamelled black and bearing initials, dates and symbols – seed pearl crosses, forget-me-nots – and simple inscriptions such as IN MEMORY OF . . . . Hair was also placed under crystal in round or oval locket bezels, and so were portraits. A fine locket ring commemorating Victor Emmanuel II (d. 1878) has a black lid with his crowned diamond cipher; inside is his miniature, covered by glass. By this date it was more usual for photographs to be inserted in memorial lockets and rings: one was in the collection of memorial jewelry which Queen Victoria distributed after the death of Prince Albert in 1862.

pp. 186–87

p. 185

PRESENTATION RINGS

Gifts of jewelry were the usual means by which royal persons acknowledged services. Dr Thomas Evans, the American dentist who attended the Emperor Alexander and Empress Marie of Russia in 1858, received valuable rings from them: some bore a crowned cipher, others were set with important stones in massive gold. Queen Victoria and her family liked to be remembered by portrait rings. This type is exemplified by a group made by Garrard for the visit of the Prince of Wales to India at the time of the proclamation of Queen Victoria as Empress in 1875. The locket bezel is set with his enamelled portrait framed in a diamond Garter, and there are leaves and roses on the shoulders.

POLITICAL THEMES

In Continental Europe citizens wore rings expressing resentment of foreign rule and invasion. *Queen* in 1867 reprinted an ordinance from the Russian Governor of Petrikan in Poland:

> for some time past the authorities have remarked among a certain number of persons a tendency to wear revolutionary emblems such as a particular kind of ring. . . . I warn the public that all such persons who shall exhibit such objects will incur a severe punishment and will be placed under the surveillance of the police.

In 1871 *Queen* noticed rings made by the firm of Froment-Meurice commemorating the German bombardment of Paris during the Franco-Prussian War:

> Some rings have been recently introduced which the fair Parisiennes are purchasing to present to their husbands as a souvenir of the siege and foreigners are buying as a souvenir of Paris. These rings which are very wide are of oxydised silver: a coronet

of laurel leaves is chased all round them: on one side the arms of the City of Paris are chased and on the other an escutcheon with the words TOUS AU DANGER TOUS A L'HONNEUR 1870–1871 (United in danger, united in honour).

Patriots showed their objection to the German annexation of the provinces of Alsace and Lorraine in 1871 by wearing rings stamped with the initials AL, the emblems of the sword and the cross, coats of arms, and the motto ESPOIR (Hope).

The conflict between Republicans and those desiring the restoration of the monarchy is also illustrated in French rings. The fall of President Thiers in 1873 was followed by a time of uncertainty during which the way was open for the accession of the Bourbon Pretender, the Comte de Chambord. Rings with his cipher HV and shield with the crowned Bourbon lily were worn by Royalists in token of their desire to see him back. However, his insistence on the principle of Divine Right cost him the crown, and the Republic once again established itself in popular favour. By 1889 the centenary of the Revolution could be celebrated with great rejoicings, and citizens showed their approval by wearing rings bearing the evocative symbol of the Cap of Liberty.

ECCLESIASTICAL AND DEVOTIONAL RINGS

The most interesting development was the introduction of Christian imagery into episcopal rings, both in Roman Catholic and Protestant countries. The massive bezels are set with an amethyst or a sapphire – flanked by long crosses in a ring made by Köchert, the Viennese court jeweller, in 1890 (Schatzkammer, Vienna). Two guardian angels stand at the shoulders of an amethyst ring made for Chaumet of Paris in 1889. When the Anglican Bishop Harold Browne transferred from the see of Ely to that of Winchester in 1875 he was given a ring in which the heads of the respective diocesan patrons, SS. Etheldreda and Swithin, look out from oval recesses on either side of an uncut sapphire. (This is preserved in the Treasury of Winchester Cathedral.)

p.175

Rings made for private devotional purposes in Roman Catholic countries fall into two categories: there are the rosary rings, often given at a First Communion, and those bought as souvenirs of pilgrimages to shrines, stamped with cult images such as those of St Anthony of Padua, the Black Virgin of Le Puy, and Our Lady of Lourdes.

SIGNETS

Looking for a gift which would keep her always in his thoughts, Lucy Lyttleton chose an onyx signet for Lord Frederick Cavendish when they became engaged in 1864. It was the mark of a gentleman everywhere. In the novel *The Dodd Family Abroad* (1872), C. Lever describes the favourable impression made on the English by Signor Giacomo Lamporeccho, 'a tall fine looking man of about forty dressed in very accurate black with a splendid chain of mosaic gold across his ample chest, opal shirt studs and waist coat buttons and a very gorgeous looking signet ring designed to show off a stylish look'.

Portrait of Princess Marie of Baden, Duchess of Hamilton. As a relative of Napoleon I and wife of one of the richest men in Europe, she was a very grand lady; yet her rings, which epitomize the taste of the Romantic period, are small and symbolic, indicative of sentiment rather than wealth.

The rings become more solid and more uniform in design, with square, oval or shield-shaped bezels; these are engraved with monograms or initials in Roman, Lombardic or Gothic characters and with coronets, crests, and coats of arms, with or without mottoes. Some were left plain. The substantial settings, which were reduced in scale around 1890, were available in a range of stock patterns. An advertisement for T. Moring of London includes no less than nine different designs.

CAMEOS AND MOSAICS

Discussing Parisian fashions in 1863, *Queen* observed the strong preference for cameo rings: 'one Duchess will wear upon her finger a ring which to all appearances is worth nothing but in reality has cost 1,200 francs being an engraved stone of the time of Henri II (d. 1559) – cameos take the first rank they have no rivals for toilettes worn during the day.' p. 176

Much cheaper were the cameos carved from shell and Vesuvian lava which travellers brought home from Italy. In Rome, where glass mosaics were a speciality, they also acquired brightly coloured miniature reproductions of the monuments which, like the cameos, could be set in rings, where they were both ornaments and reminders of happy adventures or pilgrimages abroad. p. 192

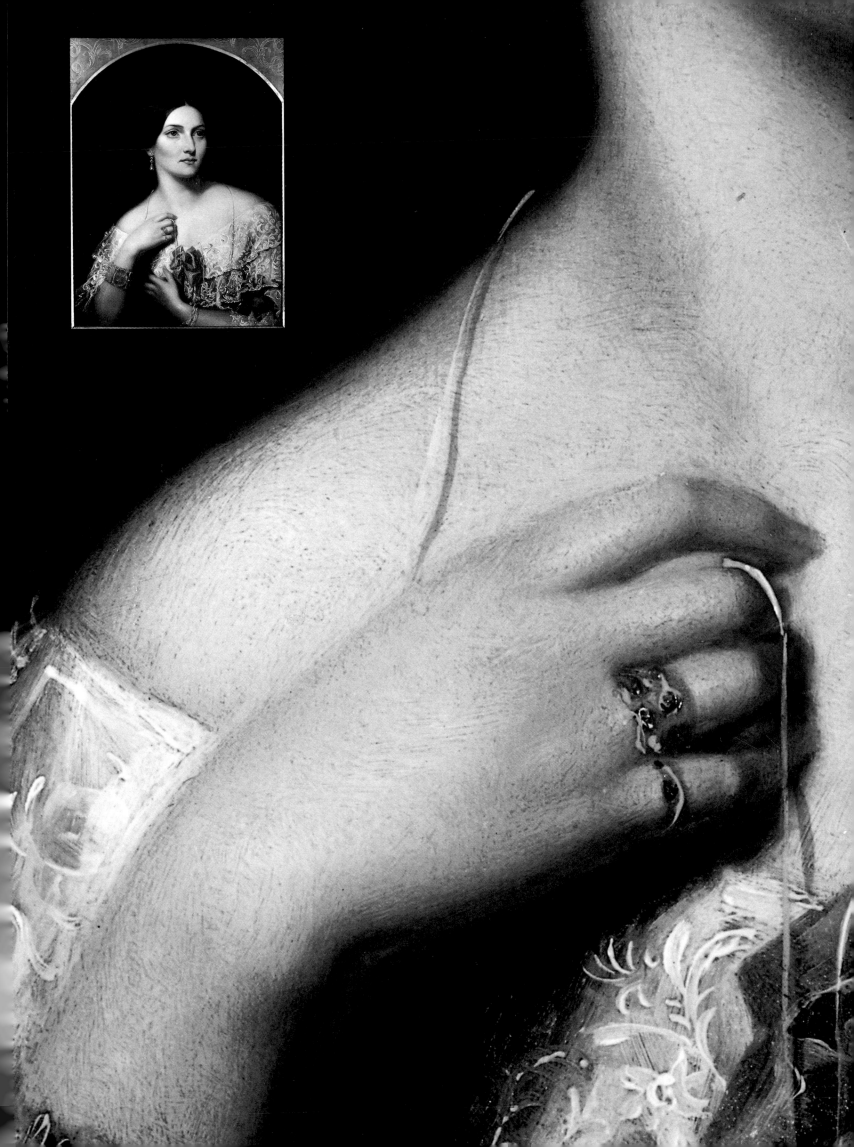

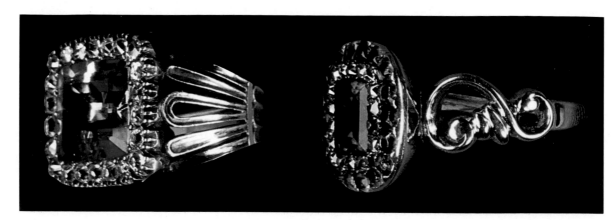

1600   1601   1602   1603

1604   1605   1606   1607

1608   1609   1610   1611

1612   1613   1614   1615

1616   1617   1618   1619

1620   1621   1622   1623

1624   1625   1626   1627

1628   1629   1630

A PASSION FOR COLOUR

Left: Early 19th-century sapphire, emerald and turquoise rings, of characteristic substantial shape, but varied design. The first two are edged with brilliant-cut diamonds; the massive chased setting of the third is inscribed inside, NEI GIORNI FELICI RICORDATE DI ME (Think of me when you are happy).

Below: Standardized late 19th-century patterns, from the catalogue of E. W. Streeter of New Bond Street, London, *c*. 1896. All the most popular styles are shown: hoops, half-hoops, clusters, single and united hearts, marquise and cross-over bezels. The emphasis is on the stones, which are set *à jour* (without enamel or foiling); coloured stones are always accompanied by diamonds or pearls.

THE NILE AND ANCIENT ROME

With the turn-of-the-century conquests in Egypt first of Napoleon and then of Nelson, Neo-Classicism took on an exotic flavour. Two crocodiles, symbolic of Egypt and the Nile, form the hoop and shoulders of this ring set with an onyx cameo head of the Roman Emperor Otho.

Above: Three rings in ancient Roman style by Castellani, the 19th-century Roman jeweller famous for the archaeological correctness as well as the beauty of his creations. They come from a casket of his jewels presented by the people of Rome to Princess Maria Pia of Savoy, daughter of Victor Emmanuel II, on her marriage to the King of Portugal in 1862. The casket is crowned by a figure of the wolf suckling Romulus and Remus, founders of the city.

Right: The Parisian version of an ancient Roman ring, signed by Jules Wièse, *c.* 1880: the uncut emerald is set in an oval bezel gripped by two snakes.

RENAISSANCE REVIVAL

From the revival of antiquity, designers moved
on to other, more recent, styles. Stimulated by
exhibitions and museum collections of
Renaissance art, the public looked back to that
period as a golden age. Architects recreated the
16th-century *palazzo* and jewellers revived the
rings, resplendent with sculpture and enamels, of
the type illustrated by Pierre Woeiriot in his *Livre
d'Aneaux d'Orfèvrerie* of 1561 (see p. 64). This
group of Neo-Renaissance rings in the style of
Paul Robin comes from the Parisian jeweller
Joseph Chaumet. The two cabochon gems flanked
by busts of women and bearded masks would have
been worn with the richly coloured day clothes of
the 1870s. The faceted amethyst ring of 1889 (*far
right*), flanked by guardian angels, may have been
designed for a bishop by the ecclesiastical
goldsmith Armand Calliat, also working on
commission for Chaumet.

Right, above: A Neo-Gothic ring
designed *c*. 1860 by the English
architect William Burges, perhaps
for his own use. It is of gold,
decorated with trefoils, and set with
a cabochon sapphire, the most
popular stone in the Middle Ages.

Right, below: A Renaissance onyx
cameo, in a setting whose split
shoulders and shell ornament echo
Rococo designs such as that of
Prince Eugene of Savoy's leopard
ring (p. 150); made by Picot for the
Parisian firm of Frédéric
Boucheron, 1872.

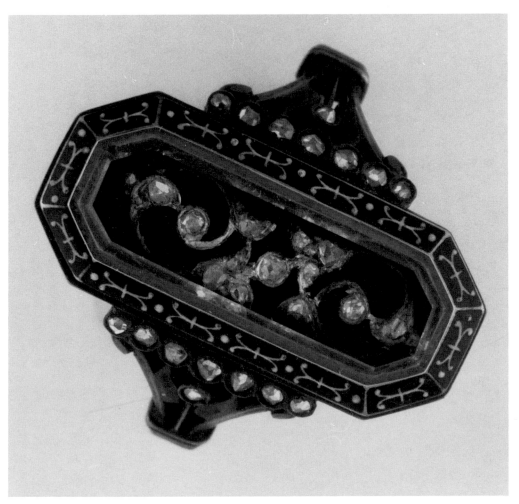

Two rings from Frédéric Boucheron inspired by 18th-century models. *Above*: A design of 1887 with an openwork bezel consisting of the interlaced initials AB bordered by leafy branches; as in a Rococo jewel, the rose diamonds are set in silver. The initials in this type of ring might be those of a single individual or of a pair of lovers; often they are so interwoven as to be impossible to identify. *Left*: A mourning ring of 1879, in a standard geometric Neo-Classical form. The black enamelled setting surrounds a cavity for hair, with the letter S in diamonds.

SYMBOLS OF SENTIMENT

This page:
In some rural areas, particularly in Ireland, Normandy and Austria, the symbolic *fede* ring remained an essential part of the ritual of courtship and marriage. This silver-gilt ring with the *fede* at the base of the hoop, and bezel set with coloured pastes amidst berries, comes from the South Tyrol.

Opposite page:
Forget-me-nots, for memory, and snakes, symbols of eternity, could serve equally for love or memorial rings.

Above right: A gold ring with bezel in the form of a lover's knot between turquoise forget-me-nots; a third forget-me-not decorates the heart-shaped locket, which contains hair.

Above left: A forget-me-not in rose diamonds embellishes the bezel of a black-enamelled memorial ring; the inscription inside reads JOHN WILLIS MD OBT 23 SEPT 1835 AET 83.

Below right: A snake with diamond eyes and scales drawn in black enamel, commemorating Nathaniel Meyer de Rothschild, founder of the British branch of the family, who died in 1836.

Below left: A sumptuous serpent ornamented with a line of diamonds between rubies.

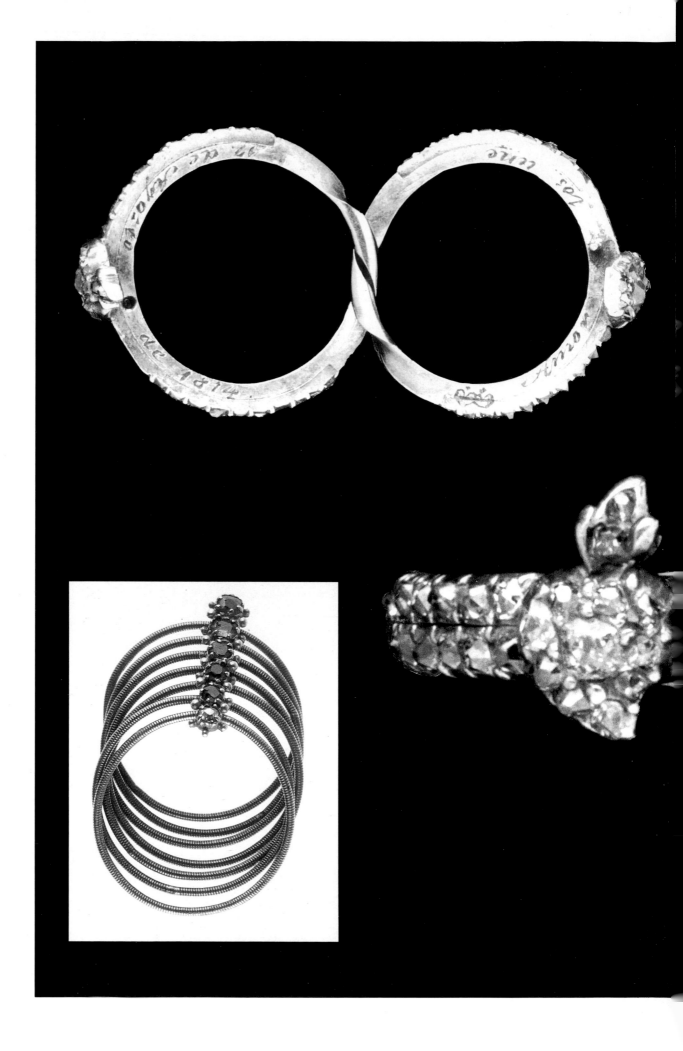

HEARTS, HANDS AND COMPLIMENTS

Below and left: Closed, this gimmel ring shows a pair of flaming hearts united; they and the hoop are all paved in tiny diamonds. Inside, it reveals its purpose at a wedding, with the Spanish inscriptions AMOR LOS UNE / 12 DE AGOSTO DE 1814 (Love unites them / 12 August 1814).

Bottom left: A new version of the multiple-hoop ring, said to have been invented by the Parisian jeweller Mellerio before 1811, used stones to spell out a message by means of the first letter of their name. In this example, seven ribbed hoops support seven stones to form the word REGARD – ruby, emerald, garnet, amethyst, ruby again, and diamond.

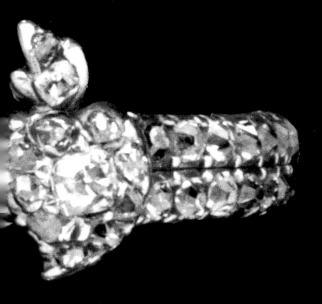

Right: Three versions of the traditional motif of hands offering a gift: gold hands and a pearl forget-me-not; diamond hands and heart surmounted by a Russian-style mitre crown; and a single gold hand offering in its palm a ruby heart to a lover, by Castellani of Rome.

PATTERNS OF LOYALTY

Right: When the armies of Napoleon invaded Portugal, Cardinal Caleppi as Papal Nuncio used his diplomatic skills to safeguard the rights of the Church. His reward from Pope Pius VII was this magnificent ring, in which the skills of the early 19th-century Roman cameo-cutter and jeweller are combined. The Pope is shown in profile, his name inscribed in gold letters on the orphrey across his shoulder. The bezel swivels to reveal a paved diamond back bearing a processional cross and the word PAX (Peace) above the arms of the Pope's family, Chiaramonti, in the form of a stylized mountain. The shoulders are adorned with small cameos of his family crest, a blindfolded blackamoor.

Left, below: After the death of Napoleon at St Helena in 1821 admirers wore rings to commemorate him. In this dramatic example a coffin opens to reveal a figure of the Emperor in general's uniform.

Left, top and centre: This ring with a diamond fleur-de-lis proclaimed its wearer as a supporter of the Bourbons in exile after the revolution of 1830. The hoop is ornamented with branches of laurel and olive, symbolizing wisdom and peace. Inside is the inscription MON DIEU MON ROI ET MA DAME, pledging allegiance to God, to 'Henri V' – the Comte de Chambord, Pretender to the throne – and to the Pretender's mother, the Duchesse de Berri.

PATRIOTS AGAINST NAPOLEON

Below: Admiral Lord Nelson, many times victor over the French, was commemorated after his death at Trafalgar in 1805 by this red jasper signet, on which his profile is surrounded by the famous signal he had given before the battle: ENGLAND EXPECTS EVERY MAN TO DO HIS DUTY. As befits a naval hero, the ornament chosen for the shoulders is anchor chains.

Left: Two views of a ring with a swivel bezel in the form of the Iron Cross, the great Prussian military decoration instituted in 1813. The cross itself, set in silver, is made of iron; on one side it bears the date – DIE ZEIT 1813 – and on the other a rose and EISERN IST (It is iron). Prussian citizens who had given their jewels to finance the war received iron jewelry in return, made in the Berlin foundries.

COMMEMORATIVE PORTRAITS

Opposite, left: Provision was made in wills for memorial rings, containing portraits, to be given out after a person's death. Those bequeathed in 1832 by Jeremy Bentham, the English social reformer, held a lock of hair and a silhouette made by the virtuoso John Field, who had developed a technique of providing colour (here in the hair) by the use of substances such as bronze powder. One of the friends to whom a ring was sent was the Guatemalan politician José Cecilio del Valle; it was proudly added to his portrait, painted some ten years earlier.

Opposite, right: A memorial ring to Victor Emmanuel II of Italy (*d.* 1878), probably made for a member of the Italian royal family. The outside of the black-enamelled bezel bears his crowned cipher of gold and diamonds. Inside is a miniature portrait. By this date commemorative rings often contained photographs rather than hand-made images.

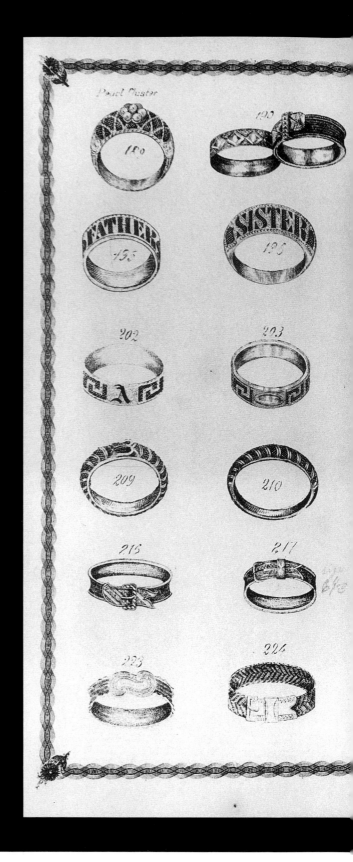

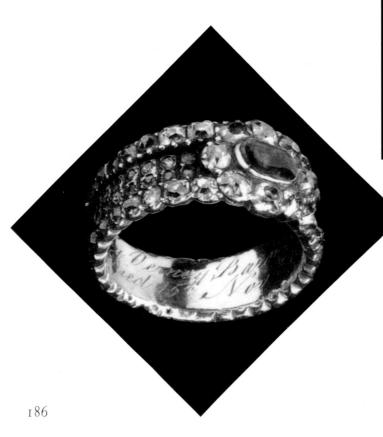

MEMORIAL RINGS

Above left: Two views of a diamond and pearl ring commemorating Lady Harriet Eliot and her brother, the statesman William Pitt. Her hair, with gold wire initials HE, is set in the bezel, which is inscribed on the back LADY HAR ELIOT OBT 25 SEPT 1786 AET 28. The enamelled hoop bears the inscription RT HONBLE WM PITT OB 23 JAN 1806 AE 47. More luxurious than the standard memorial ring, it may have been made after Pitt's death for his niece, Lady Harriet's daughter, Lady Hester Stanhope.

Left: A diamond dog-collar ring with ruby-set cluster bezel inscribed with the name of Mary Verney, Baroness Fermanagh, who died unmarried at the age of 76 in 1810.

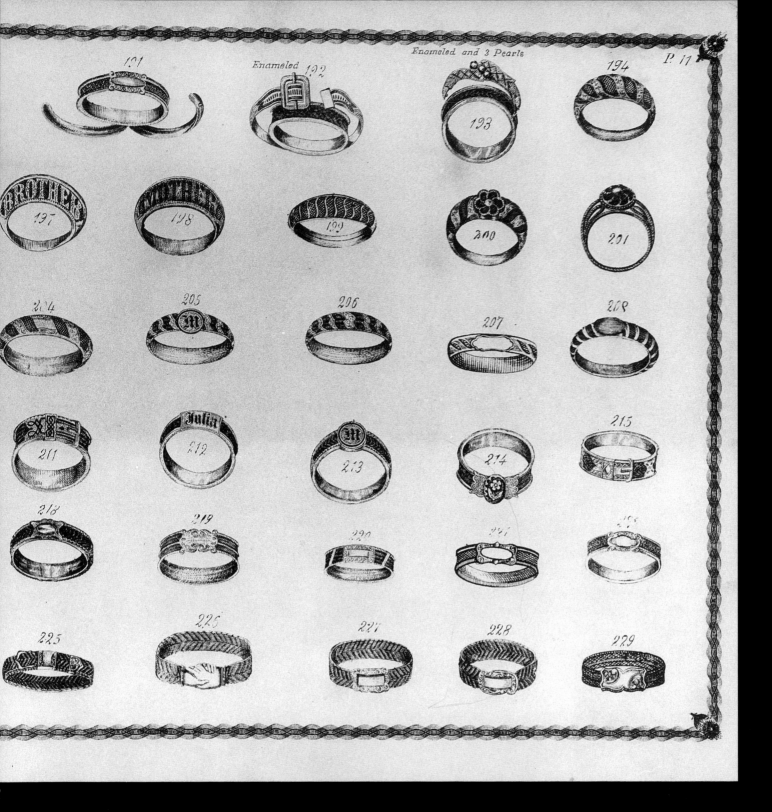

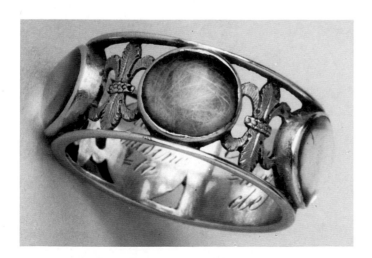

Above: A page from the catalogue of a firm specializing in hair jewelry, *c.* 1840. Designs illustrated include simple braided hoops with a plaque for initials or a *fede* motif, and others more complex, with forget-me-nots, names, initials or kinship appellations; in three the hair is concealed within a casing.

Left: A memorial ring to Louis XVI and Marie-Antoinette, commissioned by Louis XVIII after the Restoration of 1815. Fleurs-de-lis alternate with lockets containing the hair of the King and Queen and their children.

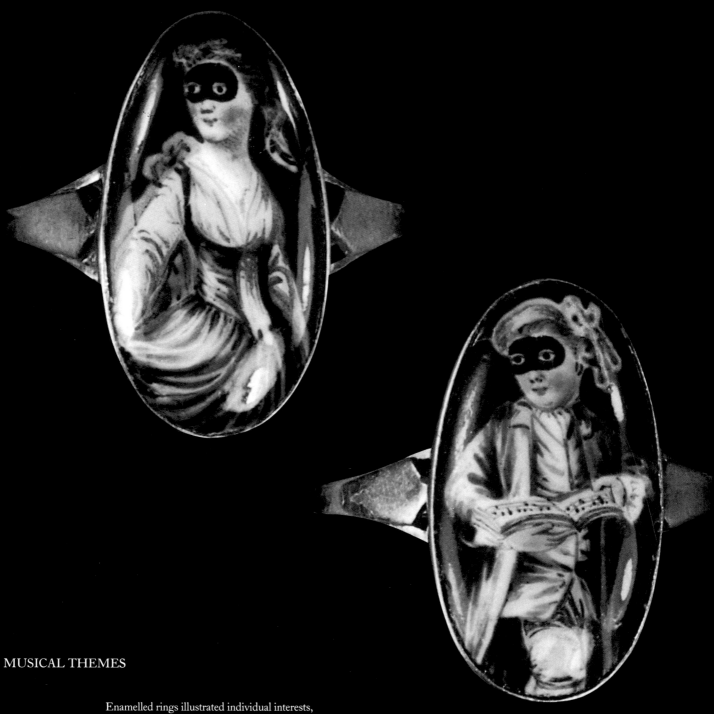

MUSICAL THEMES

Enamelled rings illustrated individual interests, such as hunting and, more rarely, music. The two rings *above* represent a young couple at a masquerade: he sings, holding a book of music in his hands, and she dances, skirts billowing to the movement.

Opposite: A lyre in filigree, studded with coloured stones spelling out a message whose meaning is now lost. This filigree style was introduced around 1830.

Date		N°		Description	Prix		Vente	
1879 Juillet	1	208	Châtelain	1 Bague Jonc or mat M 78			86 Janvier	5
				1 saphir étoilé 100, E 1	183	"	"	"
" 8bre	25	209	Fouquet	1 " Diadème Saphir 1c 3/32 F 15. 13 Bte			RN 1-1100	
				1 c à CFS roses ES M&E COS	815	"		
Xbre	10	210	Pelletier	1 " double main or mat	45	"	85 Sept	19
80 Mars	25	211	Desbazeille	1 " Sardoine carrée or &	58	"	85 Juin	15
Avril	25	212	Châtelain	1 " Jonc anglais grenat Cab 2 Bte			86 Avril	30
"				1/2 à OSK M.ER, E 1	203	"	"	"
"	25	213	Martin	1 " perle 8gr 1/2 à ci, 2 Bte 11/16 à			96 Avril	4
"	"			OSK, M&E 15	318	"	NFS 1560	"
"	"	214	Pelletier	1 " perle 12g 1/2 à oi, 12 Bte 2c 9/32			1890 février	4
				à OSK M&E, RI	865	"	90S juillet	1
Mai	31	215	Fleury	1 " In. à roses sur 3 corps	23	"	88 xbre	31
"	"	216	Vincent	1 " Serbe or & plat. 5 R.	25	"	02.40	
Sept bre	25	217	Martin	1 " 2 Bte poires 13/16 à CRS 3 Bte 5/16			91 Sept	30
				à CIS M&E 1F Bague cœur	245	"	01S "	"
Déc	1	218	Châtelain	1 " Jonc anglais saphir Cab. 4c 11/16 à RS			85 Janvier	15
				2 Bte 9/8 à OSK M&E CSK	700	"	"	"
1881 Janv.	15	219	Occasion	1 " 5 corps 1 Bte 2 Sap. 2 Rub. 2 Edes & roses			88 8bre	27
				m. or	200	"	01S "	"
"	"	220	Gillot	1 " Marq. 23 Bte 4c 5/16 à OSK, 36 roses			86 mai	15
				7/32 M&E. EU	990	"	"	"
"	"	221	"	1 " Marq. 17 Bte 2c 1/32 à OSK 17 roses			88 Juillet	26
				3/32 à coi M&E TE	505	"	01S "	"

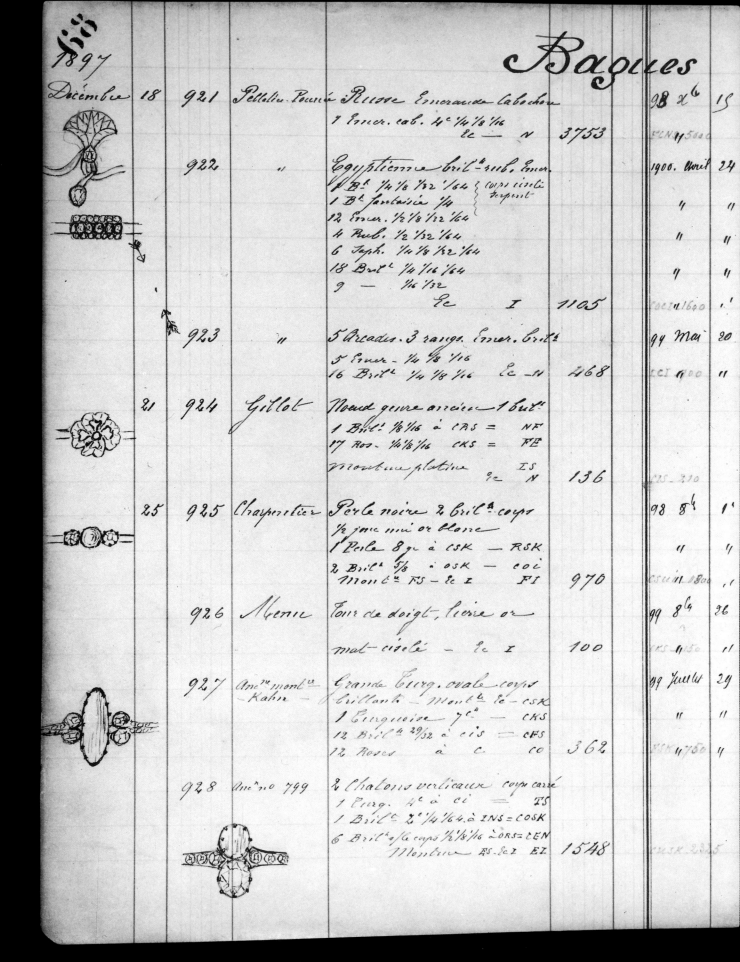

Décembre 18   921   Pellotier-Pournie Russe   Emeraude cabochon   98 x⁶ 1S

       1 Emer. cab. 4ᶜ ¼ ⅛ 1/16
             Ɛc — N   3753

922   "   Egyptienne bril⁴ᵉ rub. Emer.   1900. Avril 24
1 Bᵗ ¼ ⅛ 1/32 1/64 } cops incli
1 Bᵗ fantaisie ¼   serpent   " "
12 Emer. ½ ⅛ 1/32 1/64   " "
4 Rub. ½ 1/32 1/64   " "
6 Saph. ¼ ⅛ 1/32 1/64
18 Bril⁴ ¼ 1/16 1/64   " "
9 — 1/16 1/32
            Ɛc   I   1105

923   "   5 Arcades 3 rangs Emer. Bril⁴ᵗ   94 Mai 20
5 Emer — ¼ ⅛ 1/16
16 Bril⁴ ¼ ⅛ 1/16   Ɛc —N   468   "

21   924   Gillot   Nœud genre ancien —1 bril⁴ᵗ
1 Bril⁴ ⅛ 1/16 à CRS =   NF
17 Ros. ¼ ⅛ 1/16 CKS =   FE
   Monture platine
           Ɛc   IS N   136

25   925   Charpentier   Perle noire 2 Bril⁴ᵃ corps   98 8⁴ 1'
½ jonc mi or blanc
1 Perle 8 gr à CSK — RSK   " "
2 Bril⁴ ⅝ à OSK — COI
   Mont⁴ᵉ FS — Ɛc I   FI   970

926   Menu   Tour de doigt, lierre or   99 8⁴ 36
mat -ciselé — Ɛc I   100   "

927   Ancⁿᵉ montᵉ   Grande Turq. ovale corps   99 Juillet 24
—Kahn—   brillanté — Montᵗᵉ Ɛc —CSK
1 Turquoise 7ᶜᵈ — CKS   " "
12 Bril⁴ 29/32 à cis = CFS
12 Roses à c   CO   362

928   Ancⁿ n° 799   2 Chatons verticaux corps carré
1 Turq. 4ᶜ à ci   TS
1 Bril⁴ 2ᶜ ¼ 1/64 à INS = COSK
6 Bril⁴ à/c corps ½ ⅛ 1/16 à ORS= CEN
     Monture FS Ɛc I EZ   1548

These record rings sold in a particular year, with the names of suppliers. The page for 1879–81 shows cluster and marquise bezels, smooth gypsy settings, a multiple-hoop style, and an unusual design by Alphonse Fouquet (top left) – a sapphire set in a diadem bezel outlined in rose diamonds. The page for the Christmas season of 1897 records an elaborate Egyptian-style ring (top) set with diamonds, emeralds, rubies and sapphires; a Rococo revival ribbon bow knot in platinum; and designs with stones set along or across the finger, all combining diamonds with other stones – emeralds, a black pearl, a large turquoise, and a smaller turquoise twinned with a diamond.

PIETY AND PILGRIMAGE

Top: A rosary ring of *c*. 1830, studded with a decade of turquoises for private meditation.

Centre: A ring set with a micromosaic picture of St Peter's in Rome, brought back as a souvenir by a pilgrim.

Bottom: The cross of Faith encircled by the serpent of Wisdom. The design – in gold, diamonds, rubies, and dark blue enamel for the serpent – is similar to that of a ring made by the Parisian jeweller Fossin for the Duc de Montebello in the 1840s.

6

The 20th century:
high fashion and
the return of imagination

In 1901 the *Illustrated London News* observed that 'it is actually the fashion in Paris and therefore becoming so here to wear a large ring on every finger, two or three rings on some of the fingers.'

Influences from the 18th century predominated, with J. W. Benson in 1910 advertising 'Old English cluster rings reproducing those worn in the time of Queen Anne' and 'Marquise rings, reproductions of the beautiful French models worn by the noblesse of the eighteenth century'. They were quite different from the originals, for not only were the stones cut differently but the platinum millegrain settings were much lighter than p. 209 gold or silver. An innovation was platinum latticework which filled the marquise- or cartouche-shaped bezels and provided an almost invisible support for the stones, which were usually diamonds. Thanks to modern calibré cutting, coloured stones could now be p. 208 cut into shapes of measured neatness far more precisely than hitherto.

The gem-set ring was the principal concern of jewellers. *Queen* in 1905 regretted that 'rings, the preeminent symbols of friendship, love and married life are no longer designed in regard to the significance of the gift but in reference to the intrinsic worth or exchange value.' This view is borne out by the order books of Hennell's in London, which show that diamonds were the favourite choice for engagements, the largest (1–10 carats) being mounted as solitaires, the smaller as clusters or paved into marquise shapes. Many officers got married before leaving for the front so from 1914 the demand for engagement rings increased noticeably. Coloured stones are only occasionally recorded. Sometimes a symbolic heart is requested, brought up to date with slender platinum millegrain settings and calibré-cut rubies and diamonds framing the diamond heart.

Queen continued: 'even the wedding ring which should be honoured as the most significant jewel in my lady's casket is worn by the smart woman of today as narrow and insignificant as possible.' Yet the Hennell order books indicate that sentiment had not entirely vanished: the inscriptions on the circles of flat gold sometimes record more than just the names of the couple and marriage date. They include the Biblical MANY WATERS CANNOT QUENCH LOVE and TILL DEATH US DO PART, and the heartfelt declarations MY OWN DARLING and WIFIE 1904 FOR EVER AND AYE. The American jewelry historian George Kunz, in *Rings for the Finger* (1917), discusses platinum hoops encircled with crowns of ivy and oak, and gimmel hoops – one of gold, the other platinum – bearing the names and the dates of the engagement and marriage respectively. For staunch Protestants with a sense of history the London firm of Watherston reproduced the gimmel ring of Martin Luther. Kunz, in touch with the social changes of his time, suggested that 'in view of the great number of divorces now granted we might well introduce the custom of giving divorce rings. This might be differentiated from the old-fashioned wedding ring by substituting the inscription ABC *from* DEF for ABC *and* DEF.'

Queen also declared that 'the mourning ring has died as a memento and the custom of leaving money in wills for it.' The tradition was revived by Cartier after the sinking of the *Titanic* in 1912 when relatives of the victims had their diamonds outlined in black onyx or

p. 209enamel to great effect. With the outbreak of World War I and the casualties which followed, this 'demi-deuil' (half-mourning) style continued to meet the needs of society well into the 1920s, though by that time it was not necessarily a sign of bereavement.

The symbolic snake continued to be worn by both sexes. Leila von Meister remembered how in 1903 the Crown Prince of Germany, godfather to her baby son, had given her 'a ring of two serpents entwined with diamond and sapphire heads. He begged me to wear it and give it to Willy when confirmed saying he thought it nice for a boy to have something his mother has owned.'

The man-about-town liked to wear a plain gold or platinum signet with his crest or initials and another ring set with a stone. One client of Hennell's in 1909 ordered 'a piece of labrador spar deeply cut as a monkey's head to be mounted in a plain gold ring for a gentleman's little finger' with plenty of colour and diamond eyes. George Kunz mentions the enormous numbers of rings made in the United States for members of societies, Freemasons, trade unions, and college and school fraternities, the emblems enamelled or encrusted with gems. The Massachusetts firm of L. G. Balfour continues to produce one million such rings yearly.

An alternative to conventional jewellery was proposed by René Lalique as part of the Art Nouveau movement which crystallized in Paris at the Exposition Universelle of 1900. Like the Renaissance goldsmith, he proved that jewels need not be the sole preserve of the stone-setter: they could be created from figurative elements wrought in gold, enamelled and highlighted with a mere sprinkling of diamonds. Lalique rings are miniature versions of his naturalistic pendents and brooches. Thistles, ears of wheat, ivy, papyrus, anemone and chrysanthemum flowers, and the wings of insects frame and enclose Baroque pearls and stones such as opal, topaz and agate, chosen for their decorative quality rather than their intrinsic worth. This Lalique style emphasizing art rather p. 204 than money is epitomized by the ring commissioned by the courtesan Liane de Pougy for her friend, the American heiress Natalie Barney (nicknamed 'Moonbeam'), where chased silver bats frame a heart-shaped moonstone. For the sophisticated gentleman who wished to establish his aesthetic credentials Lalique made even more striking designs, set p. 205 with pearls and uncut amethysts flanked by golden-haired nymphs and by lovers dancing or embracing. What is new about Lalique's reinterpretations of these themes – previously executed by Robin of Paris – is the vitality that emanates from the figures.

In France Lalique's numerous followers included Eugène Feuillâtre, who excelled at exotic orchid bezels with tiny diamond dew drops glistening on the petals, and Lucien Gaillard, whose asymmetrical flowers derive from the art of Japan. Others were Henri Vever, Georges Leturcq and Georges Fouquet, who in collaboration with the artist Alphonse Mucha made a spectacular snake bracelet with ring for the actress Sarah Bernhardt, whose fingers were always covered in rings. In America, Tiffany and Marcus were both strongly influenced by Art Nouveau but found they could not prevail against the desire of their well-to-do clients for precious stones that proclaimed their wealth.

ARTISTIC STYLES

Among the Continental jewellers who struck out on their own was the Viennese firm of Roset & Fichtmeister, who had a reputation for men's rings modelled in relief with grotesque masks and half figures: these, like Lalique's versions, stemmed from the Renaissance tradition. In Copenhagen Georg Jensen from 1904 expressed his talents in silver and semi-precious stones for the middle-class market and thereafter adapted that formula to the successive changes in 20th-century art, invariably producing unmistakably contemporary designs.

In Britain jewellers joined the Arts and Crafts Movement which had originated in the 19th century, inspired by the protests of John Ruskin and William Morris against the encroaching industrialization which threatened the survival of the hand worker. All believed that design and execution were inseparable and had to be the creation of a single mind. Each had his own individual style. The leader among the metalworkers, Henry Wilson, was inspired by medieval art and by nature herself; when making a ring, he recommended in his text-book, *Silverwork and Jewellery* (1912), 'remember always to have a bit of the natural foliage beside you as a guide, never do anything in the way of ornament without reference to nature.' Then there was C. R. Ashbee, founder of the Guild of Handicrafts, whose design album contains sketches of a ring enamelled with Masonic symbols and a modern version of the Rococo *giardinetti* type. Arthur and Georgie Gaskin, a husband and wife team who had a great following in Birmingham, centre of the mass-produced jewelry trade, made silver studded with moonstones, amethysts and pearls their particular medium. Nor were rings neglected by Charles Rennie Mackintosh of the Glasgow School or by the Manxman Archibald Knox, whose openwork creations derived from Celtic art were sold by Liberty's. The partnership between Omar Ramsden and Alwyn Carr between 1898 and 1918 produced many good things including a medievalizing sapphire ring made for Archibald Robertson on his appointment as Bishop of Exeter in 1903 (British Museum, London, Hull Grundy Collection 1004). Highly abstract jewels, one of them a ring, were made by the sculptor Sir Alfred Gilbert from twisted strips of silver or gilt wire (Royal Academy of Arts, London).

Whereas the Art Nouveau style on the Continent was a spent force by 1914, the British Craft Revival proved a much hardier plant, perhaps because it was so strongly rooted in ideology. It flourished for several more decades, with the emergence of Sybil Dunlop, George Hunt and Dorrie Nossiter. Then it revived again with a tremendous wave of enthusiasm in the 1960s, fostered by Goldsmiths' Hall and the Diamonds International Awards organized by De Beers (see below, p. 200).

1920–1930

Conventional jewelry underwent a dramatic change with the emergence of the Art Deco style, which took its name from the 1925 Paris Exposition des Arts Décoratifs. In *Vogue* that year, Raymond Templier, himself an avant-garde designer, traced its origin to Paul Iribe's jewels, particularly his rings. What was new about them was not only their huge size, but the daring colour contrasts and virtuoso mixture of modern cuts in geometrical patterns – triangles, hexagons, trapezes – which broke away from tradition. p. 202

The new cuts were outlined by calibré-cut coloured stones, by tiny brilliants or by the long rectangular baguette diamonds which were also introduced at this time. In addition to the contrast of precious and semi-precious, opaque and transparent, faceted and uncut stones, lacquer – black, red, white, green – and bright red coral, onyx, lapis and rock crystal were dramatically juxtaposed. In the hands of the Art Deco jeweller even the traditional episcopal ring was geometricized into a solid angular block. The influence of Eastern art is reflected in rings set with Chinese jade and Mughal carved stones.

p. 208
p. 203

Harper's Bazaar summed up the fashionable look for evening in 1929: 'One no longer sees each finger covered with two or three rings. The chic Parisienne wears a diamond hoop wedding ring and a large solitaire and perhaps one other coloured ring – an emerald, turquoise or sapphire – to carry out the tone of her dress. But all are large and mostly single stones.' By day an elegant woman would usually wear a wedding circlet of plain platinum. An innovation launched by Cartier was the Trinity ring, consisting of three hoops of red, yellow and white gold, fitting and twisting neatly into each other like the gimmel and puzzle rings of the past. They were not used exclusively for wedding rings and might be worn with matching bracelets. After Steichen photographed one for *Vogue* in 1925 the ring was taken up by the interior decorator and hostess Elsie de Wolfe, and it has been in fashion ever since.

p. 202

During the 1920s and 1930s a group of French designers – Jean Desprès, Jean Fouquet, André Léveillé and Raymond Templier, all followers of the architect Le Corbusier – interpreted the modern style with much more rigour than the makers of fine jewelry. Their rings are not only large: they are severely abstract designs of chrome, steel, silver, lacquer and hardstones from which all ornament has been eliminated. Deliberately, they evoke the world of the machine – the ball-bearing, the aeroplane engine – and of modern industry instead of nature and tradition.

p. 210

An early example of Cartier's Trinity ring, 1937.

1930–1950

In the 1930s the geometric outlines of the Art Deco ring are dramatized and exaggerated. At first angularity was emphasized; then with the emergence of a more plastic style, curves were developed into volutes, barrel-, fan- and turban-shaped bezels. Scale continued large and imposing. Those rich enough to disregard the Depression wore important sapphire, ruby and emerald solitaires whose perfect cut and colour was shown off by discreet platinum mounts polished to mirror surface. Barbara Hutton, the Woolworth heiress, who could afford everything, chose the smartest ring of all on her engagement to Prince Mdivani in 1933: a wonderful black pearl from Cartier. Paul Flato won a reputation among the screen stars of Hollywood for diamond solitaires, one of which was worn by Clare Boothe Luce in 1936 to a rehearsal of her play *The Women*, where she was observed by the columnist Ilka Chase: 'as cool as the Snow Queen on her way to a dinner party, gowned by Hattie Carnegie, sabled by Jaeckel and on her finger flashed one of Paul Flato's ice-cubes.'

pp. 210,
212

After the successful diamond jewelry exhibition held in Paris at the Palais Galliéra in 1929 the 'all-white' look was adopted by fashionable women. Circular and baton-cut diamonds stud the hoops and sides of massive wide bezels and are dotted across the surfaces – frosted or clear – of rock crystal rings carved into great ice-like chunks. For one ring Cartier filled a wide octagonal bezel with six alternate rows of round and rectangular diamonds rising in steps to a single large brilliant at the top; another was covered with a smooth diamond mass, domed like a snowball. Paved diamond spirals overlap the asymmetric bezel of a ring designed by Charles Bruno for Hennell in 1936. Peter Hinks has p. 210 credited the Parisian firm of Mauboussin with the invention of the internationally imitated three- or five-row tube ring, 'a short cylinder of platinum and diamonds into which the finger slipped naturally and comfortably, the front pavé with diamonds, orthodox brilliants and baguettes and the whole gamut of fancy cuts – triangle, trapeze, keystone, obus and lunette. The back was fretted out to a mere skeleton outline.' It was the contrast of the different cuts, each contributing its own particular fire to the whole, which saved the all-white look from monotony.

There were many alternatives to expensive coloured stone solitaires. Star sapphires, huge slabs of citrines, aquamarines, amethysts, turquoises and burnt topazes were mounted in skeleton platinum settings with a sprinkling of diamonds, sapphires or rubies at the shoulders, contrasting with the huge mass of colour. Then very small stones, precious and semi-precious, were massed together into the new bulky styles. Cartier made fan- and turban-shaped bezels paved with tapered rows of rich colour for the little finger. One such, with three lines of cushion-shaped rubies and three of sapphires rising p. 202 across the domed surface, was given to Mrs Simpson by the Duke of Windsor in 1937 to mark the completion of her divorce and the end of their separation. An innovation from Van Cleef and Arpels of Paris in 1933 for domed or bombé-shaped bezels was the invisible setting, in which stones are massed into a mosaic of pure colour secured by wires out of sight at the back. It remained in production until the 1960s; other jewellers, noting the technique's success, made versions of their own. p. 203

The jewelled hoop or eternity ring worn as an alternative to or next to a plain platinum or gold wedding ring now came in variants. Some were designed as chains, ribbons, or as minute hexagonal motifs with a gem in the centre of each. One of Cartier's was hung with six diamond balls, each the size of a pea, which scintillated with every gesture of the hand. The Duchess of Kent, who married in 1934, chose three eternity rings which struck a patriotic note, each band – of rubies, diamonds and sapphires – representing one of the colours of the British flag.

The chunky ring, formed as if hewn from solid rock or carved from a block of wood, was particularly suited to men's wear. Some were set with precious or semi-precious stones; others, such as the one Paul Flato designed for himself, bore a personal p. 211 monogram.

Gold, which had returned to jewelry in 1935, became the principal material during World War II when platinum was requisitioned. Through alloys of copper and silver different shades of pink, green and yellow could be obtained. Further touches of colour were added by synthetic and semi-precious stones, particularly topazes and citrines. In

New York, Fulco di Verdura, a Sicilian nobleman who had trained with Coco Chanel in Paris and then collaborated with Paul Flato, began to make a reputation for bold and imaginative designs that owed nothing to Art Deco.

The New Look launched by Christian Dior in 1947 brought a return to feminine clothes and stimulated the desire for showy jewelry to wear with them. The rings of this period have been classified by Melissa Gabardi according to the shapes of the large gold bezels dotted with small diamonds and coloured stones into five types: bridge, open book, Turk, turban and ribbon bow. There were also lighter styles inspired by wrought-iron patterns, using plain or twisted wire sprinkled with small gems or lines of calibré rubies topped by emeralds.

The prosperity of the post-war years coincided with a period of security which encouraged ostentation. Precious stones were available once again. Worn by day as well as by night, they could never be too big or too grand for the fingers. The three great historic family diamonds which had blazed from the heads of two successive Duchesses of Westminster were remounted into rings by the New York jeweller Harry Winston, who bought the Westminster tiara in 1959.

1950–1990

Rings were of two kinds: the intrinsically valuable, like those set with the Westminster diamonds, and the imposing but moderately priced 'cocktail ring'. The classic engagement ring was usually bought as an investment and so belonged to the first category. Few brides considered any stone other than the diamond of the very latest cut, mounted – if large – into conservative solitaire, cross-over or three-stone designs in barely visible platinum to give the fullest play of light. Important sapphires, emeralds, rubies and pearls were similarly set and flanked by shoulders built up with diamonds to enhance colour or sheen. Smaller stones contrasting in size, colour and cut with a larger central gem were mounted in variations on the cluster design.

p. 206 The smartest dress or cocktail rings came from Fulco di Verdura. He cradles large semi-precious stones – translucent green peridots, purple amethysts, pink tourmalines – in gold, ruby or diamond fronds, repeated in layers at the shoulders. For what *Vogue* called his 'bird in a gilded cage look' he twisted gold wires into rope edge borders or placed them across the gem in a network of lines. Often his gems are secured with ribbons criss-crossed into an X. The X was also used by Verdura's rival, the French designer Jean Schlumberger of Tiffany, to tie together multiple cable twist wedding p. 214 bands. Mellerio and Boucheron truss up tiny emeralds, amethysts, topazes and diamonds with gold rope into reticulated high-domed bezels combining an effect of lightness with importance. Cartier's version of this style mixes coloured stones with diamond p. 212 stripes in swirling patterns squared off by thin cords of platinum or gold wire. Another Cartier success introduced in 1951 was the dress ring consisting of thick ribs of coral alternating with diamond bands.

The grandest triumph of Jeanne Toussaint, Artistic Director of Cartier in Paris, was p. 212 the creation of the sculptural panther ring, a miniature version of the clips and bracelets

The fashionable woman of 1938, drawn for
the cover of *Queen*. She wears one large
ring, as recommended by *Vogue*: 'no meek
little ones will do. Insignificance is the only
sin.'

made for the Duchess of Windsor and for Nina Dyer, wife of Prince Sadruddin Agha
Khan. The two beasts confronting each other across the bezel of the first models are
succeeded by just one, with sapphire spotted diamond body encircling the finger.

In the 1960s the explosive effects of Abstract Expressionism changed the appearance
of jewelry. Stones were mounted in splintered motifs which seem to have been created
more by chance than design. The movement is epitomized by the work of Andrew Grima p. 214
in London, who discovered ways of texturing metal, hammering it into bold and daring
shapes and setting it with dramatic slices of opal, turquoise or tourmaline with only the
lightest sprinkling of diamonds, or with diamonds alone. At the same time, a generation
of artist-jewellers emerged internationally who showed an awareness of developments in
modern art and a willingness to experiment with the new technology and introduce acryl-
ics, titanium and plastics into their work alongside the traditional precious materials. In
England these talents – Gerda Flöckinger, Wendy Ramshaw, Jacqueline Mina, David p. 207
Thomas and Kevin Coates – owed much to the encouragement of Graham Hughes, who
as Artistic Director could give the patronage of Goldsmiths' Hall. They belong to the
Arts and Crafts tradition, for they are masters of their medium as well as of modern
design.

Artists, too, have involved themselves with jewelry design in the 20th century. They
include Karl Schmidt-Rottluff, Alexander Calder, Salvador Dalí, and the brothers
Arnaldo and Giorgio Pomodoro. Georges Braque collaborated with Henri-Michel
Heger de Loewenfeld in the 1960s: one of their rings is set with a sardonyx cameo head
of the Greek enchantress Circe, while another shows the most haunting image of the
artist's late work, a bird, symbolic of light, space and movement. p. 207

In the 1980s the supremacy of the great French houses was challenged by Bulgari of
Rome. Until recently motifs have come from the architecture, painting and mosaics of
the churches and palaces of that city, but 1991 saw the introduction of motifs derived
from nature. All are executed in yellow gold in preference to platinum, use uncut rather
than faceted stones, and have strong colour contrasts accented by the gleam of baguette
diamonds. Bulgari's speciality is archaeological jewelry: the rings are set with ancient p. 206
coins and intaglios in distinctively striking designs.

Another strong contender is Joel Rosenthal, New York-born and Harvard-educated,
who has won an international reputation from his shop in the Place Vendôme, citadel of
Parisian jewelry. His highly individual approach is rooted in a connoisseur's love of pp. 214–15
stones and knowledge of art history. Sometimes he takes a pearl or stone as his point of
departure and decides on the cut and setting which will show off the particular water,
colour and brilliance best. His particular forte is creating dramatic three-dimensional
designs massing diamonds together to form miniature sculpture. Equally masterly is his p. 207
revitalization of traditional themes – twinned hearts, the pansy, the fleur-de-lis – which
emerge from his hands sparkling and rich, as jewelry should always be, but also bold,
as the spirit of our times requires.

GEOMETRIC PRECISION

The rings of the 1920s and 1930s are large, dramatic, and abstract in design. Stones are cut and mounted in new ways, reflecting the modernist passion for bold geometrical forms. Brilliant colour and exotic associations ensured the popularity of carved stones from India and China.

This page:
Top: Novel geometric cuts as well as stark black and white contrast in this diamond, onyx and white gold ring made in 1925, the year of the 'Art Deco' exhibition in Paris.

Bottom: Charles Bruno's design for a sapphire solitaire flanked by emeralds at the shoulders mounted in platinum, 1929. The ring was made by Hennell's of London for Gwen, wife of the Hon. Henry Mond, the future Lord Melchett.

Centre: A wide domed turban-style ring made by Cartier to be worn on the little finger, paved with six tapered rows of rubies and sapphires. This was a present from the Duke of Windsor to Mrs Simpson celebrating the completion of her divorce. Inside is the inscription OUR REUNION IN CANDE, together with the dates of their separation, 3-XII-36 to 3-V-37.

Opposite page:
Two rings from Boucheron of Paris. The one *above*, of *c*. 1930, sets a piece of carved jade in platinum with millegrain edging; at the shoulders are rose diamonds and a curved motif made of blue enamel on gold. *Below* is a chunky 'bridge'-style ring of 1938, displaying diamonds and sapphires, the latter in the invisible setting invented by Van Cleef and Arpels five years earlier.

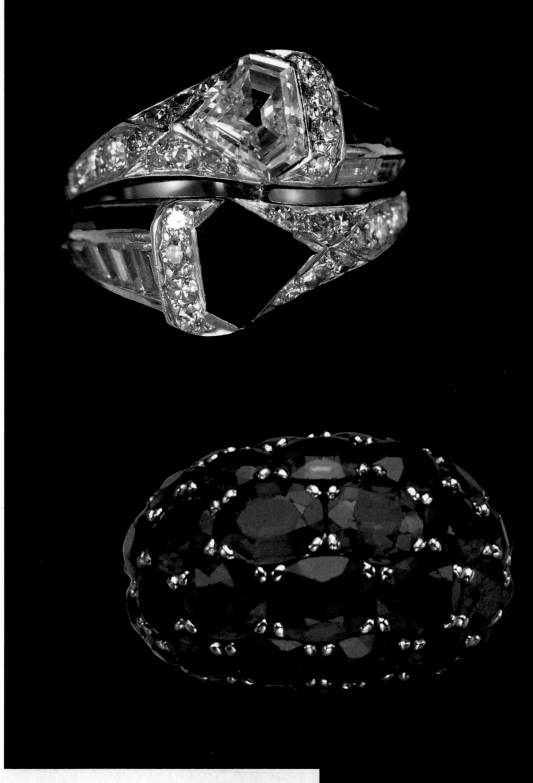

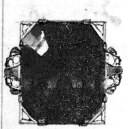

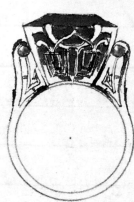

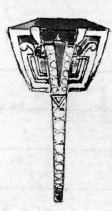

See N° 474 for colour of sapph.
MS. 285.

8111

28. 5. 29

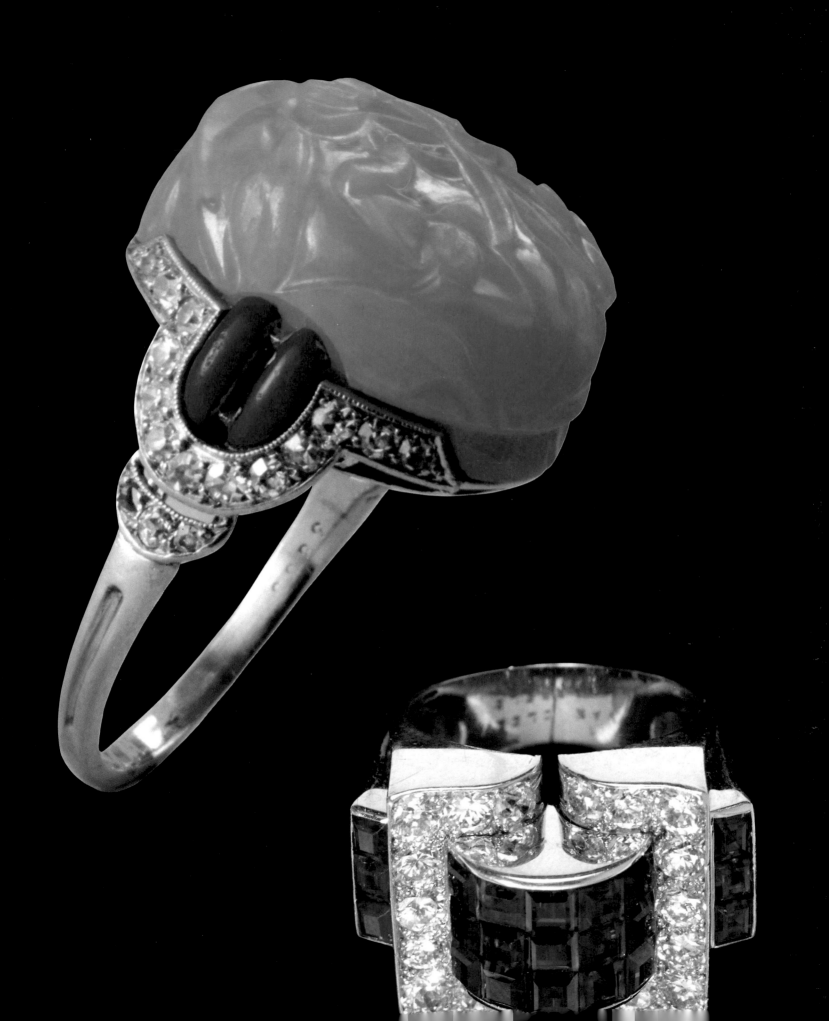

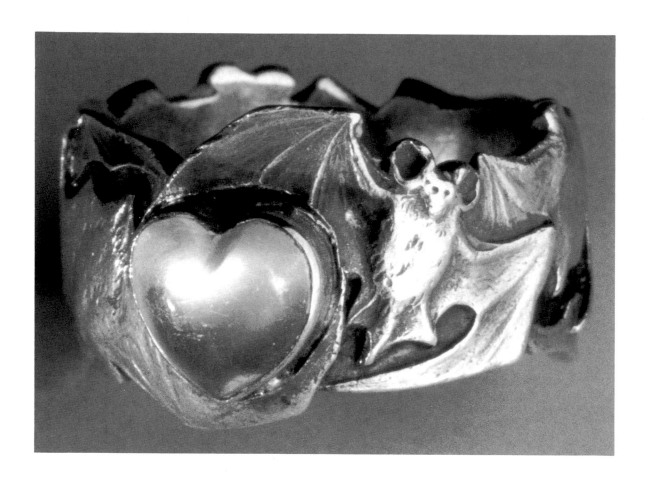

ARTISTIC RINGS

Above and right: Unlike most Art Nouveau jewellers who found the miniature scale of the ring too small a canvas, René Lalique succeeded brilliantly in adapting his sculptural designs to it. *Above* is a ring made in 1899 as a gift from Liane de Pougy to her friend, the American heiress Natalie Barney, nicknamed 'Moonbeam'. It is set with a moonstone and ringed with silver bats against a blue enamel ground. Inside is the message: TANT ME PLAIT QUE TU SOUFFRES DE ME COMPRENDRE ET DE M'AIMER L. (It delights me that you should suffer in understanding and loving me). The ring on the *right*, with two pairs of golden lovers supporting a baroque pearl, was designed *c.* 1899–1901 for an artistically-minded man to wear.

Left: A clear acknowledgment of French admiration for Japanese metalwork technique is this gold-inlaid steel hoop patterned with bats flying amidst clouds, made by Provost-Blondel for Boucheron in 1916.

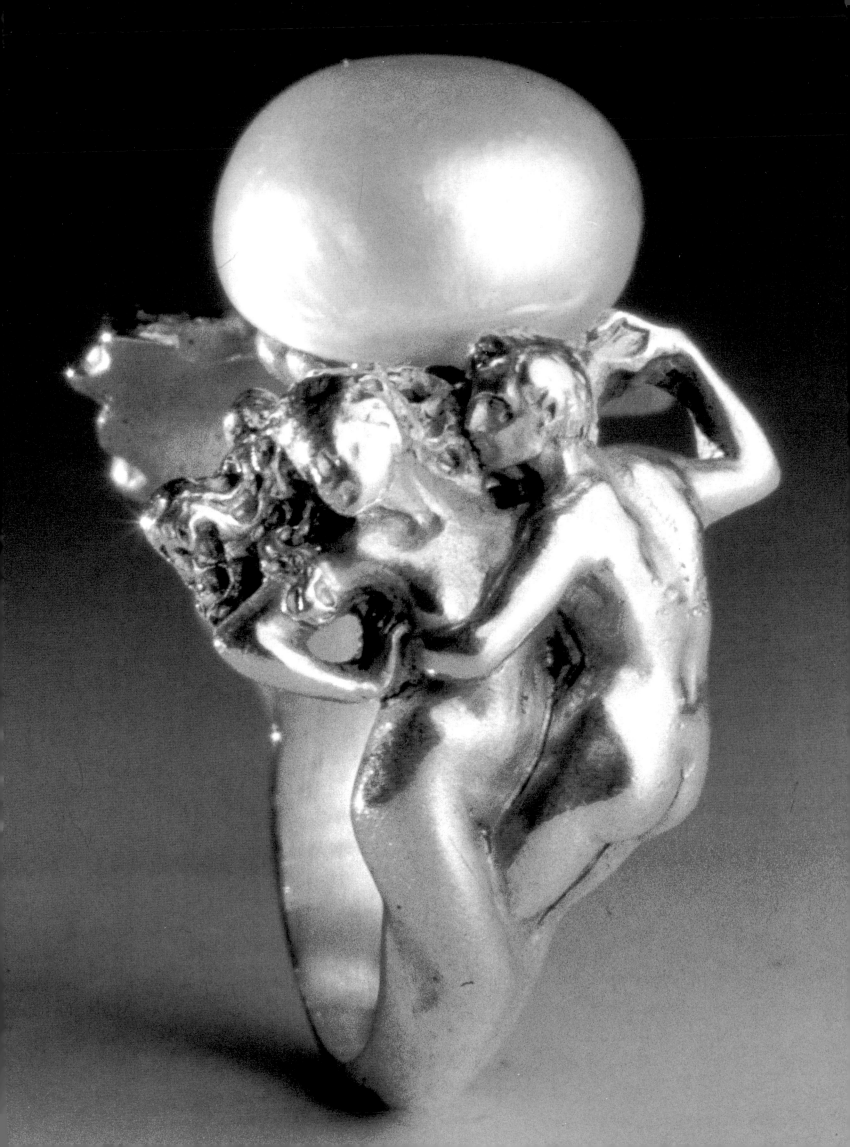

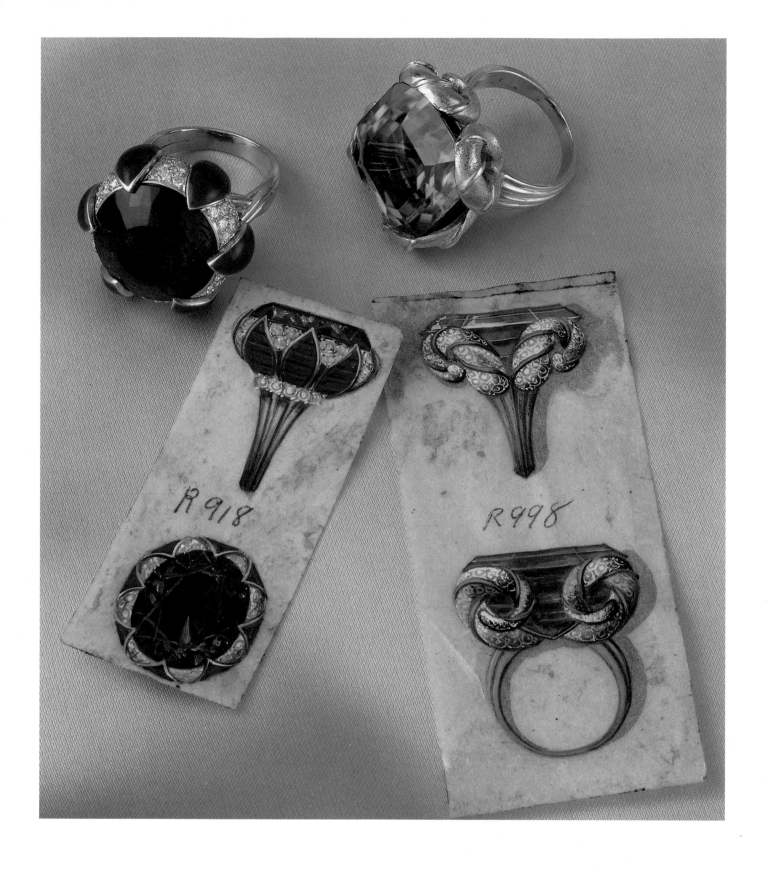

FORTY YEARS OF DIVERSITY

This page:
Above left: A bird in flight by the painter Georges Braque, realized in calibré-cut rubies and gold by Baron Héger de Loewenfeld, 1962–63.

Left: Paved diamond swan ring, part of a suite made by Joel Rosenthal in Paris, 1987.

Above: Black South Sea pearl mounted in textured gold highlighted with diamonds, by Gerda Flöckinger, London, 1989.

Opposite page:
Above: Cocktail rings of the 1950s by the leading exponent of the genre, Fulco di Verdura of New York, who set large semi-precious stones – here a green peridot and pink tourmaline – in elaborately worked bezels standing high above the hoop. The finished rings differ slightly from the designs.

Below: Three distinctive gold rings by Bulgari of Rome: cabochon rubies outlined with diamonds (centre), and double-bezel rings set with late Roman cornelian intaglios and with classical Greek silver coins. These archaeological designs were introduced in the 1960s.

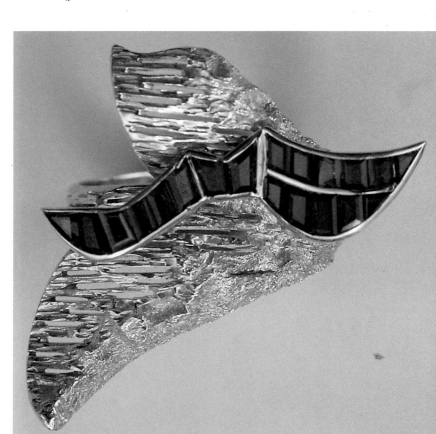

Left: A signet ring by Boucheron, 1900. The seal is a diamond engraved with a French baron's coronet; it is outlined in calibré-cut sapphires and set in platinum and gold. Diamonds engraved by C. Bordinckx were a speciality of Boucheron around this time. The ring was made by Pelletier, who also executed designs for Cartier.

Left, below: An ecclesiastical ring in Art Deco style by Cartier, 1928. The massive gold setting has a cardinal's insignia on the shoulders, flanking an amethyst.

Above: Three Cartier versions of late 18th-century marquise and octagonal bezels. The upper one, paved with diamonds, dates from *c*. 1910. The other two are set with pearls on onyx in the 'demi-deuil' (half-mourning) style introduced after the sinking of the *Titanic* in 1912; there are tiny diamonds on the edges of the ring at the left.

TRADITIONAL
PURPOSES AND DESIGNS

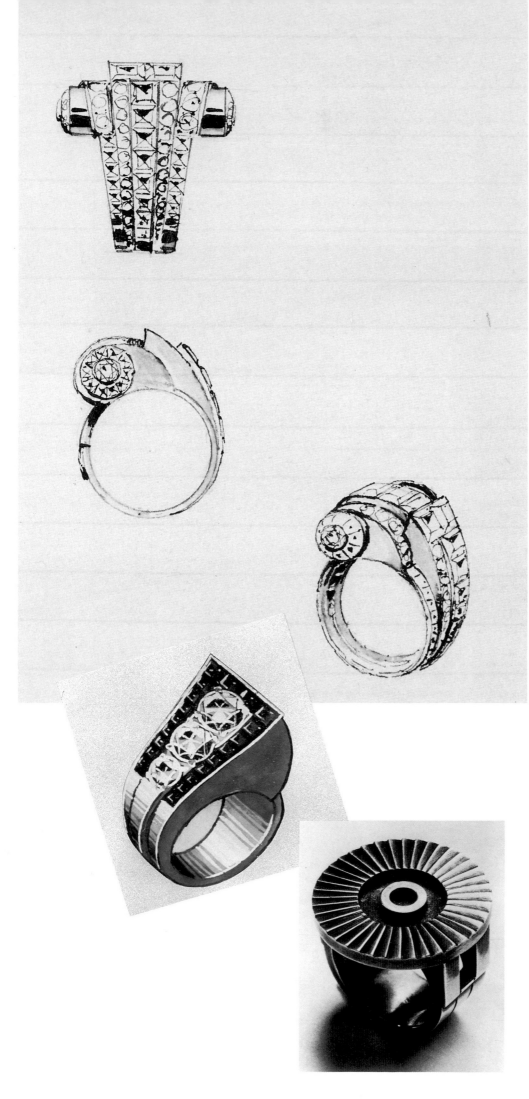

THE THIRTIES AND FORTIES

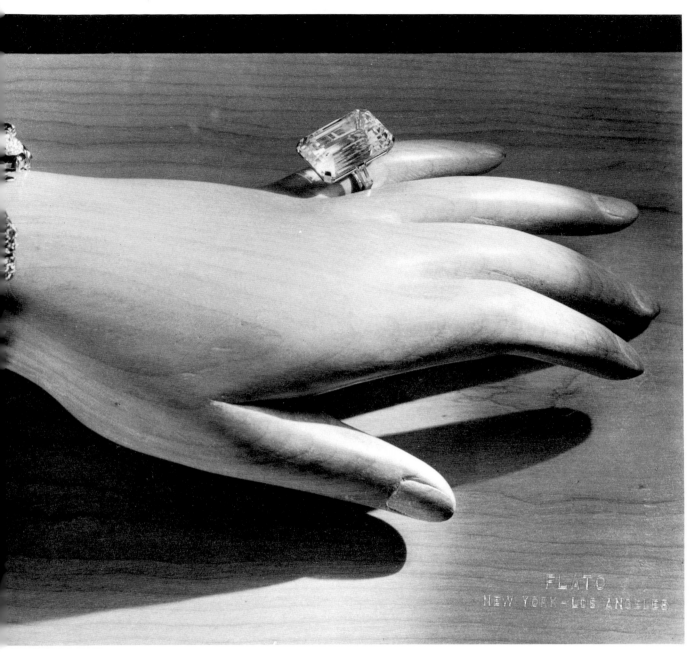

The angularity of Art Deco was succeeded by asymmetrical curves. *Left, above*: A design by Charles Bruno for a platinum ring for Hennell's client Mrs Pershore, 1936; small round diamonds pavé volutes overlapping the asymmetrical bezel. *Left, centre*: a Boucheron design of 1942 for a bulky dramatized version of the asymmetrical bezel, with three brilliants bordered by calibré-cut sapphires.

Left, below: The machine aesthetic. This silver ring by Jean Desprès, a follower of Le Corbusier, suggests the fan blades of an aeroplane engine; *c.* 1930–36.

Above and right: Paul Flato, jeweller to the stars of Hollywood, specialized in large solitaires, known at the time as 'ice-cubes'. He showed the same concern for bulk, angularity and volume in the ring made for himself, with his initials cut out of gold. Both designs, of *c.* 1938, are shown in his own publicity photographs.

CARTIER
IN LONDON, PARIS
AND NEW YORK

Opposite: An advertisement for
the London shop, 1933,
showing an elegant couple
choosing their engagement ring
from the window display in
New Bond Street.

Above left: An Art Deco-style
platinum ring from Cartier's,
New York, 1933. Three
cylinders, of onyx flanking coral,
tipped by coral flanking onyx,
form the bezel; they are
brightened by bands of brilliants
which also highlight the coral
shoulders.

Above right: An asymmetrical
peacock feather design of 1946.
Gold wire alternates with bands
of calibré-cut coloured stones.

Right: The first appearance of a
Cartier classic – the panther
ring, devised in Paris in the late
1940s by the artistic director,
Jeanne Toussaint. Two panthers
grip a large cabochon gem in
their paws. In later versions
there is just one panther,
modelled with increasing
realism.

Cartier Ltd
LONDON

Social
Occasions

ENGAGEMENT
RINGS
from £30

A MARRIAGE HAS BEEN ARRANGED

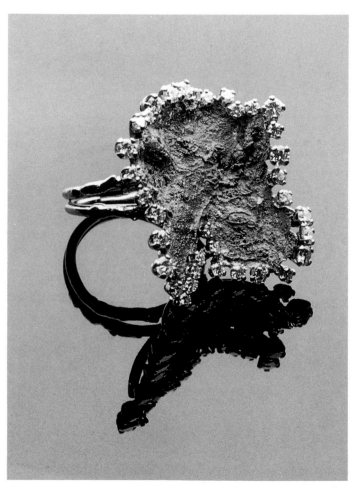

1950–1990

Far left, top and centre: Designs for cocktail rings in the characteristic Boucheron style of 1950, with light openwork gold wire bezels. In one, a cabochon emerald surmounts a dome sprinkled with coloured stone clusters; in the other, a brilliant-cut diamond is flanked by sapphire, emerald and ruby flowers within cable-twist borders.

Far left, below: During the 1960s Andrew Grima of London adopted a style in which the shapes seemed to be there by chance rather than calculated design. This ring, the bezel of gold textured like rough bark, with jagged edges set round with diamonds, won the Duke of Edinburgh's Prize for Elegant Design in 1966.

Left: Five rings of the late 1980s showing the versatile talent of Joel Rosenthal. On the left-hand cylinder: a ring in Indian style with tasselled bezel, combining gold, diamonds, rubies and a large pearl. On the centre cylinder: two all-white rings, the upper one set with a square-cut diamond bound in twisted diamond cords, the lower with a large central diamond surrounded by triangular moonstones, in diamond borders. On the right-hand cylinder: a ring with sapphire bezel and amethyst-set hoop, the stones held by claws encrusted with diamonds, and a diamond ribbon tied in a knot with an emerald drop.

ECHOES
OF THE COLD WAR

These two rings, in quite different ways, reflect the rivalry between the Eastern and Western blocs after the Second World War. The one *above* appears to be of massive gold, but the bezel contains a camera lens, and the ring was allegedly used by a Soviet spy in the 1950s. The one *below* is Cartier's reaction to the launch in 1957 by the USSR of the *sputnik*, proclaiming Russia's technological superiority; the broad bezel is studded with projections set with diamonds, emeralds, sapphires and rubies, in allusion to the projecting antennae of the first earth satellite.

Glossary

bezel: focal point of a ring as seen from the top of the finger.

brilliant cut: diamond cut comprising an octagonal top table with fifty-eight facets above and below the girdle, or widest part.

cabochon: unfaceted stone with rounded surface and flat back.

calibré: precise cutting of small coloured stones so as to fit neatly together in a row or cluster.

cloisonné enamel: technique by which cells formed from strips of metal soldered to a surface are filled with enamel.

collet: receptacle for the stone; may be either cup-shaped or made from strips of metal bent to the shape required.

damascening: technique of inlaying patterns of gold on steel.

doublet: a thin sliver of gemstone backed by or placed between thicker layers of glass or crystal to appear like a genuine gem.

engine-turning: machine engraving on metal used to produce various patterns including stars and wavy lines.

filigree: fine gold wire, plain, twisted or plaited.

foil: paper-thin sheet of metal placed behind a stone in the collet so as to improve colour and lustre.

habillé (of cameos): embellished with gemstones.

hogback cut: rectangular roof-shaped diamond cut.

hoop or *shank*: the part of the ring which encircles the finger.

millegrain: effect obtained by breaking up a platinum rim into tiny light-reflecting beads.

niello: a black substance made from an alloy of lead and sulphur, fused into the lines of engraved decoration to make it stand out clearly against the metal ground.

point cut: diamond cut based on the natural octahedral form of the stone.

rose cut: multi-faceted diamond cut with domed upper surface and flat back.

rose diamond: small and relatively unimportant rose-cut diamond.

Schwarzornament: minute symmetrical patterns derived from strapwork or similar ornament, executed in black enamel.

shank: see *hoop*.

shoulders: junction of hoop and bezel.

table cut: diamond or coloured stone cut with the top faceted flat.

Acknowledgments

It is a pleasure to thank the friends who introduced me to rings by inviting me to study their collections: Ian Lowe of the Ashmolean Museum, Oxford; Richard Randall Jnr. of the Walters Art Gallery, Baltimore; Graham Pollard of the Fitzwilliam Museum, Cambridge; Isabel Godinho of the Ajuda Palace, Lisbon; and Richard Camber and High Tait in the British Museum, London. I have learnt much from dealers, especially from Martin Norton who gave me the enjoyable task of cataloguing exhibitions held at S. J. Phillips, London, in 1976, 1977, 1978 and 1988, and also from Edward Donohoe, Brian Norman, Nicholas Silver, Isabelle Fellas, Joel Rosenthal and Pierre Jeannet in Paris and Ward Landrigan of Verdura in New York. Elizabeth Mitchell has kindly let me examine rings sold by the Works of Art Department at Sotheby's, and at Christie's Mary Feilden has generously shared her many discoveries. John Goodall, FSA, has not only advised me on medieval rings, but as archivist made the records of Hennell's available. Similarly, Teresa Buxton and Betty Jais of Cartier in London and Paris have taken endless trouble over my enquiries and provided illustrations. My thanks are also due to Béatrice de Plinval for allowing me to publish material from the stock books of Chaumet, which begin in 1838 with Jean-Baptiste Fossin. At Boucheron Françoise d'Elbreil and Michel Tonnelot looked after me most efficiently. I am grateful to the owners who have let me illustrate objects in their possession, especially the Princess Corsini, the Countess of Rosebery, Lord MacAlpine of West Green, Chantal Brasseur, Mr and Mrs Ronald Kellet, Irene de Marghalaes, Major Malcolm Munthe, MC, and Benjamin Zucker. For help in obtaining photographs and for special photography, my particular thanks go to Michael Bell of S. J. Phillips, A. C. Cooper, Prudence Cuming, Peter Day, Keeper of the collections at Chatsworth, Susanna van Langenberg, Irina Laski, Klaus Müller of Bonn, Christopher Phillips and Robert Wilkins, FSA. Timothy Wilson and Arthur

Macgregor of the Ashmolean, Julia Poole at the Fitzwilliam, Richard Edgecumbe and Michael Dillon of the Victoria and Albert Museum and Judy Rudoe at the British Museum have all been most kind, as has Dr Aileen Ribeiro of the Courtauld Institute. To Barbara Scott I owe some of my most apposite quotations from memoirs and from French and English literature. At Thames and Hudson, the designer entered into the spirit of the book, grouping the illustrations imaginatively together so as to emphasize each particular theme. Finally, I had the great good fortune of being assigned an editor who not only approached the project with enthusiasm but applied her wide art-historical knowledge to the study of rings, and succeeded in resolving some iconographical puzzles that had eluded generations of cognoscenti.

For specific illustrations, the publishers and I would like to acknowledge and thank the following individuals, institutions, and sources. [a = above, b = below, c = centre, l = left, r = right] Walters Art Gallery, Baltimore 61bl, 71, 72a, 90–91ac, 129 – Boucheron 176b, 177, 214a, c – Chantal Brasseur 95, 101a, 110–11 – Bulgari 206b – the Syndics of the Fitzwilliam Museum, Cambridge 67, 97, 100–101b, 145, 146a, 147a, c, 172 – National Museum of Wales, Cardiff 68–69c – Cartier Archives 190–91, 208b, 209, 212–13 – Chaumet Museum 174–75 – Christie's (London and Geneva) 33b, 34–35, 75, 92, 93b, 95r, 98br, 99bl, br, c, 102l, 107b, 130b, 134b, 141b, 149al, ar, 152ar, b, 182al, 183, 186al, 192c, 207a, 216a – the Chatsworth Settlement Trustees, Devonshire Collection, Chatsworth, 31br, 139a, 171a – Donohoe Antiques 58b, 179a – Gerda Flöckinger 207b – Galleria Corsini, Florence (photo Alinari) 54, 108b – Andrew Grima 214b – His Grace the Duke of Hamilton, Lennoxlove (photo Tom Scott, © The National Galleries of Scotland) 169 – Harvey & Gore 138l, 151 – Hennell's 202b, 210a – Hereford Cathedral Library 40c – Mr and Mrs Ronald Kellett 142ar – Irina Laski 202a, 203b, 216b – Lady

Victoria Leatham, Burghley House 179cl – Ajuda Palace, Lisbon 173a, c – in London: The Bentham Project, University College London 185al, bl; British Museum 29a, 32a, c, 48, 108a, 109a, 144a, 147b, 152al, 180bl; Museum of London 77, 90c, 91c, 142b; the Trustees of the National Gallery 25ar, b, 28–29a, 32b, 57al, b; The Pennington Mellor Munthe Charity Trust, Southside House 59a; Ranger's House, Blackheath 90b; the Board of Trustees of the Victoria and Albert Museum 47, 86, 112, 118, 124, 132–33, 152c, 176a – Prado, Madrid 72b – Irene de Marghalaes 182a, c – Yves Mikhaeloff 140–41c – Bayer. Verwaltung der Staatl. Schlösser, Gärten u. Seen, Munich 66a – The National Magazine Company Ltd 201 – His Grace the Duke of Norfolk 102b – in Oxford: Ashmolean Museum 10, 23, 24, 26al, b, 27, 30, 31al, ar, bl, 37a, 40bl (inset), br, 62, 63, 66b, 68l, 78, 79, 98l, 102–3a, 103b, 109c, 116, 131, 134a, 135, 139b, 140b, 141a, 143ar, b, 146b, 178, 184a, c, 185r; Bodleian Library (Douce 133) 56, 61, 64 (Douce 366) 40a; New College 38–39 – in Paris: Bibliothèque Nationale 97l, 99a, 138r; Louvre (inv. OA 952U), © Photo R. M. N. 33a; Musée des Arts Décoratifs 205 (courtesy Lalique), 204a, 210b – S. J. Phillips 28–29bc, 33c, 37b, 59b, 64b, 65ar, 70, 96bl, 107a, 142al, 143al, 144b, c, 148l, 149br, 150, 170al, ar, 173b, 179b, 180–81al, c, 181ar, 184b, 186bl, 188, 189, 192b, 207c – Royal Naval Museum, Portsmouth (photo J. A. Hewes) 158 – Private collection 58a, 94 and inset, 96al, r, 130a, 136–37, 170–71b, 186–87a, 192a – The Earl of Rosebery 179cr – Joel Rosenthal 207c, 215 – Royal Collection, St James's Palace, © 1993 Her Majesty the Queen 91b – Salzburger Museum Carolino Augusteum 121 – Nicholas Silver 211a, b – Sotheby's (London and Geneva) and Sotheby Parke Bernet 25al, 140c, 149bl, 159, 187b, 202c – the Marquess of Tavistock and the Trustees of the Bedford Estates 89 – Tiffany & Co. 163 – Cathedral Treasury, Trier (photo D. Tomassin) 36 – Verdura 206a – Kunsthistorisches Museum, Vienna 29br – Wartski 148ar – Windsor Castle, Royal Library, © 1993 Her

Majesty the Queen 104*a, c*, 105 –
Benjamin Zucker (photos © Peter
Schaaf) 61*br*, 97*a*, 181*rc, rb* (photo
Christie's) 106

O. M. Dalton, *Catalogue of the
Finger Rings in the British Museum*
(1912) 14, 19, 40*bl*, 48, 69*r*, 81,
100*a* – F. W. Fairholt, *Rambles of*

an Artist (n.d.) 53, 161 – J.
Szendrei, *Catalogue . . . de la
collection de bagues de Madame
Gustave de Tarnóczy* (1889) 155

Bibliography

Abbreviations used in the text

B   BURY, S., *An Introduction to
     Rings* (1984)
D   DALTON, O. M., *Catalogue of
     the Finger Rings in the British
     Museum* (1912)
O   OMAN, C., *Catalogue of Rings,
     Victoria and Albert Museum*,
     London (1930)
OBR —*British Rings 800–1914*
     (1974)
T&S TAYLOR, G., and D.
     SCARISBRICK, *Finger Rings
     from Antiquity to the Present
     Day* (1978)

General

BOARDMAN, J., and D. SCARIS-
BRICK, *The Ralph Harari
Collection of Finger Rings* (1977)
BULGARI, C., *Argentieri, Gemmari
e Orafi d'Italia*, 1 and 2
(1958–59)
CHADOUR, A. B., and R. JOPPIEN,
Schmucke II, Fingerringe
(Kunstgewerbemuseum, Cologne,
1985)
CHRISTIE'S, sale cat., *Rings from
Antiquity to the Present*, 5 Oct.
1988 and 4 Oct. 1989
— *Medieval and Renaissance
Jewellery*, 13 Dec. 1989
— *Rings, Antique and Historical
Jewellery*, 3 Oct. 1990
— *Jewellery, Antique Jewels and
Rings*, 2 Oct. 1991
DELOCHE, M., *La Bague en France
à travers l'histoire* (1929)
EVANS, J., *English Posies and Posy
Rings* (1931)
JONES, W., *Finger Ring Lore* (1890,
repr. 1968)
KUNZ, G., *Rings for the Finger*
(1917, repr. 1973)
MULLER, P., *Jewels in Spain
1500–1800* (1972)
PENTINI, S. ALUFFI, *I Gioelli delle
famiglie romane dal Barocco al
Romanticismo* (unpub. degree
thesis, Rome 1987)
RICCI, S. DE, *Catalogue of a Collection
of Ancient Rings formed by the late
E. Guilhou* (1912)
SCARISBRICK, D., *The Power of
Love, Six Centuries of Diamond
Betrothal Rings* (1988)
— *2500 Years of Rings* (1988)
— *Ancestral Jewels* (1989)
— *Jewels in Britain 1066–1837*
(1993)
— 'Rings in the Fortnum
Collection', *Connoisseur*, Oct. 1978
— 'Precious Chains of History, the
Cavendish Family Jewels', *Country
Life*, 9 and 23 June, 7 July 1983

— 'Joining Hands in a Ring, 2000
years of Love and Marriage
Rings', *Country Life*, 24 July
1986
SZENDREI, J., *Catalogue de la
collection de bagues de Madame
Gustave Tarnóczy* (1889)
WARD, A., and J. CHERRY, C. GERE
and B. CARTLIDGE, *The Ring from
Antiquity to the Twentieth Century*
(1981)

Chapter 1: 1100–1500

ARMSTRONG, E. C. R., *Catalogue of
the Finger Rings in the Collection of
the Royal Irish Academy* (1914)
CAMUS, J., *La Venue de Valentina
Visconti, Duchesse d'Orléans et
l'inventaire de ses joyaux apportés de
Lombardie, Miscellanea di Storia
Italiana*, ser. 3, V (1898)
DALTON, O. M., *Medieval and
Personal Ornaments from Chalcis in
the British and Ashmolean Museum,
Archaeologia* 62, 1962
EVANS, J., *Magical Jewels of the
Middle Ages and Renaissance*
(1922, repr. 1976)
HINTON, D., *Medieval Jewellery*
(1982)
LABARTE, J., *Inventaire du mobilier
de Charles V* (1879)
LABORDE, L. DE, *Les Ducs de
Bourgogne*, I, II, III (1849–52)
LA BORDERIE, A. DE, *Inventaire des
meubles et bijoux de Marguerite de
Bretagne, Bull. de la Soc.
Archéologique de Nantes et du
Département de la Loire Inférieure*,
IV (1864)
MÜNTZ, E., *Les Arts à la cour des
papes pendant le XV* et le XVI* siècle*
I and II (1878–82)
ORIGO, I., *The Merchant of Prato*
(1963)
PANNIER, L., *Les Joyaux du duc de
Guyenne* (1873)
SCARISBRICK, D., 'A Fifteenth
Century Iconographic Ring',

Christie's Review of the Season
(1973)
— 'A Signet Ring of Pope Paul II',
Burlington Magazine, May 1985
— 'Episcopal Jewellery, The
British Tradition', *Sotheby's
Preview*, Mar. 1991
SEIDMANN, G., 'Marriage Rings,
Jewish Style', *Connoisseur*, Jan.
1981
WATERTON, E., 'The Ring of the
Fisherman', *Archaeologia* 40, 1856

Chapter 2: The 16th century

CELLINI, B., *The Treatises of
Benvenuto Cellini on Goldsmithing
and Sculpture* (tr. C. R. Ashbee,
1898, repr. 1967)
— *The Life of Benvenuto Cellini* (tr.
G. Bull, 1956)
HACKENBROCH, Y., *Renaissance
Jewellery* (1979)
HIMMELHEBER, I., and K.
STOLLEIS, *Die Gewänder aus der
Lauinger Fürstengruft mit einem
Beitrag über die Schmuckstücke*
(1977)
MONTÉGUT, H. DE, *Inventaire des
bijoux de Jeanne de Bourdeille,
Dame de St. Aulaire et de Lanmary,
Bull. de la Soc. Historique et
Archéologique du Périgord*, VIII
(1881)
SCARISBRICK, D., 'Mirror of
Tragedy, the Jewels of Mary
Stuart', *Country Life*, 3 and 10
June 1982
— 'Queen Elizabeth's Jewellery',
*Handbook of the International Silver
and Jewellery Fair*, London
(1989)
— 'For Ever Adamant, A
Renaissance Diamond Ring',
*Journ. of the Walters Art Gallery,
Baltimore*, 1982
SOMERS COCKS, A., ed., *Princely
Magnificence* (1981)
TAIT, H., *Catalogue of the Waddesdon
Bequest in the British Museum: The*

Jewels (1986)
WOEIRIOT, P., *Livre d'Aneaux
d'Orfèvrerie* (1561, repr. 1978
with introduction by D.
Scarisbrick)

Chapter 3: The 17th century
ALDENBURG, C. A., *Memoirs* (1913)
BOYLE, R., *An Essay on the Origins
and Vertues of Gems* (1672)
BRAMSTON, SIR J., *Autobiography*,
Camden Soc. (1897)
BRUEL, F., *Deux Inventaires de
bagues, joyaux, pierreries et dorures
de la Reine Marie de Médicis,
Archives de l'Art français*, ns II
(1908)
CERMAKIAN, M., *La Princesses des
Ursins* (1969)
GAUTHIER, J., *Le Portrait de
Béatrix de Cusance et l'inventaire de
ses joyaux en 1663*, Académie des
Sciences, Belles lettres et Arts de
Besançon, Procès Verbaux et
Mémoires (1897)
Inventaire après décès of Philippe I,
Duc d'Orléans, 1701–3: Paris,
Archives Nationales, 300 AP I
746, 747
Inventory of Marie-Louise
d'Orléans, 1699: Madrid,
Archivo General de Palacio, Real
Bureo, vol. 5269, registro de
escrituras de D. Francisco
Arévalo
KIELMANSEGG, A. C., *Mémoires de
la Comtesse de Kielmansegge sur
Napoléon I* (1927)
LICETO, F., *De Anulis Antiques
Librum Singularem* (1645)
LOWENTHAL, M., *The Memoirs of
Gluckel of Hameln* (1932)
PROMIS, V., *Due Inventari del secolo
XVII, Miscellanea di Storia
Italiana*, XIX (1880)
SCARISBRICK, D., 'Anne of
Denmark's Jewellery, The Old
and the New', *Apollo*, Apr. 1986

— 'Anne of Denmark's Jewellery',
Archaeologia 109, 1991
SHARP, A., 'Notes on Stuart
Jewellery', *Proc. of the Scottish Soc.
of Antiquaries* 57, 1922–30
VERNEY, F. P., ed., *Memoirs of the
Verney Family* (1925)
WHEELER, M., *The Cheapside
Hoard in the Museum of London*
(1928)
YOGEV, G., *Diamonds and Coral*
(1978)

Chapter 4: The 18th century
ALLEMAGNE, H. D', *Les Accessoires
du costume et du mobilier depuis le
13ème jusqu'au milieu du 19ème
siècle* (1928)
BAPST, G., *Inventaire de Marie-
Josèphe de Saxe, Dauphine de
France* (1883)
HAEDEKE, H. U., 'Ringe des 18
Jahrhunderts', *Kunst und
Antiquitäten* (1987)
HAVARD, A., *Voltaire et Madame du
Châtelet* (1863)
HERZ, B., *Catalogue of the Collection
of Pearls and Precious Stones formed
by Henry Philip Hope* (1839)
PROSCHWITZ, G. VON, *Gustave III
par ses lettres* (1986)
SCARISBRICK, D., 'The Jewellery of
Madame de Pompadour, Queen
of the Dressing Table', *Handbook
of the Antique Dealers Fair at
Grosvenor House*, London (1983)
— 'A. M. Zanetti and the Althorp
Leopard', *Apollo*, Dec. 1979
— 'The Jewellery of Treason',
Country Life, 10 Mar. 1988
TAIT, H., ed., *A Catalogue of the Hull
Grundy Gift to the British Museum*
(1984)

Chapter 5: The 19th century
ATKINSON, C., 'The Bentham
Ring', *UCL Bulletin*, University
College London, VI, 11, 1986

BARRERA, A. DE, *Gems and Jewels*
(1860), for the inventory of Mlle
Mars
BLANCHE, J.-E., *Portraits of a
Lifetime 1870–1914* (1937)
CHRISTIE'S, sale cat., New York,
Jewellery, 25 Oct. 1983, for rings
of Dr Thomas Evans
GARY, M.-N. DE, *Anneaux et bagues,
dessins*, Paris, Mus. des Arts
Décoratifs (1992): designs of the
Robin firm, with introduction
GERE, C., and G. MUNN, *Artists'
Jewellery* (1989)
MARQUARDT, B., *Schmuck
Klassizismus und Biedermeier
1780–1850, Deutschland,
Österreich, Schweiz* (1983)
MASSON, F., *L'Impératrice Marie-
Louise* (1902)
SCARISBRICK, D., 'Emma Hamilton
and her Jewellery', *Handbook of the
International Silver and Jewellery
Fair*, London (1985)
— 'Maria Pia and her Jewellery',
Country Life, 4 June 1987
VEVER, H., *Histoire de la bijouterie en
France au 19ème siècle* (1906, repr.
n.d.)

Chapter 6: The 20th century
BARTEN, S., *René Lalique* (1977)
BECKER, V., et al., *Jean Schlumberger*
(1991)
GABARDI, M., *Gioielli degli anni '40*
(1982)
HINKS, P., *Twentieth Century British
Jewellery* (1983)
MEISTER, L., VON, *Gathering
Yesterdays* (1967)
NADELHOFFER, H., *Cartier* (1984)
NERET, G., *Boucheron* (1988)
RAULET, S., *Bijoux Art Déco* (1984)
SNOWMAN, K., ed., *The Master
Jewellers* (1990)
SOTHEBY'S, sale cat., *The Jewels of
the Duchess of Windsor*, Geneva,
2 Apr. 1987

Index

Anfossi, Giacomo 55
Angoulême, Marguerite of 50, 60
Anjou, Louis of 12
Anne, Queen of England 86
Anne of Austria, Queen of France 86
Anne of Cleves, Queen of England 52
Anne of Denmark, Queen of England 76, 80, 87
aquamarine 13, 46, 119, *139*, 156, 198
Arre, Monsieur d' 80
Ashbee, C. R. 196
Atholl, Charlotte Strange, Duchess of *130*
Augustus, Emperor 7
Augustus the Strong, Elector of Saxony and King of Poland *139*

balloons 123
Balzac, Honoré de 156
Barbo, Cardinal Pietro: *see* Paul II
Barney, Natalie 195, *204*
Bavaria, Albrecht, Duke of 50, *66*
Beefsteak Club 128, *152*
Benson, J. W. 194
Bentham, Jeremy 159, *185*
Berqhen, Robert de 76–79 *passim*
Bernhardt, Sarah 195
Blanche, Jacques-Emile 162
Blancourt, H. 80
Blücher, Marshal 160
Boleyn, Anne 45
Bonzanigo, G. M. 123
Bordinckx, C. *208*
Borromeo, St Charles 55
Boucheron 162, 163, *176–77*, 199, *203*, *204*, *208*, *210*, *214*
Bourchier knot 17, *33*
Boyle, Robert 88
Bowen knot 46
Braque, Georges 200, *207*
Braschi, Don Luigi 122
Brittany, Marguerite, Duchess of 11
Browne, Harold, Bishop of Ely and Winchester 167
Browning, Elizabeth Barrett 165
Bruno, Charles 198, *202*, *210*
Buchanan, George 42
Bulgari 6, 200, *206*
Bunyan, John 85
Burch, Edward 126
Burges, William 163, *176*
Burgundian goldsmiths and gemcutters' work 11, 24, *29*, *33*, *37*, *66*
Burgundy, Jean Sans Peur, Duke of 14, 17, *33*
Burgundy, Mary of 11, *29*
Bury, Lady Charlotte 156
Butz, Johan 56

Calder, Alexander 200
Caleppi, Cardinal 161, *183*
calibré cutting 194, 197, *207*, *208*, *210*, *212*
Calliat, Armand *175*
cameos 6–8 *passim*; (1100–1500) 13–14, 23, *33*, *34*; (16c.) 42, 47, 50, 53, *55*; (17c.) *81*, 83, 85, 86, 87; (18c.) 118–19, 120, 126, 127, *138*, *148–50*; (19c.) 158, 159, 160, 161, 168, *172*, *176*, *183*; (20c.) 195
Caradossi, Cristofano 55
Carlistle, 4th Earl of 119
Carr, Alwyn 196
Cartier 8, 162–65 *passim*, *190–91*, 194–95, *197*, 198, 199, *202*, *208–9*, *212–13*, *216*
Casanova, Giovanni Jacopo 114, 119, 121
cassolette rings 157
Castellani 162, 163, 165, *173*, *181*
catseye 13, 79, 115, 164
Cavalli, Mario 42
Cellini, Benvenuto 6, 44–47 *passim*, 55, 155
Chalcis Hoard *10*, 11, 12, 14, 15, 18, *26–27*, *30*, *31*, *40*
Chambord, Comte de 160, 167, *182*
Charles I, King of England 45, 58, 59, 80, 81, 86, *102*, *104*, 120
Charles II, King of England 80–81, 86, *105*
Charles V, Emperor 44, 49–50
Charles V, King of France 11, 12, 13, 15
Chaucer, Geoffrey 17
Chaumet 163, 167, *174–75*
Cheapside Hoard 77, 81, *90–91*
Chéron 116
chiastolith 87
Chicheley, Sir John 85
Child, Sir Francis 77
Childeric I 7
chrysoberyl 77
chrysolite 46, 122
chrysoprase 13, *36*, 51, 156, 161
claddagh rings 164
Clement IV, Pope 19
Clement of Alexandria 7
Coates, Kevin 200
coin rings 9, 200, *206*
Colmar, ghetto *13*, *19*
Colonna family 125
coral *48–49*, 87, *102–3*, 158, 197, 199, *212*
cramp rings, 24, 56
Cromwell, Thomas 46
crystal 13, 47, 48, 79, 85, *103*, *139*, 197, 198
Cusance, Béatrix de 78, 79

Dalí, Salvador 200
damascening 157
Dante 18
Datini, Francesco 18
Desprès, Jean 197, *210*
Devonshire, Christian, Countess of 82
Devonshire, Elizabeth, Dowager Countess of 88
Devonshire, 2nd Duke of 114, 118, *139*
Devonshire, 6th Duke of 161
devotional rings 8; (1100–1500) 21–24, *23*, *37*; (16c.) 53, *55*; (17c.) 87–88, *108*; (19c.) 167, *192*
diamond (1100–1500) 11, 13, 18, *28–29*; (16c.) 43–45, 46, 48, 49–50, 59–61, *66*; (17c.) 75, 76–77, 78, 79, 82, 83, 86, *90*, *94–98*, *102*, 106, 107, *109–12*; (18c.) 114–15, 117, 122, 125, 127, *130–31*, *134–35*, *138*, *141–44*, 147, *150*; (19c.) 157, 162, 163, 164, *170–71*, *177*, *179–83*, *185*, *186*, *190–92*; (20c.) 194, 197–98, 199, 200, *202–3*, *206–10*, *212*, *214–16*
    coloured 76, 114–15, 117; cuts 11, 76, 197–98; engraved 48, 80, *104*, 117, *208*; relative value 46, 77; rosettes 11, 45, *66*, 76–77, *97*; symbolism 11, 18, 43–44, 50, *60–61*
Dickens, Charles 186
D.M.T. 114
Dioscourides 7, *149*
Donne, John 87
Doria, Cardinal Giorgio 120–21
Doria inventories: *see* Aldobrandini, Pamphilj
doublets, 13, 47
Dunlop, Sybil 196
Duvaux, Lazare 116
Dyer, Nina 200

ecclesiastical rings (1100–1500) 19–21, *34–36*, *38–39*; (16c.) *54*, 55, *70–71*; (17c.) 87–88, *108*; (18c.) 120–*121*; (19c.) *161*, 167, *175*; (20c.) 196, 197, *208*
Edward III, King of England 11
Edward VII, King of England 165, 166
Egypt and Egyptian Revival 6, 8, 160, 162, *172*, *191*
Eleanor of Aquitaine, Queen of England 12
Elizabeth I, Queen of England 42, 44–48 *passim*, 55
emerald (1100–1500) 12, 18, 20; (16c.) 45, 46, 47, 51, *65*; (17c.) 56, 77, 78, 85, 87, *93*, *99*, *107*; (18c.) 115, *130–31*, *134*; (19c.)